RAISING A HYPERACTIVE CHILD

RAISING A HYPERACTIVE CHILD

Mark A. Stewart, M.D.
and Sally Wendkos Olds

HARPER & ROW, PUBLISHERS

NEW YORK
EVANSTON
SAN FRANCISCO
LONDON

Designed by Sidney Feinberg

Library of Congress Cataloging in Publication Data

Stewart, Mark A.
   Raising a hyperactive child.
   Bibliography.
   1. Hyperkinesia.   2. Exceptional children.
I. Olds, Sally Wendkos, joint author.   II. Title.
[DNLM: 1. Hyperkinesis—In infancy and childhood.
WS 350 S851h   1973]
RJ506.H9S73   618.9'28'5   72-79696
ISBN 0-06-014121-2

This book is dedicated
to all children—
the ones who are called "hyperactive"
and the ones who aren't—
but most especially
to Nancy, Jenny, and Dorie
and
Sarah, Anne, and Duncan

CONTENTS

Introduction   **xi**

PART I

The Nature of the Problem

1. WHO IS THE HYPERACTIVE CHILD?   3
2. HOW DID HE GET THIS WAY? SOME THEORIES
   OF THE ORIGIN OF HYPERACTIVITY   11
3. HYPERACTIVITY AS A NORMAL VARIANT
   OF TEMPERAMENT   25
4. WHO CAN HELP?   34

PART II

How to Help Your Child at Home

5. HELPING YOUR CHILD TO LIKE HIMSELF   59
6. ESTABLISHING A HEALTHY CLIMATE
   IN THE HOME   91
7. HOW CHILDREN LEARN TO BEHAVE   101
8. RULES AND REGULATIONS   117

9. HELPING CHILDREN TO ACQUIRE GOOD HABITS
   AND LOSE BAD ONES   127
10. SOME SPECIAL PROBLEMS AND WHAT TO DO
    ABOUT THEM   135

PART III

How to Help Your Child in School

11. SCHOOL PROBLEMS   191
12. THE POWER OF POSITIVE TEACHING   212
13. SPECIAL EDUCATION   222
14. DRUGS AND THE HYPERACTIVE CHILD   232

PART IV

Stages Through Life

15. THE FIRST FIVE YEARS   253
16. THE HYPERACTIVE ADOLESCENT   268
17. ALL'S WELL THAT ENDS WELL   281

   Epilogue: A Final Word to Parents   286
   References   287
   Index   293

To be what no one ever was,
To be what everyone has been:
Freedom is the mean of those
Extremes that fence all effort in.
—Mark Van Doren,
"Freedom," *Collected Poems*

INTRODUCTION

This is a book for parents, but we hope that it will also help teachers, grandparents, babysitters, and anyone who has to care for and raise hyperactive children. Our purpose is to restore parents' confidence in themselves by explaining the nature of the problems presented by hyperactive children and by describing practical ways to deal with them.

It is only natural for the parents of a hyperactive child to blame themselves for their child's bad behavior; they think that it is due to their not having given the child enough attention or not being firm enough, to the mother's going out to work, or to the father's being out of town too often. Unfortunately, grandparents, friends, neighbors, teachers, physicians, and even the stranger in the supermarket who sees a child act up are very ready to reinforce parents' guilt by saying that their child is spoiled, or neglected. It is also usual for the parents to "try everything" and find that nothing works; they allow their child to do whatever he wants "to take off the pressure"; they become stern and punish the child frequently and severely, but neither approach works. Their failure leads to shame and embarrassment in front of friends and neighbors, and in public places like stores. It puts a strain on their marriage, as one parent begins to blame the other, saying, "If only you would . . ."; it sends the mother to bed at night crying with frustration and exhaustion. Parents become so upset and exasperated that they have times when they hate their child and may beat him cruelly in an explosion of anger; they then feel disgusted with themselves.

There are many such parents who deeply need to be understood and to have practical help. This book is meant for them. What we have written comes from hundreds of conversations with parents of hyperactive children, the experience of treating children and watching them grow up, our own research and others',* and the wisdom of many parents, teachers, and physicians. It is not another theory on how to raise children; this would be the last thing that parents need.

---

* Throughout the book we make many references to the valuable work of others. Instead of interrupting the text with innumerable footnotes or numbers, we have collected all the references in the back of the book, keyed to the numbers of the pages and of lines on the pages to which they refer.

PART I

The Nature of the Problem

Say of him what you please, but I know my child's failings. I do not love him because he is good, but because he is my little child.

—Rabindranath Tagore
"The Judge," *Collected Poems and Plays*

1   WHO IS THE HYPERACTIVE CHILD?

"He is hyperactive" has become a familiar phrase on the lips of parents, teachers, and doctors in the last ten years. There certainly were hyperactive children before, but people had very different attitudes toward them, based largely on ignorance. As long ago as 1848, a German family doctor wrote some stories for his children, one of which told a sad incident in the life of "Fidgety Phil," surely a typical hyperactive child. Probably the first scientific description was published by an English pediatrician named George F. Still at the turn of the century. Only recently, however, has our society turned its attention toward the problems that children have in school because of behavioral, emotional, or perceptual handicaps. The result of this attention has been a great spurt of research and growing understanding. We can now talk intelligently about children who are "hyperactive" or who have learning disabilities or other problems at home and in school, instead of labeling them lazy, undisciplined, spoiled, or just plain bad, as people tended to do in the past.

Who is the hyperactive child? We can define him simply as a child who is persistently overactive, distractible, impulsive, and excitable in the eyes of his parents and his teachers. Other kinds of behavior are also typical of hyperactive children, but these seem to be the cardinal signs. We will usually refer to the hyperactive child as "he" because there are many more boys with this kind of behavior, perhaps as many as eight boys for every girl.

3

An important part of the definition is that the typical behavior pattern has been present for years, and usually from an early time in the child's life. There are periods when his behavior is much better or much worse, the latter often associated with emotional stress, but basically the restlessness and other traits are there all the time. A child whose behavior changed strikingly at, say, seven or eight, and who became hyperactive then without having shown any signs of such behavior before, should have a careful medical examination. This unusual development might well be the result of an illness, such as hyperthyroidism, or a lesion in the brain.

In addition, the intensity of the over-all problem varies greatly. At one end of the spectrum is a youngster like Roger, whose behavior is so extreme that he is dangerous to himself and to those around him. He sets fires; he locks his mother out of the house; he hits out violently at his little brother. For the sake of everyone's safety, Roger, at eleven, requires residential placement. At the other end of the scale is a child like Julie, who, at eight years of age, is getting along well in most areas of her life. She does have a tendency to talk too much and to have problems completing school assignments, but she is otherwise a lively and bouncy charmer.

The child with a mild "case" of hyperactivity can hardly be distinguished from an average child. Much depends on the expectations and tolerance of the child's parents and teachers, and on the way he is raised. If parents can put up with messiness, boisterousness, and a lot of tearing around the house, the problem will not be so severe as if they are quiet, highly organized people themselves. The behavior of hyperactive children is the same kind of behavior displayed by all children, but to a different degree. As one mother put it, "George is a regular boy—only magnified a thousand times."

A Close-up of the Problems

The characteristics of the syndrome of the hyperactive child can be roughly divided into four principal categories: overactivity, distractibility, impulsiveness, and excitability.

Overactivity labels the child's excess of energy, his restlessness, fidgetiness, never getting tired. This child moves more than other children, and his activity is different. Studies of these children show that their activity tends to be purposeless and inappropriate. They cannot turn their motors off. They squander their energy in activities that have no focus. They do not concentrate on a task at hand.

The hyperactive child has a passion for touching things: he leaves behind a trail of breakage, spillage, and disorder. He pokes and touches other children until a brawl results. He experiments with electric light plugs, opens and closes drawers, and takes apart everything in sight. He is so hard on clothing that he wears out the knees of his jeans by the second washing, and one mother has lamented, "Stevie would ruin a suit of armor by the end of the first day!" His baby crib is likely to be thrown away rather than handed down.

He fidgets, jiggles, and rocks on his chair at the dinner table until he falls off. In class, during a lesson, he jumps and runs around the room. He never walks when he can run and never sits still when he can be up and about. He is not ready to go to bed at a "reasonable" hour; yet he is up in the wee hours of the morning, disturbing everyone else's sleep or getting into trouble.

Distractibility is his short attention span, particularly in the performance of some task. While he may be able to sit and watch television for hours or to curl up with a book and read for a long time, this ability to concentrate disappears when he has to make any kind of active effort. He will begin to do his homework, notice a fly on the windowsill, and find that catching that fly is the most important aim of the moment. Once that is accomplished, he may go back to his work for a couple of seconds—until he encounters some other distraction.

It will take days and as much as a dozen starts for him to write a three-sentence thank-you note to his grandparents for a birthday present. A few minutes after beginning a card game with his brother, he flings his cards around the room. Midway through listening to a story, he gets up and goes to the water fountain.

While everyone else in his math class is conscientiously laboring over a page in the workbook, he becomes absorbed in the flight of birds glimpsed through the window. When parents and teachers give him directions, he tries to listen, but "tunes out" after the first two or three words.

He loses everything, because he forgets that he took off his new jacket to mark second base, that he rode his bicycle to the park and left it a few feet away, or that he put down his books to get a drink of water.

His *impulsiveness* makes him a stranger to fear or inhibition. In class, he blurts out the answer to a question directed at another student, interrupts the teacher's lesson to ask his own question, or loudly comments in the middle of a quiet period. He leaps before he looks—unmindful of the consequences for himself or for others. He jumps into the deep end of the pool without knowing how to swim, takes a drink from a bottle without knowing what is inside it, or takes apart a clock without knowing how to put it together again. He darts into the street on foot or bicycle, lets out secrets he has sworn to uphold, or buys candy with money he has been saving for a fishing rod.

Because he does not think before he acts, he is more prone to get into trouble: to lie, to play hooky, to commit an act of vandalism, to run away from home. If he sees small change lying about the house, he may pocket it without stopping to remind himself that it belongs to someone else. If his eye catches a pack of matches, he forgets that he has been forbidden to play with them and, in fact, has already received several spankings for this very activity.

He gets into trouble with reading because he cannot force himself to stop to figure out, or "sound out," words but will, instead, guess wildly. When he realizes that this approach gets him nowhere, he gets discouraged and gives up on the whole business.

Excitability: he is easily upset. His low frustration tolerance may cause him to destroy a toy that he cannot get to work properly, to pitch a temper tantrum when rain forces postponement of a picnic, or to punch a friend who does not feel like playing ball at the same instant he does. He is like a snowball; once he gets started, he just can't stop. He gets so keyed up at birthday parties—his own and his friends'—that they usually end up as catastrophes marked by crying and fighting. He cries at a later age and for less cause.

He is subject to moods of excruciating irritability. Someone comes up to say "good morning" and is immediately in an argument with him about what kind of day it is. When he is in one of these moods, which are unpredictable and may last anywhere from a few hours to several months, nothing pleases him and nothing can shake him out of his irritability.

Excitability is particularly troublesome to parents for two reasons. First of all, the emotional swings of the hyperactive child create a tense atmosphere in the home, heavy with screaming, fighting, and copious tears. His parents resent him, and come to feel guilty, as a result. Second, his babyish behavior makes it difficult for him to make and keep any friends. Parents grieve to see their child, who can often be good-natured and affectionate, become lonely and disliked.

Effects on Child and Parents

A description of the typical characteristics of a hyperactive child gives clues to the problems he experiences in daily life. Because of his unpredictable, uncontrollable behavior, the hyperactive child is often caught in a downward spiral of defeat and worsening self-image, till he says, "Why was I born this way? I'm just a weirdo!"

When a mother has to put a sixteen-month-old child back in his crib for the twenty-second time in one evening, or when she comes down in the morning to find the contents of every box and bottle in the kitchen strewn all over the floor, or when she has to listen to a neighbor complain that seven-year-old Sammy covered Mr.

Jones's garage with mud for the third time in a week, she may realize that she dreads having this child around. As one mother said, "We never stopped loving Billy, but for a long time I just didn't like him. I would go to bed at night, absolutely quivering, and wish we had never been blessed with this child."

Billy's mother recognized her ambivalent feelings toward her son and could express them. Many fathers and mothers, however, cannot. They want to love their child, and yet it seems that he thwarts them at every turn, making it almost impossible for them to respond to him in any positive way.

"Every night I would go to bed thinking 'tomorrow is going to be different,'" said one father. "I would promise myself that tomorrow I wouldn't scream at Donny; I wouldn't yell; I wouldn't nag; I wouldn't hit; I wouldn't ruin both our days before we left the house in the morning. And yet, every morning, there we were. Donny would say something or do something, and the two of us would be at each other's throat every waking moment we were in the same house."

The child, meanwhile, is convinced not only that his parents do not love him but that he is unlovable. Aside from his feelings of rejection, he is burdened with guilt, since he knows what he is doing to distress them. He may hear his parents quarrel over him all the time and feel sure that if it were not for his existence, the household would be happier. He senses that his brother and sister consider him a nuisance most of the time and are relieved when he is not around. Pathetically, no matter how much he wants his family to be happy with him and proud of him, he has little control over his behavior.

He is likely to have few friends, since the other children become disgusted with his constant poking and hitting and his silly, show-off behavior. In school, his classmates resent his interruptions in class, his failure to complete a game, and the way he bangs into their desks. Because he does not get along well with the other children, he may develop a "chip-on-the-shoulder" attitude, which then leads to fighting, bullying, and further trouble. Or he may desperately try to win friendship by telling boastful stories, giving out candy or money, or being the class clown.

School is his worst affliction. He has trouble with his schoolwork, not because he does not have the ability to learn the work, but because he cannot concentrate on it and cannot show what he does know. He loses his books, fails to complete tests, forgets to do his homework. Because of his tendency to guess at answers rather than puzzle them out, he has trouble with reading and math.

And, of course, he usually has trouble with his teacher. Annoyed because this child seems bent on disrupting the class, a teacher often throws up her hands. He seems to defy her every effort and to frustrate her at every turn. The child's parents often blame her for their child's poor progress in school. She feels inadequate and unappreciated, especially since she feels she has put forth extra effort for this child. She may end up using him as a scapegoat, blaming him for everything that goes wrong.

Yet, such a child may be basically outgoing and friendly. "There's not a mean bone in his body," said the mother of one hyperactive boy, "and everybody likes him—at times." If there is a prize for selling the most candy for the Little League team, he is likely to win it. If there is a hard, dirty job to do, he will most likely volunteer for it. If he is kept after school for acting up in class, he will probably help the teacher straighten all the books, help her on with her coat, talk her ear off, and walk off the best of friends. "If he were only like this all the time!" she sighs when she describes the afternoon to his mother.

Happily, parents and teachers can do more than sigh and hope for the best. They can recognize that even though they did not cause the child's problem, they can do much to solve it. They can be assured that inadequate parenting or teaching did not make this child hyperactive—but that super-parenting and super-teaching can make things better. As one mother put it, "A hyperactive child requires hyper-parenting." Parents and teachers can help a hyperactive child learn to control his behavior, develop his potential to the fullest and emerge from childhood no worse adjusted than his more "normal" brothers and sisters. That is what this book is all about.

This face you got,
This here phizzog you carry around,
You never picked it out for yourself,
    at all, at all,—did you?
This here phizzog—somebody handed it
    to you—am I right?
Somebody said, "Here's yours, now go see
    what you can do with it."
  —Carl Sandburg
    "Phizzog," *Good Morning, America*

2   HOW DID HE GET THIS WAY? SOME THEORIES ON THE ORIGIN OF HYPERACTIVITY

One of the first questions parents ask when they learn that their child is hyperactive is "What caused this?" What they often are thinking is "What did we do wrong?" When parents are besieged by experts telling them how to raise their children, they all too readily take the blame for their children's problems. One mother expressed the feelings of many when she said, "Eric is now twelve years old. He first started to make me feel a complete failure as a mother when he became mobile at fifteen months—and I have been feeling more and more inadequate with every passing year."

It is easy to blame yourself when you see that many other parents do not seem to have the same troubles in bringing up their children. But you should not feel guilty. Neither clinical findings nor research studies suggest that the behavior of parents can cause hyperactivity by itself.

What does cause hyperactivity? We have clues to its origins and believe that it may often be due to several causes working together, but we cannot yet be precise about the causes of the "hy-

peractive-child syndrome." This chapter, which sets forth some
of the theories that may explain hyperactivity, is full of qualifiers
like "maybe," "it is possible," and "we suspect."

Abnormalities of Brain Function

The brain is an unbelievably complicated organ, consisting of mil-
lions of different kinds of cells. The intricate connections between
the various groups of nerve cells almost defy description and make
telephone exchange wiring look like a nursery-school toy. We
know relatively little about the ways in which different parts of the
brain are involved in the expression of feelings such as pleasure
and anger, in the experience of different moods, and in the regu-
lation of activity level, aggressiveness, attention span, and perseverance. We think that the emotional quality of responses is
determined by nerve cells in two parts of the cerebral cortex and
in the hypothalamus, a small but crucial region lying at the base
of the two great lobes of the brain. Some cells in these various
centers probably provide the raw stuff of emotions, while others
tend to inhibit or modulate the expression of emotions. The frontal
cortex probably provides the fine control of emotions and actions
that one expects of people who follow our social conventions.
People who have had accidental injuries to the frontal cortex tend
to behave in crude and uninhibited ways.

Problems in Brain Development

The anatomical and biochemical development of the brain is
complex. The actual cells are laid down during growth of the fetus
or in the early stages of infancy, but their full development takes
years and may not be complete until the end of the first decade of
life. Given the complexity of this process, there are obviously
many ways in which the course of development may go wrong.
Inherited defects in metabolism, prenatal infections, and abnormal
chomosomes are some of the factors that can affect development.

The more obvious errors of development have marked effects on behavior and intelligence. It seems possible that some less severe problems in learning and behavior may be caused by inherited abnormalities in development of the brain. For example, some children of normal intelligence do not develop speech until after the age of four but then acquire nearly normal speech after the course of two or three years. Many of these children come from families in which there are other affected members. It seems reasonable to suppose that in these families there is an inherited problem in the development of that part of the brain which underlies the function of speech. Using this condition of "developmental aphasia" as an analogy, we can reasonably theorize that "hyperactivity" may also be a sign of delayed development in a particular part of the brain or a lack of proper co-ordination of development in several centers of the brain.

Injury to the Brain

Hyperactivity has been referred to as the "brain-damage syndrome," since it does sometimes follow some trauma to the brain. In 1902, Dr. George F. Still first reported an association between behavior problems of children, which he quaintly called a "morbid defect of moral control," and such diseases as brain tumor, meningitis, epilepsy, and head injury. Dr. Still's descriptions of these children deficient in "moral control" sound remarkably like descriptions of present-day hyperactive children. There were the six-year-old boy who was unable to keep his attention even on a game for more than a short time, the nine-year-old boy who stole small amounts of money and committed other indiscretions, for which "no amount of punishment seemed to have any deterring effect," and the seven-year-old girl who "flew into a rage, seized a stick, and deliberately smashed the window" on a day when she was not permitted to go outside.

Twenty years later, Dr. Franklin G. Ebaugh and Dr. Edward A. Strecker of Philadelphia reported severe hyperactivity in a group of seventeen children who had suffered attacks of encephalitis during the 1918 epidemic and had been seen subsequently at the neuropsychiatric clinic at Philadelphia General Hospital.

Among the children who recovered from the acute phase of encephalitis, many later showed a catastrophic change in personality: they became hyperactive, distractible, irritable, unruly, destructive, and antisocial. Many of the children had been referred to the hospital clinic by school authorities because they were "unmanageable" and were not making progress in school. "Frequently, they had disturbed the whole class," Dr. Ebaugh reported, "since they were very quarrelsome and impulsive and often left the school building during class exercises. Nor did these children respond to discipline."

Brain injury seemed implicated as the cause of these children's unruly and difficult behavior, since a majority of the patients had changed completely from a condition of good adjustment in home and school. On recovering from the acute illness, the children showed marked swings of mood, seesawing between irritability and affability, quarrelsomeness and overaffectionateness.

Since that time there have been many more reports of hyperactivity following presumed brain injury, most commonly some difficulty at birth. Few of these studies have been adequately controlled. The general truth seems to be that children who have suffered injury to the brain are more likely to have behavior problems than other children, though many of them behave quite normally. The kinds of problems range from hyperactivity to underactive and withdrawn behavior.

Most children who are hyperactive do not have anything in their medical histories that suggests injury to the brain. Only about one out of ten hyperactive children who come to a psychiatric clinic has any history suggesting brain injury. By and large, the mothers of hyperactive children have had uneventful pregnancies, the birth experiences have been normal, and the children's early years have been free from illnesses and injuries known to damage the brain. Complications of pregnancy and delivery are no more common among hyperactive children than among children in the general population.

Even when such complications are present, they are not necessarily significant. In a follow-up study of all 750 children born on the island of Kauai, Hawaii, within a year, researchers concluded that children are not generally affected by difficulties in pregnancy, labor or delivery, or by neonatal illness. There was no difference in terms of learning or behavior problems between children who had had smooth sailing in infancy and those who had experienced trouble. By the age of ten, most of the children who had experienced severe perinatal stress were doing satisfactorily in school and at home.

In spite of this evidence, it is still possible that damage to a specific part of the brain may be followed by hyperactivity. Perhaps an association between perinatal stress and hyperactivity does not show up in large-scale studies, because there are so many common disorders of pregnancy and delivery that do *not* have any effect that the specific association we are looking for might be getting lost in the welter of statistics. An example is the relationship between prematurity and later behavior problems, which is currently under investigation.

Because evidence of injury to the brain is lacking, a number of professional persons have turned to the term "minimal brain dysfunction" to explain hyperactivity, as well as an assortment of other childhood behavior disorders. This "umbrella" term is used to describe a wide range of "learning or behavior disabilities," and therein lies the trouble with the term. While it covers the syndrome of hyperactivity, it is also used to cover underactive children, those with reading problems, and those with speech and coordination problems. Saying that a child suffers from "minimal brain dysfunction" is, in fact, like describing a child with a sore throat or a skinned knee as having "minimal physical impairment." The description is not precise—and in some cases it is not even apt. For example, a severely hyperactive child whose behavior constitutes such a problem to himself and to others that he requires residential schooling suffers from more than *minimal* brain dysfunction.

Another problem with the term is that the words "brain dysfunction" often turn into "brain damage" in the minds of the parents offered this diagnosis of their child. Their first reaction is shock at hearing that they have a child whose brain has been damaged in some mysterious way. Their second reaction is often resignation: since the damage is already done, they are powerless to repair it. Nothing could be further from the truth.

Let us, then, recognize the fact that some hyperactive children may have suffered some insult to the brain, that when the child's past history or present symptoms seem to point to such a possibility, a neurological examination may be indicated (see page 44). For the majority of hyperactive children, however, introducing the idea of brain injury or dysfunction is neither helpful nor justifiable.

Chemical Imbalance in the Brain

The idea that hyperactivity has a biochemical basis is suggested by the fact that in approximately half the diagnosed cases of the syndrome some of the most distressing symptoms can be dramatically relieved by giving stimulant drugs (more about these in Chapter 14). The hyperactive child becomes quieter, attends longer, perseveres more with his schoolwork, and is generally easier to get along with. Why should these drugs, which are stimulants, have such an apparently paradoxical effect?

A possible explanation for the effectiveness of stimulant medication—and maybe for the occurrence of hyperactivity—may lie in the brain's "neurotransmitter" substances, so-called because the release of these chemicals at the endings of one nerve cell seems to trigger an impulse in the next nerve cell. Researchers presently believe that the parts of the central nervous system that control emotional reactions, appetite, and such basic qualities of behavior as activity level have many cells which produce the chemical norepinephrine as a transmitter substance. Norepinephrine is probably involved in mood, arousal, hunger, thirst, temperature control, and sexual activity. Another chemical, serotonin, seems to be produced by other cells and to be associated with inhibitory effects, such as those on sexual behavior and in the onset of sleep.)(These assumptions are speculative and are the subjects of a great amount of research.)

It is possible that a relative lack of functioning norepinephrine at the endings of nerve cells may be responsible for hyperactivity. Amphetamines and other stimulant drugs raise the level of norepinephrine at nerve endings and thus increase activity in the networks of nerve cells that use this substance as a transmitter agent.

It seems likely that amphetamines and other stimulants have this effect on those parts of the brain that mediate and regulate feelings and activity levels. We do not know for sure that this is true, but it is a reasonable hypothesis that the feelings of well-being and the greater ability to concentrate produced by stimulants in normal adults and the calming effects seen in hyperactive children are due to the increased release of norepinephrine.

There is no hard evidence that a chemical imbalance in the brain causes hyperactivity, but the astonishingly specific changes brought about by the stimulants make it seem a strong possibility. We know that stress leads to the release of norepinephrine in the brains of experimental animals; we also know that the effects of stimulant drugs often mimic the effects of situations that are stressful for the hyperactive child. For example, a child who has been described by his mother as a demon may be an angel when he is in a strange situation, such as a psychiatrist's office. Or he may be subdued and submissive when he goes to the doctor's office for an allergy shot. The explanation may lie in a stress-induced release of norepinephrine in the brain cells. Thus a state of anxiety may produce the same effect as a dose of a stimulant drug—through exactly the same mechanism—to correct a chemical imbalance in the nervous system.

Problems in Prenatal Development

Recent research conducted by Mary Ford Waldrop and Charles F. Halverson, Jr., of the Child Research Branch of the National Institute of Mental Health has suggested the possibility that hyperactivity may be associated with a defect in early fetal development. Studies of several groups of children showed that hyperactive boys have an unusually large number of minor physical anomalies. (Since the conclusions from these studies were rather contradictory for girls, we shall discuss them only as they apply to boys.)

Waldrop and Halverson examined 132 two-and-a-half-year-olds, most of whom had been judged free from complications of pregnancy and birth, 62 seven-and-a-half-year-olds who were among the two-and-a-half-year-olds of the original study, and 90 elementary-school children ranging from kindergartners through sixth-graders. Observers rated the children for characteristics of hyperactivity. Other examiners checked the children closely to detect such physical anomalies as a head circumference significantly larger or smaller than the average, very fine "electric hair," skin folds partially covering the corners of the eye, unusually wide-set eyes, low-set or unusually shaped ears, a curved little finger, a certain type of crease in the palm of the hand, webbing between the toes, and a big gap between the first and second toes. The investigators found that the more minor anomalies a child showed, the more likely it was that he would be considered hyperactive. The relationship between high anomaly scores and hyperactivity held true over the years for those children who were seen twice, at two and a half and seven and a half.

A minor infection incurred in the first three months of prenatal life may have caused both the physical anomalies and the hyperactivity. It is also possible that subtle irregularities of the chromosomes (the tiny particles that contain the genes and that are passed on through the sperm and the egg to each new being) caused both phenomena, though no one has yet demonstrated such abnormalities. At Washington University we found no chromosomal abnormality in a group of hyperactive children, but the development of more sensitive techniques for analyzing chromosomes may lead to such anomalies being found.

Before we take a close look at our youngsters, we have to remember, however, that none of the minor anomalies described above is important in itself. Many normal individuals have more than one, and many of the hyperactive boys examined had low anomaly scores.

Sex-Linked Factors

One noteworthy fact about hyperactivity is its marked preponderance among boys. Every study of the syndrome that has ever been published has found many more hyperactive boys than girls in the general population. This ratio ranges from a low of 2.5 boys to every girl, through a more common proportion of four to six boys to every girl, up to a high figure of nine boys to every girl. These findings mirror the preponderance of boys seen with such disorders as autism, reading disability, and delayed speech development. For some reason, females are a more or less protected class with respect to these and other problems.

A possible explanation for these disparities of sex-influenced incidence is that male hormones make the development of the nervous system less stable. Both boys and girls have small amounts of male hormones circulating in their bodies from birth (boys have somewhat more than girls), and it is conceivable that hyperactive boys and girls have unusually high levels of these hormones. Another is that girls have a general biologic advantage because they receive X chromosomes from both parents while boys necessarily get Y chromosomes from their fathers and their single X's from their mothers. This means that girls receive a more mixed set of genes than boys, a fact that tends to give them a biologic advantage analogous to the vigor of a hybrid.

Emotional Disturbance

While many doctors, teachers, neighbors, and relatives who see a hyperactive child in action feel that the child is suffering from an emotional disturbance—and do not hesitate to tell this to the parents—the truth seems to be that hyperactivity leads to emotional problems, rather than being a symptom of them.

In the next chapter we will discuss the several aspects about hyperactivity that make us feel that the syndrome is usually inborn and not due to emotional upset. There *are* some children who seem tense and "wound up," or who have difficulty concentrating on their schoolwork, or who behave impulsively and excitably because of conflicts at home or inability to express deep-seated feelings. Their disturbed behavior generally shows up at a later age— usually about eight or nine—than does physiological hyperactivity. Emotionally based "hyperactivity" is milder, related to specific situations, and less consistent than biological hyperactivity, which goes on all the time to a greater or lesser extent.

When the basic temperament of a hyperactive child manifests itself immediately after birth—or even in the womb—it is difficult to see how emotional deprivation could be playing a part. It is common to hear a mother say that her hyperactive child was much more active than her other children even before birth or that he manifested his restless nature in his first few days of life.

One mother has said, "When I was in the hospital, I used to hear one baby crying in the nursery all day and all night. I used to think, 'Oh, that poor mother—what she's going to have to go through when she gets home!' A few days later I found out that that poor mother was me! From the day we got home from the hospital, Ellen was awake and crying twenty hours out of twenty-four. Right from birth, she was completely different from my first child, who had been one of those dreamy babies who do nothing but eat and sleep for the first few weeks." While not all hyperactive children show their personality at such an early age, so many of them do that we cannot ignore the evidence pointing to hyperactivity as an inborn constellation of personality traits. More about this in the next chapter.

When children who are emotionally disturbed are brought into a psychiatrist's office or into a child-guidance clinic, the professional consultant can often immediately spot some obvious problems in the home—long-standing conflict between the parents, for example, or obvious lack of love toward the youngster, or an extremely chaotic home situation. With most hyperactive youngsters, however, this is not the case. The parents of hyperactive children seem to treat their children just as most other parents do; the home situations are, by and large, as stable; the children, for the most part, have had no more unfortunate experiences in life than has the average child. Also, the fact that there is usually only one hyperactive child in a family argues against the condition having been caused by something the parents have done.

Parents and homes are never perfect, of course. Every family situation has its own unique and unusual set of characteristics. Someone who is looking for a cause of emotional disturbance can usually find it, and many parents of hyperactive children tell of having been told by pediatricians, psychologists and psychiatrists that they are somehow to blame for their youngsters' problems. One couple were told that if they slept in the same bed, their child would be more secure and would not act up so much. Another couple were told that they should be more creative parents; another that they were not consistent enough; another that their child was reacting to the knowledge that he had been adopted; and so on and so on and so on.

All these comments may have contained a germ of truth; parents are rarely as creative, as consistent, as understanding, as skillful as they would like to be. Yet the great majority of children learn to adapt to minor shortcomings in their environment and to grow up healthy in spite of us flawed adults.

The other side of the coin is that the hyperactivity itself often causes emotional problems in both the child and the parents. A high activity level, an impulsive and thoughtless nature, a tendency to be restless and distractible, and an emotionally volatile temperament definitely make a child a prime prospect for psychological problems, since other people tend to react negatively to him. In the wee, small hours of the morning, a harassed mother may confess to herself that she dreads having this child around and cannot bear facing him in the morning. A father may be unable to hide his disappointment with this child, who can't play a game of ball without dissolving in tears or who can't get A's in school. A teacher may become so frustrated with the child's inability to do his own work and his propensities for disrupting her class that she takes a strong dislike to him. Other children, annoyed by his silliness, his inability to finish a game, and his constant fighting may brand him as a "retard" or an "oddball." Rejection from all corners of his world takes its toll from the child's self-esteem, leaving him feeling defeated and inadequate, till he may say, as did one unhappy ten-year-old, "I have nothing to live for."

The worse the problems get with the child, the worse they become with the parents. It is a strain to raise normal children; it is a double strain to raise a child with a special problem; and it is a triple strain to raise a hyperactive child, whose problem has no obvious physical stigma and is usually blamed on the parents' mishandling. The parents, then, have the extremely difficult task of living with and raising this "impossible" child, and they also have the worry that maybe, somehow, without meaning to, they are causing his problems. Under these tensions, they quarrel between themselves, one blaming the other for being too lenient, too harsh, too indifferent, too blind. The atmosphere in the home becomes heavy with discord, affecting everyone in the family: the child himself who feels guilty because he knows he is the cause of his parents' quarrels, his brothers and sisters who resent both the trouble he causes and their parents' extra concern for him and, of course, the parents who become overwrought and sick with worry. By the time they seek professional help, the problem is indeed highly emotional—but an emotional problem that has been caused by the presence of hyperactivity and not the other way around.

If parents can recognize and understand their child's hyperactivity and then embark on a therapeutic program to help him, they can go a long way toward avoiding the development of reactive emotional problems in themselves and their child. Even if emotional troubles have already appeared, all is not lost. Much can be done to alleviate them and to help everyone involved—the child, the parents, the siblings, the teachers—understand and deal with the underlying hyperactivity and the emotional overlay.

Atmosphere in the Home

When Dr. George F. Still first described hyperactivity at the turn of the century, he looked for causes. One of the causes he considered was "deficient training" in the home. Dr. Still went on to urge physicians to take the home environment into careful consideration in each individual case. There are some homes in which children are raised so permissively or so haphazardly that they are never taught how to listen to someone else, how to stick to a task, or how to control their impulsive behavior. Such children will, of course, be at a disadvantage when they venture outside the home— to school or to other children's homes or in other situations where they are expected to exert some controls over their behavior.

If a child has been brought up in a very unstructured environment, without a reliable pattern to depend on, in a chaotic home atmosphere, he will tend to exhibit some of the traits of hyperactivity—a high activity level and a general lack of self-control, a tendency to flit from one activity to another, to "tune out" on verbal instructions, to act impulsively without considering consequences, and to become easily bored.

This is not true hyperactivity as we have been discussing it, and yet children whose apparently hyperactive behavior stems from a lack of proper teaching can benefit from many of the techniques of management discussed in this book, such as an emphasis on structure and routine, programs of verbal training and impulse control, and rewards for good behavior.

Other Theories

It would be impossible for us to discuss in one book all the theories attempting to explain hyperactivity. We would like to say a word or so, however, about three beliefs currently being propounded in some circles.

Some people attribute the behavior problems in some children to the presence of hypoglycemia, a condition in which the sugar level in the blood is abnormally low. Yet it is hard to see how the kind of constant hyperactivity we are talking about could be due to this condition, which tends to occur in attacks and to be associated with seizures and other physical symptoms. Others claim that vitamin deficiencies or food sensitivities are causing hyperactivity. At the present time, however, there is absolutely no good evidence to suggest that any of these factors is responsible for hyperactivity, and it seems unlikely that any will be uncovered.

One other explanation for hyperactive behavior—a constellation of inherited behavior traits—seems such a strong possibility that we feel it needs a chapter all to itself.

There is a luck of faces and bloods
Comes to a child and touches it.
　　　　　—Carl Sandburg
　　　　　The People, Yes

3　HYPERACTIVITY AS A NORMAL VARIANT OF TEMPERAMENT

A number of characteristics which everyone has, to some degree
or other, are more marked in hyperactive children, suggesting that
hyperactivity is a normal variant of temperament, rather than an
illness or emotional disorder.

What is a person's temperament? We mean a person's inborn
characteristic style of behavior; his or her tempo, emotional re-
sponsiveness, aggressiveness, sociability, impulsiveness. In *Tem-
permanent and Behavior Disorders in Children,* psychiatrists Alexander Thomas and Stella Chess and pediatrician Herbert G. Birch
offer a particularly good definition of temperament:

> Temperament may best be viewed as a general term referring to the
> *how* of behavior. It differs from ability, which is concerned with the
> *what* and *how well* of behaving, and from motivation, which seeks
> to account for *why* a person does what he is doing. When we refer
> to temperament, we are concerned with the *way* in which an individual
> behaves. Two children may each eat skillfully or throw a ball with
> accuracy and have the same motives in so doing. Yet they may differ
> with respect to the intensity with which they act, the rate at which
> they move, the mood which they express, the readiness with which
> they shift to a new activity, and the ease with which they will approach
> a new toy, situation, or playmate.
>
> Thus, temperament is the *behavioral style* of the individual child—
> the . . . term used to describe the characteristic tempo, rhythmicity,
> adaptability, energy expenditure, mood, and focus of attention of a
> child, independently of the content of any specific behavior.

25

Evidence that a particular style of behavior was common, that it could be identified early in a child's life, that it remained stable over much of his life, and that it was determined genetically would tend to support the idea that the pattern was one of temperament.

Prevalence

The very prevalence of hyperactivity attests to its normality in the range of human behavior. A study done by Ray Miller, principal of a school in Webster Groves, Missouri, showed the prevalence to be 8 per cent of boys and 1 per cent of girls in suburban elementary schools.

The 1965 study of ten-year-old Hawaiian children referred to earlier found that about 6 per cent of the youngsters (9 per cent of the boys) were considered hyperactive by their parents or teachers. These children represented a variety of ethnic groups and all socioeconomic levels present on the island of Kauai. It seems more reasonable to suppose that this high proportion of boys is part of normal variation than that they are sick.

Early Onset of Symptoms

As we noted before, many hyperactive children display their characteristic behavior at an early age. They often are colicky and experience difficulty settling down to a particular formula. They do not sleep well or regularly, and they are generally cranky, fussy babies. They also exhibit inordinate amounts of energy and may be precocious in their physical development. These are some of the ways parents have described their hyperactive children as babies:

"As an infant, Richie was constantly on the move. By the time he was eight months old, his crib mattress was a total wreck. My sister had passed her crib mattress down to her third child, so I knew right away we would have our hands full with this fellow!"

"David has always been overactive, impulsive and difficult to control, from the time he was an infant. He never would nap for more than fifteen or twenty minutes at a time during the day, was almost impossible to get to sleep at night, and was always up bright and early in the morning."

"When Kitty was an infant, I couldn't turn my head away for a second while I was diapering her. She squirmed and wriggled so much that she would have been on the floor in a split second. Even while I was nursing her, she was never relaxed but was constantly shifting position, waving her arms about and kicking."

The above parental observations are borne out by a research project conducted by the three New York physicians quoted earlier, Alexander Thomas, Stella Chess and Herbert G. Birch. They have followed 231 children from birth through adolescence and found that the children differed markedly as infants with regard to a variety of personality characteristics. The characteristics studied included level of activity; regularity of biological functioning (whether they tended to get hungry and sleepy at about the same times each day); characteristic responses to new situations; adaptability to changes in routine; sensitivity to sensory experiences such as noise, light, wetness, pain, or even the feel of their clothes; prevailing mood; intensity of their emotional responses; ability to concentrate; and persistence. The main finding was that children who developed behavior problems, such as hyperactivity, could be distinguished from other children as infants.

Stability

Once hyperactivity has made its appearance—which is often in infancy but may not be obvious or troublesome until the youngster reaches school—it tends to be relatively stable. The same child will exhibit different problems at different ages, all of which reflect his basic personality.

That bouncy, never-sleeping infant grows into a toddler who is always on the run and into everything. His curiosity is unslakable; his impulsiveness may lead him to drink poison or to dart into the street. He is up in the night, has a terrible temper, and hits or bites other children. In nursery school he is disruptive, is hard on the toys, ignores the teacher's instructions, does not listen to a story, does not finish his pictures.

In elementary school his problems magnify. He struggles unsuccessfully with the tasks of sitting for long periods of time, staying with projects, and producing neat written work. At home he will not conform to limits and fights constantly with his brother and sister.

The hyperactive adolescent may have less trouble with excessive physical activity, but he is likely to continue to be restless and impatient, distractible, impulsive, and more irritable and quarrelsome than the average teen-ager. He is also more defiant, more rebellious and more adventurous.

At Washington University we followed up eighty-three boys and girls between the ages of twelve and sixteen who had been diagnosed as hyperactive children some years earlier. Gabrielle Weiss and her colleagues at Montreal Children's Hospital did a similar study and found the same results. At the time of our follow-up contact, about half the young people had definitely improved in their behavior and schoolwork, another quarter had probably improved somewhat, and the behavior of the rest presented as much of a problem as ever. The picture is encouraging in that *most* of the youngsters were behaving fairly normally, even though they still tended to be restless, impatient, impulsive, and more irritable and quarrelsome than other youths.

Most of these young people had apparently learned to recognize and work within the confines of their personalities. They found constructive outlets for their surplus vigor, learned how to plan their work to allow for their restlessness, and developed controls over their impulsiveness. The traits that had been such a liability to them in their earlier years were being balanced in part by their energy and ambition and by their usually outgoing, aggressive, relatively uninhibited natures. These youngsters will probably find a niche in adult life where they can use their personality to advantage, and so become happy and useful citizens in spite of their difficult years in school.

On the other hand, the picture was not all rosy. Three out of four of these teen-agers were giving their parents a great deal of trouble because they would not obey rules in the home; many of them were moody and suffered from a lack of self-esteem accompanied by a "chip on the shoulder"; many were still having trouble in school. A minority—eighteen out of the total of eighty-three, or one in five—had more serious troubles: long histories of lying, stealing, fighting, destructiveness, and other antisocial behavior.

It is only fair to point out that the youngsters in this study may have been worse off than most hyperactive youngsters, since they had been referred for psychiatric counseling. Furthermore, they had not received the kind of treatment that we would regard as adequate today. They were seen rather infrequently at the clinic; their parents received little guidance on the practical matters of day-to-day life; and very little contact was made with the schools. We relied much more on medication than we do today and less on trying to help the children in other ways. Finally, at the time of follow-up, these teen-agers were still in school, the most difficult environment for the hyperactive personality.

Family Incidence

Additional evidence for ascribing hyperactivity to inborn temperament is the finding that in some cases it seems to be familial.

We were struck by the many anecdotes we had heard about the relatives—usually the fathers or uncles—of hyperactive children and decided to look into the families of the children who were coming for treatment to our clinic at St. Louis Children's Hospital. We studied the families of fifty hyperactive children and of fifty children matched for age, sex, and socioeconomic background who had come to the hospital for other reasons—tonsillectomies and so forth.

We found that the relatives—especially the male relatives—of hyperactive children were more likely to have had a history of difficulties in childhood that suggested hyperactivity than were the relatives of the control group of children. The finding is consistent with the impression of many people who work with these young-sters that their fathers or mothers are hyperactive children grown up, that is, they are restless, superenergetic, and given to snap judgments and outbursts of temper. Sometimes the "hyperactive-child syndrome" passes from one generation to the other. Our find-ings have recently been confirmed by Dr. Dennis Cantwell of the University of California at Los Angeles.

We have also studied the legal parents of adopted hyperactive children. There had been no more childhood or adult psychiatric problems among the adoptive parents and other relatives than there were among parents and relatives of the controls. This led us to conclude that hyperactivity passes from parents to children more through genes than through training or some other psychological process.

We have presented some of the evidence suggesting that hyper-activity is a kind of temperament and that therefore it can most often be considered a normal variant of personality, though cer-tainly a difficult one for parents and teachers to cope with. We do not mean that the behavior of a hyperactive child and his fate can-not be changed. There is a widespread but mistaken assumption that behavior determined by inheritance, or by damage to the brain, cannot be influenced. This is not true. If it were, we would not be writing this book. We know that hyperactive children can be taught self-control, can be made to follow directions, and can be raised to think of themselves as worthwhile.

We particularly want to qualify what has been said in this chap-ter about inheritance. We found a higher incidence of adult prob-lems, such as heavy drinking, in the families of hyperactive chil-dren. This does not mean that the children inherit "bad genes" or that they will necessarily have such problems themselves. Rela-tives who were hyperactive children may have had unhappy experiences that in turn caused emotional problems more serious than the hyperactivity itself.

Mrs. Smith is afraid that her seven-year-old behaves as her brother did as a boy; the brother is now an alcoholic. As a child he was loving and affectionate, but at times he was wild. At six, he turned over the baby carriage in which his little sister was sleeping, and, at ten, waving a butcher knife, he chased the family maid out of the house. Unfortunately, little was done to control his wildness. His distressed parents did not know what to do. Eventually, they more or less "wrote him off" and lavished their love on Mrs. Smith. The brother's behavior became worse. He alienated more people, thought less of himself, and ended up with a serious drinking problem.

The brother's history followed a sad and familiar pattern. Over and over again we hear this kind of story about a delinquent or antisocial relative of a hyperactive child. When we look closely into the story, we find evidence of hyperactivity in childhood and evidence that this individual did not get the "hyper-parenting" that might have helped him to grow up healthy and happy.

We have no evidence to prove that antisocial behavior can be prevented by following the guidelines we set forth, but we have observed that spirited children who grow up in well-disciplined but kindly homes seem more likely to develop positive goals than do children growing up in homes where parents are confused and uncertain about how to handle them.

Implications for Parents of the Causes of Hyperactivity

It is obvious that we cannot ascribe hyperactivity to a single cause. Hyperactivity is a general term that can be applied to very different children who happen to share some patterns of behavior, which are probably determined by many different factors. In any case, no matter what caused your child's hyperactivity, several things should be clear to you, the most important of which are, first of all, that there is no cause for guilt, and, second, that there is cause to believe that you can help your child lead a happier life.

Suppose you suspect that your child's hyperactivity can be traced to problems with your pregnancy and the baby's birth—or to some illness or injury in his early life. Instead of berating yourself for having allowed these things to happen, concentrate on the present and on what you can do for your child now. Remember—today is not only the first day of the rest of your life but of the rest of your child's life as well.

Suppose your child's temperament is so much like yours that you are convinced he got your "hyperactive genes." Suppose further that you are giving your child an example of hyperactive behavior by the way you yourself act. Even if the first supposition is true, remember that you did not consciously set out to pass on your child's genetic legacy. You had no control over your genes and none over those you passed on to your child. You are what you are, and he is what he is. You do, of course, have much more control over the second supposition. But you still have to remember that just as you cannot magically change your energetic, restless, impatient child into someone with an entirely different personality, you cannot make yourself over completely, either. You can make yourself aware of those things that you are doing that are not helpful in your family situation, and you will be surprised to realize how much you can change. But there is no point in berating yourself for having failed as a parent, for having "made a mess" of your child. Guilt and self-blame will not help you to help your youngster.

Feelings of guilt come only too naturally to the parent of a hyperactive child. After you have started off the day with a tirade, when you had promised yourself to be more patient, after you have lost your temper for the tenth time in a day for something you know deep down your youngster cannot help, after you have fought with your spouse because neither of you knows what to do next—you are likely to feel you are making a bad situation worse and to worry because you cannot see a way out. All parents have ambivalent feelings toward their children; all parents say and do things they wish they had not; most parents fight with each other over their children. The parents of the hyperactive child—a "regular boy, only more so"—do all these things, only more so, and end up feeling more guilt. The guilt holds you back from being effective with your child.

Once you stop burdening yourself with self-recriminations, you can start to act. You do not have to be a superwoman or superman to be a superparent. But you do have to invest more time and thought in raising this child than with any of your other children. You can help your child cope with his own special personality; you can help him to maintain, or to restore, a good self-image, so that he will act in accordance with his self-esteem. You can influence his innate characteristics in a positive direction with loving care, firm handling, and an awareness of specific techniques that bring results.

Children must, if they are to grow, feel certain that their parents are strong enough to protect them against their own wayward impulses.

—Harold Loukes
Friends and Their Children

4   WHO CAN HELP?

It was an unexceptional morning in five-year-old Eric's life. He had started to finger-paint in his room, until the walls, floor, and furniture were spotted with red, yellow, and blue daubs. Then he decided to polish Daddy's shoes. Eric wondered how the brown shoe polish would look on the beige walls in his father's bedroom. He found out. As his mother was preparing lunch, Eric was scattering his own scuffed shoes and sneakers on the sidewalk below his window. When he went downstairs to get them, he decided to take his two-year-old sister for a walk—during which the two tots crossed a heavily trafficked street.

Eric's parents were at their wits' end. Nothing in their lives had prepared them for bringing up this child. None of the child-rearing books they had read said anything about a child like Eric. None of their friends or relatives were able to give them any helpful advice. They longed for September, when Eric would be in kindergarten—yet dreaded the calls from the teacher that they feared would come. Husband and wife quarreled constantly about the boy, blaming each other for not handling him right. "If only you would . . ." was the refrain.

At the end of a particularly trying day—which most days seem to be with a child like Eric—a father and mother are likely to look at each other, sigh, and say, "We have to do something." In some cases, that "something" may involve a realization that this child is different from most other children and requires a special type of

34

parenting. Some parents may be able to step back and take an objective look at their child and their responses to him. They may be able to spot specific problems and change their methods of dealing with their child, according to guidelines set forth in Part II of this book. Others may need more help.

The typical hyperactive child, like Eric, is not "sick." His care need not be turned over to a medical or psychological specialist but is better left in the hands of his parents. However, in the many cases when parents are overwrought and worried about their child and cannot agree on how to help him, it is a good idea to seek professional help.

There is no precise criterion for telling when it is wise to seek a professional opinion about a child. The most important measure is the way the parents feel. If you feel you have a problem, you do. You may take your fears to a professional, only to have them allayed and to be told that whatever has been distressing you is but a normal stage of growing up. Or you may be told that you do indeed have a problem, but one whose solution is in your own hands. On the other hand, your child's behavior may be symptomatic of a deeper problem that requires evaluation and treatment by an expert.

Very often, it is the parent who spends the most time with a child—usually the mother—who recognizes first that the child needs extra help. The father of a hyperactive child tends to resist the notion that anything is wrong. He may object strenuously to the notion that his son is different from the average child. He may actively resist professional guidance, especially from a psychologist or psychiatrist. Meanwhile, the atmosphere in the house becomes more and more tense. If one parent feels that the child needs help, that parent has an obligation to herself (or himself) and especially to the child. *Even if the other parent does not agree on the seriousness of the situation, it is vital to look for help and to continue seeking until you reach someone who can tell you whether your child really has a problem.*

Some hyperactive children do need special attention before they get to school. If you are concerned about the behavior of your preschooler, there is nothing to be lost by seeking professional advice. If the problem is mild, you will be reassured, and if the problem is more severe, the sooner you get help, the better off everyone in the family will be.

You might ask yourself several questions that will help you to decide whether your child is hyperactive.

The following questions apply to a preschooler:
- Does your child stay up half the night playing and then wake up at the crack of dawn, so that you hardly get any sleep yourself?
- Is he far more active, restless, and energetic than other children his age?
- Does his attention span seem much shorter than that of other children his age?
- Does he throw temper tantrums for trivial reasons and do this regularly and often?
- Is he so hard on things that he has worn out or broken his playpen, crib, or tricycle?
- Is he persistently impulsive, running into the street, playing with electrical sockets, jumping from dangerous places like the top of the refrigerator, or drinking household cleaners?
- When he is outside, do you have to supervise him much more closely than the other parents on the block watch their children, for fear he will run off or do something wild?
- Does he bite, kick, and scratch other children, or attack them often?
- Is he unusually willful and disobedient?

These questions apply to a school-age child:
- Is it very hard for him to be still? Does he seem to have boundless energy?
- Does his attention span seem much shorter than that of other children his age, especially for things requiring an effort?
- Does he talk, fidget, rock, drum his fingers a lot?

- Do his emotions swing rapidly from excitement to anger? Does he cry easily and often?
- Is he hard to get to bed at night?
- Does he continually get up from the table or play during meal-times?
- Is he having trouble in school, either with his academic work or because of his behavior?
- Does he usually leave projects unfinished?
- Does punishment seem to have no effect on his behavior?
- Does he seem unhappy much of the time? Is he whiny and irri-table? Does he complain that "no one likes me"?

If you are answering an emphatic "yes" to several of the questions, you should probably seek professional counsel. You may save your family years of misery.

FINDING HELP

Pediatrician or Family Doctor

The first person consulted by parents of a hyperactive child usually is—and should be—the child's pediatrician or the general practitioner who treats the entire family. This physician knows your child and your family. He should be the person to coordinate all your child's medical care. He should make any necessary referrals to specialists and receive reports from them.

Your child should have a complete physical examination every year. When you take him to the physician because you are concerned about his behavior, the doctor may want to re-examine him, even if only a short time has elapsed since the annual checkup. This is so the doctor can rule out the possibility of any physical problems that may have developed during the last visit. Physical illness or defects in vision or hearing can affect a child's behavior.

After the physical examination, it is important for both father and mother (even if the parents are separated or divorced) to speak privately to the doctor about the child. If this poses a problem because there are no facilities for having the child cared for in another room, another appointment may have to be made to allow both parents plenty of time to tell the doctor their concerns about the child.

The physician has the experience to recognize the point at which a youngster's behavior differs markedly from that of others his age. He is usually in a better position to judge a child's behavior than the parents, whose experience is generally limited to their own children.

Your doctor will discuss *his* diagnosis with you after he has examined your child and listened to your story. He may feel that you are expecting a normally exuberant youngster to behave like an adult. He may reassure you that your child is acting in a perfectly normal way for his age.

It is possible that your doctor will tell you to relax and wait for your child to "grow out of" his current troublesome behavior patterns. If your expectations *have* been unrealistic, this is good advice. But many parents who have recognized at an early age that their child has a problem have been lulled by this type of "nonadvice," only to see their child's problems wax larger. "I can't tell you how many people told us Ricky would 'outgrow' his behavior, and the worst part of it was that we believed them and so did nothing for years, when we could have been helping this child," the mother of a thirteen-year-old boy says regretfully. If you are convinced that your child needs help *now,* do not wait. Do something—either with your doctor's help or without it.

If your doctor is knowledgeable and willing to take the time, he can be a tremendous help to you and your child by providing necessary medical care, making appropriate referrals, giving practical advice on home management, and, in general, serving as a source of understanding support to both child and parents.

If the doctor wants to refer your child to some other specialist, ask him why he is making this recommendation. It is perfectly appropriate to ask the probable cost of the evaluations, as well as anything else that may be on your mind.

If you are not satisfied with your doctor's conclusions and advice, you should feel free to discuss with him your feelings about your child's problems. You might ask the doctor what he thinks about hyperactivity. (Some physicians reject the notion completely, although most are aware of the problem.)

Mrs. Court had tried for years to have a baby and finally did have one who turned out to be hyperactive. Few physicians would be as unhelpful as the one who told her, "Well, you wanted children. Now that you have one, don't come complaining to me." But many doctors are extremely busy. They do not have the time that they would like to devote to helping parents with day-to-day problems. Also, most doctors are more confident about diagnosing and treating physical ailments than psychological ones.

If you feel that your family doctor or pediatrician does not understand your child's problem, you should try to find one who does. If your doctor is unable or unwilling to refer you to another source of help, you can look further yourself.

Finding Other Sources of Help

Someone from your child's school—a social worker, psychologist, or guidance counselor, perhaps—may be able to make a helpful referral. Your state, county, or municipal medical society may be able to refer you to a psychiatrist. Or a look at the yellow pages of your telephone directory (under "Social Service and Welfare Organizations" or "Mental Health Clinics") may help you to locate a facility that provides a wide range of services. Such a facility might be a hospital-affiliated child development clinic that offers medical, psychiatric, psychological, and social-work services. Or you might consult a learning center associated with a hospital or university that evaluates children with school problems, diagnoses the source of the trouble, and prescribes remedial programs. Helpful psychiatric and psychological services may be provided by a child guidance clinic, provided the clinic is staffed by persons who recognize that children's problems are not always due to deep-seated emotional conflicts. If you live in a small community, you might want to go first to a family service agency that is likely to be staffed mostly by social workers but also to have available the services of psychiatric and psychological consultants.

You may get information on the closest sources of help by writing to one of the following:

Association for Children with Learning Disabilities
2200 Brownsville Road
Pittsburgh, Pa. 15210
National Association for Mental Health
1800 North Kent Street
Rosslyn Station
Arlington, Va. 22209
Family Service Association of America
44 East 23rd Street
New York, N.Y. 10010

Psychiatrist

A psychiatrist is a doctor who graduated from medical school and then went on to specialize in psychological medicine. The fact that he or she has had medical training as well as education in mental illness means that a psychiatrist is equipped to recognize the physical aspects of emotional difficulties. In the case of hyperactivity, which may have a physiological origin, this is especially helpful. There are psychiatrists who specialize in working with children; they are particularly likely to be helpful to you.

Years ago, there was a considerable stigma attached to consulting a psychiatrist. Many people felt that this was an admission of "craziness" or "nervous breakdown." Today psychiatry is widely accepted. Many parents whose children have experienced difficulties have found that psychiatric evaluation and treatment have helped them and their child to get on the right road.

The problems a hyperactive child has in school, his difficulties in making friends, and the awareness of his parents' disappointment in him, chip away at his self-esteem. A psychiatrist can help a child see the reasons for such feelings, understand himself better, and recognize his assets.

The parents of a hyperactive child often derive great benefit themselves from seeing a psychiatrist. At a loss over what to do about their child, they tend to take their frustrations out on each other. A psychiatrist can help parents recognize and deal with their own feelings about their child's problems, including the burden of guilt that too many parents carry, their feelings of depression, and their eroded self-confidence. He or she can also advise parents on how best to deal with their child's difficult behavior, explain the results of psychological tests to the parents and teachers, and give specific advice to the teachers.

Before you take your child to a psychiatrist, you will want to prepare him for the visit. You might simply say to him that you feel he is having difficulties—either with school, with his friends, or within the family (whichever seems to trouble him most)—and you want him to have some help. You might also say that you want some help in understanding these problems. You can describe the psychiatrist as a doctor who helps people figure out why they are sad or angry or worried and who helps them find a way to do something about their troubles.

Psychologist

A psychologist is a person who has an advanced degree in psychology, the scientific study of human behavior. Some psychologists have been trained specifically to work with children. This person's key role in the treatment of a hyperactive child is to assess the child's intellectual capabilities and handicaps, and to observe his behavioral style. This function is especially important for children who are having trouble in school. The psychologist can provide a teaching prescription for the child's classroom teacher, spelling out the best ways to help the child learn.

The psychologist will hold a personal interview with the child and do a battery of tests. Prepare your child for his visit to the psychologist by telling him that he will probably be asked some questions, get a chance to work out some problems, and do some puzzles. Let him know that these "games," besides being fun for him, will help the psychologist find what he is best at and why he has difficulties. Avoid putting any pressure on your child to perform.

We will briefly describe some of the tests that the psychologist may give your child.

The Stanford-Binet Intelligence Scale. Performance on this test yields an "intelligence quotient," or I.Q., based on how your child does compared to the average child of his age. The Stanford-Binet asks the child to give the meanings of various words, to identify the missing parts in a picture, to trace mazes, and to show an understanding of numbers.

The Wechsler Intelligence Scale for Children. This test measures verbal and performance abilities separately and gives an I.Q. for each. The WISC provides some good clues to whether there are problems with language development (suggested by a verbal I.Q. significantly lower than a performance I.Q.) or with visuo-motor functions (if the performance I.Q. is much lower than the verbal I.Q.). In the verbal sections of the WISC a child demonstrates his understanding of what he reads and what he hears, his ability to see similarities among various items, and his memory span. The performance subtests ask him to put the finishing touches on incomplete pictures, to arrange sets of pictures in logical order, to assemble objects, to reproduce block designs, and to trace mazes.

The Jastak Wide Range Achievement Test (WRAT) measures a child's achievements in academic work—how well he reads, spells, and does arithmetic. When the psychologist looks at the scores for both the intelligence and achievement tests, he can see how bright the child is and how his performance compares with his potential.

Tests that pick up signs of possible brain injury are the Bender Visual Motor Gestalt, in which the child is asked to copy certain geometric figures, and the Benton Visual Retention Test, in which the child draws figures after having seen them for only a few seconds. The Wepman Test for Auditory Discrimination and the Illinois Test for Psycholinguistic Abilities (ITPA) pick up difficulties in perceiving visual and auditory stimuli and in responding to them.

While giving these tests, the psychologist can observe the child's behavior in a situation somewhat like the classroom. He or she can see how the youngster tackles the various tasks and can draw conclusions about the child's self-confidence, his adeptness, and his tendencies toward restlessness, distractibility, impulsiveness, and poor frustration tolerance.

A battery of tests may take about four hours to perform. The psychologist then has to go over the test results to score them and to interpret them in the light of the child's history and behavior during the testing. Because of the time and skill involved, psychological testing tends to be expensive, often costing about $200.

The psychologist's contribution is twofold: first, in giving the parents and teachers an accurate estimate of the child's actual potential, thus helping them to develop realistic expectations for him, and second, in prescribing an individualized teaching program geared to the needs of the child.

Parents sometimes overestimate the abilities of their children and form unrealistically high aspirations for them. This is particularly common in the case of a hyperactive child, who may have been precocious in his physical development and who may talk a great deal and show interest in many different activities. The fact that Stanley appears to be brighter than he actually is really aggravates his problems, because when his schoolwork does not measure up to the expectations of his parents and teachers, they blame him for not working harder. Stanley is then considered an underachiever, a lazy fellow or just plain unco-operative, when he may, in fact, have adopted some of these very postures because he himself recognizes the impossibility of meeting overambitious standards.

In other instances, parents underestimate their children. A very bright child may seem to be hyperactive in school because he is bored. Or, if he is genuinely hyperactive, his behavior may be much worse. Since he does not receive the intellectual challenge that he needs, he misbehaves to make life more interesting. Or, realizing he is not making progress, he may start clowning around to boost his morale. A youngster like this needs special stimulation in school and perhaps at home, too. He may benefit from intellectual enrichment within the classroom or even from being skipped into a higher grade, although this practice is becoming rarer and rarer in our public schools.

On the basis of the testing and interview results, the psychologist is often able to develop an individualized "prescription" teaching program for the child.

Educational Consultant

Another specialist can help a child who is having troubles in school. This person, who holds an advanced degree in education and is particularly knowledgeable about special education, may also be called an educational therapist or a psychoeducational diagnostician. Such a specialist meets with parents and child, administers tests, and makes referrals to other specialists if indicated. The consultant also goes into the child's classroom to observe the child, the teacher, and the classroom dynamics. After making an educational diagnosis, the consultant meets with the child's teacher to develop a prescriptive teaching program. Regular consultations with parents, child, and school faculty allow for an ongoing evaluation of the progress of the prescriptive program and, if necessary, for modifications of it.

Neurologist

A neurologist is a physician who specializes in diseases of the nervous system. A detailed neurological examination need not be part of the routine work-up for a child with behavior problems.

It is indicated *only* for certain specific situations—if, for example, your child has exhibited such symptoms as delayed speech or speech that is hard to understand, serious clumsiness, convulsions, double vision, continuing or severe headaches, lapses of consciousness, recurrent or continuing dizziness, an unexplainable decline in the level of school work, or a sudden change of personality. Such symptoms would raise the possibility of a brain disorder.

You can prepare your child for the neurological examination by pointing out the specific problems he has been having, that is, his clumsiness, or his hard-to-understand speech, or his troubles in school. Explain that a neurologist is a doctor who knows a lot about the brain and how we use it to control our bodies, and that he helps children with problems like your child's. Some children are comforted by knowing that the neurologist never gives shots. Tell your child what the examination will be like. He will probably be asked to strip down to his underwear, so that the doctor may see more clearly how he uses his body and how his reflexes are working. The doctor will check his eyes, his ears, and his sense of touch in a number of ways. He will ask your child to perform a wide variety of simple motions, such as raising the eyebrows, winking, standing on one foot, holding his arms straight out in front of him, tapping rhythmically, touching his finger to his nose, tying his shoelaces, and walking a straight line. He will check the child's reflexes by tapping him with a rubber hammer and also by scratching him very lightly.

During the physical examination of the child, the neurologist looks for "soft" and "hard" signs of neurological impairment. Soft signs are slight deviations from the statistical norms in the performance of certain tasks and in physical appearance. These deviations are found more frequently in persons with impairment of the central nervous system but are also found in many, many normal individuals. By themselves, they do not point to brain injury. But if soft signs are found in quantity and are accompanied by other evidence, the neurologist may suspect physiological impairment. Hard signs are those not found in normal children.

The neurologist may perform an electroencephalogram (EEG) or may send you to a laboratory where this test may be run. An EEG measures the electrical activity of an individual's brain. It sounds and looks quite complicated, since it involves apparatus with many fine wires that are either pasted to the youngster's scalp or inserted into its surface. The paste is painless but messy, which means that an EEG performed according to this procedure is usually followed closely by a shampoo. When the wires are inserted instead, there is some slight discomfort but no real pain. If your child is scheduled for an EEG, find out ahead of time how the apparatus will be attached, so that you can better prepare him for the experience. He may be cheered to know that the electrodes attached to his head are very like those worn by astronauts in space.

The electroencephalogram is particularly helpful in the detection of brain-wave patterns suggesting epilepsy.

On the whole, hyperactive children seem to show more soft signs and more abnormalities on the EEG than do children with no behavior and/or learning problems. Even so, these findings tell little about the individual child, because many children who exhibit hyperactive behavior and/or learning disabilities show no neurological abnormalities and many normal children show EEG abnormalities and soft signs. In addition, different examiners often draw different conclusions from the same electroencephalograms, casting doubt on the validity of these measures. Moreover, even when the doctor suspects some minor organic component to your child's problems, the treatment recommended may still be more psychological and educational than medical.

So, you say, why go through an expensive, time-consuming procedure like a neurological examination? Only, as we said earlier, to rule out a disorder of the nervous system that would require specific treatment. If your child does not display any of the symptoms described above, a neurological examination would probably be an unnecessary financial burden.

Speech and Hearing Specialist

If your child's speech development is slow, or if he has a marked speech impediment, or if you suspect that some of his difficulties may be due to hearing defects, you should take him to a speech and hearing specialist, who evaluates a child's hearing and language functions and can carry out corrective therapy.

Parents' Organization

Joining an organization of parents who have concerns similar to yours can be enormously helpful. It can give you the feeling that you are not alone—that others also cope with the problems that seem unique. It can provide practical assistance: you can get helpful literature, learn about educational, recreational, and medical facilities in your community, and keep informed about pertinent local, state, and federal legislation. A parents' group can be an effective lobbying force to influence governmental agencies to conduct important research and provide essential services.

One parents' organization that is particularly interested in the problems of hyperactive children is the Association for Children with Learning Disabilities (2200 Brownsville Road, Pittsburgh, Pa. 15210). ACLD sponsors an annual international conference, publishes regular newsletters, distributes literature on learning disabilities, and participates in research projects. Local ACLD affiliates usually hold regular meetings, compile information on community services, publish their own regional newsletters, and sponsor workshops for teachers.

Founded in 1964, ACLD now has more than 300 chapters in forty states, with a total membership of about 20,000 parents and professional persons. ACLD's board of directors is made up entirely of parents of children with learning disabilities, who are guided by the professional advisory board. Membership in the group ranges from parents of children with relatively mild problems in school to those who are severely brain-injured.

People and Places to Avoid

Parents who feel they have tried everything and gone everywhere are often so desperate to find help for their child that they
will seek assistance from individuals or agencies that promise much
but actually give little. One example of agencies in this question-
able category is the private learning center that is franchised to
operate as a business. Some of these centers may do a good job,
but too many others charge exorbitant fees for poor programs run
by inexperienced teachers.

To find out whether an individual or an agency is likely to offer
the right kind of help for your child, ask yourself these questions:

- Does the treatment sound like a simple solution to your complex
  problem?
- Are enthusiastic claims for success made for a specific treatment
  that cannot be backed up by reports published in respected professional journals?
- Does someone whose professional opinion you respect have a
  good word to say about the treatment? Such a person might be
  your own doctor, the school psychologist, or a child development specialist at a university or hospital.
- Are you asked to sign an expensive, long-term, unbreakable
  contract? If so, you should be extremely wary. A reputable professional person or agency charges only for services rendered
  and leaves the client free to stop participating at any time.

Never hesitate to ask a professional person or the representative of an agency for qualifying credentials. Some information you
might want to know about individuals would include the degrees
they hold from accredited universities, their memberships in professional organizations, and their experience and backgrounds. Information that can help you judge an agency would relate to its
affiliation with an accredited hospital or university and to the credentials of the professional persons on the staff.

Specific Therapies

As we have said and will continue to say, in most cases the parents and teachers of a hyperactive child can resolve the youngster's difficulties by changing their methods of dealing with him. In those cases, however, when parents and teachers are stymied about how to change or what to change, professional help can be invaluable. One or several of the following therapeutic programs can often give the child and his family a boost toward the solutions of his problems.

Counseling and Psychotherapy for Parents

Psychotherapy is a broad term covering any kind of help aiming to alleviate emotional difficulties. It usually works at two levels: a deep one, which attempts to relieve pent-up feelings of anger and fear that have been keeping an individual from functioning at optimum levels, and a more pragmatic, immediate one, which involves the individual in working rationally toward effective social behavior. Psychotherapy may be short-term, with a definite goal set in terms of time (usually up to twelve weekly sessions), or it may be more open-ended, lasting as long as the therapist and the client feel that help is needed. Counseling, which generally implies the offering of practical advice to deal with specific situations, can be an important element of psychotherapy. The type of psychotherapy most helpful to parents of a hyperactive child has a large component of counseling on day-to-day management of the child.

Psychotherapy is more valuable for the parents of a hyperactive child than it is for the child himself. This is not because the parents are emotionally "sick." But the problems they face in dealing with their child usually leave them worried, anxious, resentful, frustrated, and beset by feelings of hopelessness and inadequacy. Such feelings naturally can plunge parents into deep wells of depression. Add to this the disagreements and mutual recriminations between husband and wife that often dig a chasm between them. Psychotherapy for the parents allows both to air their feelings toward each other in the neutral setting of the therapist's office and to find out precisely how and why they disagree about the management of their child. Therapy can also offer the parents some very specific advice and help in redesigning the way they handle their child.

By the time a child's problems have loomed large, it is difficult for many parents to figure out solutions on their own. Obviously, whatever they have been doing up to this point has not helped. The parents may realize that they have been heading in the wrong direction without knowing how to change their course. Ideally, this is what psychotherapy should provide—a navigational chart that enables the parents to set a goal and steer toward it as directly as possible.

Every child benefits when his parents agree on a course of action, when there is harmony in the home, and when his parents feel assured that they are doing the right thing. Any psychotherapy that helps parents to feel surer of themselves and more secure in their own capabilities is bound to have a good effect on the child.

Parent Discussion Groups

"No matter how much the doctor tells you that your child's behavior problem isn't your fault, you keep blaming yourself, wondering what you're doing wrong, how you're failing your child. And nobody else seems to understand. Or, at least, nobody did until my husband and I came to this group," says the mother of nine-year-old Barry.

"Here in the group I know that we're not the only ones who sometimes hate our child, we're not the only ones who feel baffled because we don't know what to do. When you see other couples who seem like perfectly nice, normal, loving parents, and they have the same problems, you begin to think that you're not so bad yourselves," says the father of six-year-old Barbara.

"The problems we had with Billy were driving us up the wall, but when we spoke with other parents who had had some of the same ones and had been able to figure out ways to do something about them, it helped us. We put into practice some of the ideas that had worked for the other parents in our group, and we were thrilled to find out that some of them worked for us, too," says Billy's mother.

These comments all came from different parents who have taken part in parent discussion groups conducted by professional leaders—psychiatrist, psychologist, or social worker. Their comments fairly well sum up the benefits of taking part in such a group—the support and practical help that parents receive from being able to share their experiences with other families in the same boat. Each family benefits as much or more from hearing the experiences and ideas of the other parents as it does from listening to the psychotherapist. Hearing other parents talk about their problems, it is often possible to see what they are doing wrong, and then to come to the amazing conclusion that you have been doing the same thing. On the other hand, parents in these groups are often able to exchange solutions to similar problems. When a parent hears advice from another parent, he or she knows that the advice being given comes right from the trenches—and not from way behind the lines. The advice carries more weight; it is apt to be taken more seriously and to be acted on sooner and more vigorously.

The groups have other advantages over private counseling. Many persons feel more comfortable in a group setting than in individual therapy. And then there is the economic benefit: since several families share the cost of paying the leader, the out-of-pocket cost is much less than private counseling sessions would be.

Such a group may exist in the community where you live. If not, you might be able to get one started. If you want to organize a parents' discussion group, your best bet would probably be to find five or six other couples who would be interested—possibly through your school psychologist, your pediatrician, your local ACLD chapter, or even through a classified ad in your local newspaper. Once you have the nucleus of a group, you might approach a representative of a community mental health agency, a family service agency, your school district, your local ACLD chapter, a child guidance clinic, child development center, or a psychotherapist in private practice. Chances are that one of these sources is bound to yield a trained group leader who would be interested in conducting a parents' discussion series.

Psychotherapy for the Child

The kind of psychotherapy that aims to restructure a child's personality is, in most cases, a nonproductive drain on the emotions and finances of the entire family. Until children enter adolescence, they are rarely introspective enough to talk much about their feelings or able to try to redesign their behavior on a conscious level. A number of studies on child psychotherapy have concluded that children benefit no more from such therapy than they would from the passage of time alone. Psychotherapy and counseling for the parents who are dealing with the child on an intimate daily basis is likely to be much more fruitful.

Anthony F. Donofrio, Ph.D., a psychotherapist who has worked with children for twenty-two years in child guidance clinics and in private practice, recently concluded in an article in *Mental Hygiene* that child psychotherapy is usually a hindrance rather than a help. We agree heartily with this statement by Dr. Donofrio: "If one grants the premise that a child's psychological well-being depends on the fulfillment of his basic needs, and that his ego is still in a dependent relationship, then how can one, or even two hours a week of expensive play or interview sessions truly serve this child's ego when in the other 167 hours, the significant adults in his life are often unwittingly blocking need fulfillment by omission or commission, by misconception and confusion."

Despite the limitations of child psychotherapy, however, there is sometimes some value to having a child see a therapist. If a child suffers from very low self-esteem, it may be well worth offering him supportive psychotherapy—the chance to talk about his worries with a friendly and sympathetic person, who can reassure the youngster that he is going to come out okay. If a child is particularly introspective, he may be able to discuss his social problems and his own feelings of incompetence with a therapist. An older preadolescent or a teen-ager may profit from a combination of individual psychotherapy and of sessions that involve other members of the family, either one at a time or as a complete family. In these family sessions, realistic compromises on questions of rules and discipline can often be hammered out. Group therapy can be an important influence on a disaffected teen-ager, with peer pressures helping him to direct his behavior along more constructive lines.

If you seek a psychiatric consultation, both the parents and the child should see the therapist, so that he or she can size up the child and get some insight into the relationships within the family. The therapist may want to see the child a few more times to learn more about how the child feels about himself, his family, school, and his place in the world. Sometimes these feelings emerge in the way a child plays, the kinds of drawings he makes, or the stories he makes up. This kind of therapeutic involvement, then, is more of a diagnostic nature to help the therapist in understanding the child's situation.

Educational Remediation

After a child has been tested by a psychologist or educational consultant and has been found to have specific learning disabilities, a custom-tailored, special-education program can help his school progress considerably, and at the same time boost his self-esteem. A child *feels* more adequate when he *is* more adequate, when he proves to himself that he can make progress in school.

A remediation program will usually help a child to master those areas in which he is weak by teaching to his strengths. A child with a disability in visual perception can learn to read by concentrating on the way words sound (by learning phonics) or on the way words feel (by feeling sandpaper letters or by tracing letters with the fingers). A child who cannot remember what he hears can learn better with such visual aids as filmstrips, charts, and maps.

The modern classroom has access to a wide variety of teaching tools that can be used to help children who have problems of co-ordination, perception, and concepts of time and space. And teach-ers are often ingenious in devising new techniques to help such children. You are lucky if you live in a school district that provides classes small enough to allow for such individualized teaching and that hires teachers who are both interested and specially trained in providing special educational help. If your school district does not have such facilities, one of your highest priorities should be to work with other parents for such services. Meanwhile, you may be able to find a private educational therapist to help your child. Or you may be able to work with him yourself.

Counseling and Support for Teachers

The teacher who wants to help a hyperactive child do better in school is often just as much in the dark about what to do as are the child's parents. Too few institutions of teacher training place much, if any, emphasis on the special needs of the many restless, distractible, overactive youngsters a teacher is likely to encounter during his or her career. And even when the teacher does have a theoretical background for understanding these children, she needs practical information to help her teach them.

The teacher needs information that will help her form realistic expectations of the child's capabilities, such as the results of psy-chological evaluations of the child's personality and potential and the educational recommendations. She needs to know what kinds of techniques are most likely to help this child do well in the class-room, both academically and socially. She needs to have access to someone who can give her specific advice on managing this child.

The teacher, therefore, should be in fairly close communication with the professional person who is overseeing the child most closely—usually the pediatrician or psychiatrist. Sometimes the school social worker or guidance counselor facilitates this inter-disciplinary communication. But if you know that your child's teacher has not been informed about the assessments made about your child, you should certainly intervene. Ask the teacher to call the doctor, or vice versa. You are entitled to expect this sort of ongoing interest and concern from both your child's doctor and his teacher.

Drug Therapy

Physicians often prescribe medication for hyperactive children. The increasingly common practice of treating behavior and aca-demic problems with drugs has so many ramifications that the whole of Chapter 14 is devoted to a discussion of medication for hyperactive children: which drugs are most commonly prescribed, what the effects are, and when they are or are not indicated.

The major contribution of the professional persons cited in this chapter is their ability to give parents and teachers the tools to help a child forge a successful life. Since the child's parents and teach-ers will, by and large, be the wielders of these tools, the rest of this book is devoted to advice in dealing with the common, everyday problems of raising and teaching the hyperactive child.

PART II

How to Help Your Child at Home

The common idea that success spoils people by making them vain, egotistic, and self-complacent is erroneous; on the contrary, it makes them, for the most part, humble, tolerant, and kind. Failure makes people bitter and cruel.

—W. Somerset Maugham
The Summing Up

5 HELPING YOUR CHILD
TO LIKE HIMSELF

Throughout the first part of this book we have been repeating our conviction that parents can help their children to fulfill their potential, even when those children are so energetic, impulsive, and restless that they are called "hyperactive." The hyperactive child *is* different from the average child; his difference is, however, a matter of proportion more than kind. He is a child who requires parenting to the nth degree. *So, while the suggestions offered in this chapter and the ones to follow are applicable in the raising of any child, they are most important for bringing up the youngster at the hyperactive end of the scale.*

The most vital function of parents is establishing an atmosphere in which their children can thrive. Just as a gardener cares for a young seedling, giving it the right soil and care so that it will develop to the fullest extent, so do parents provide the nurture for the growth of their children. Recognition of the individual child's nature is essential to this process. No matter how skillful and hardworking a gardener is, he cannot make an oak sapling grow into a birch tree.

So it is with children. No matter how good we are as parents, we cannot change the temperament of a restless, impatient, irritable child into a paragon of amiability and perseverance. But we can provide the atmosphere that will help a child to make the most of his personality. We can help a youngster learn to value himself for the kind of person he is, rather than feel inferior because he is not the person we wanted him to be.

A crucial factor in a child's growing up into a happy, successful adult is the image that child has of himself. The person who thinks well of himself faces life with a happy, confident outlook. He feels that he can cope with whatever obstacles life throws in his path; he is not excessively burdened by self-doubt. Because he believes he *can* succeed in the goals he sets for himself, he generally *does* succeed. Since he radiates confidence and assurance, he is attractive to other people, who enjoy being in his company. Since he has respect for himself, he is free to respect and to love others. He is not likely to develop neurotic forms of behavior that will interfere with his successful functioning.

On the other hand, the person who thinks poorly of himself is handicapped. Expecting failure, he does not try hard to master tasks or to form relationships. His expectation of failure almost insures that he will fail. The more often he fails, the more his depressing self-image is likely to hold him back. A person like this tends to turn in on himself and become self-centered, chronically anxious and preoccupied with his own bodily symptoms because he has learned that he cannot cope with the outside world.

Parents of many hyperactive children are more distressed about their children's low level of self-esteem than they are about their children's behavior. A parent grieves to hear a child say, "Why was I born? I'm just no good," or "Why does everybody hate me? I must really be a weirdo." The mother of seven-year-old Emily expressed her feelings this way: "My main worry is to get Emily into adulthood feeling that she's a worthwhile person and that she doesn't have to do outlandish things to get people's attention."

What, then, can parents do to help their hyperactive children develop a sense of their own worth? In a book written chiefly for professionals but of importance for parents and teachers, *The Antecedents of Self-esteem,* Dr. Stanley Coopersmith, a psychologist at the University of California, tells us a great deal about the forces in a child's life that cause him to have a good opinion of himself. Dr. Coopersmith studied eighty-five ten-year-old to twelve-year-old boys, whose self-esteem, measured by various tests and rating scales, ranged from low to high. The boys and their mothers were interviewed separately to determine the relationships between self-esteem and other aspects of the boys' lives, including parental attitudes and practices.

Dr. Coopersmith suggests that an individual develops his image of himself according to his sense of acceptance, competence, virtue, and power. Acceptance implies the degree to which an individual feels he is approved of and loved by the important persons in his life; competence refers to his skills in performing tasks that he deems important and worthwhile; virtue, to his own assessment of how well he meets ethical and moral standards; and power, the extent to which he influences his own life and the lives of others. While a person may draw a favorable picture of himself if he rates high on some of these measures and low on others, the higher he rates on all four, the higher will be the esteem in which he holds himself.

We can translate these conclusions into practical terms especially for the families of hyperactive children and use them as guidelines in our thinking and in our day-to-day living.

Acceptance and Love

Acceptance of a child is of prime importance for his self-esteem. When we talk here about acceptance, we are talking about an overall positive attitude with many facets, all of which are important. Passive acceptance implies taking your child as he is, without feeling the need to make him over. More active acceptance embraces liking your child, respecting him, appreciating his good qualities, enjoying his company and, of course, loving him.

No child likes himself more than his parents do. While it is relatively easy for parents to accept bright, achieving, obedient children, it is more difficult to accept a child who seems to thwart them at every turn, who is hard to get along with, apparently intelligent but unaccountably behind in academic achievement. And while it is also relatively easy to accept the fact that a child with a broken leg cannot run races or that a youngster with defective hearing cannot heed spoken instructions, it is much more difficult to understand the limits imposed on a child by his temperament. Before a parent can accept his hyperactive child for what he is, the parent has to understand the syndrome of hyperactivity and how it affects the child's behavior. The parent needs to understand that the hyperactive child is not simply being willful when he continually misbehaves, but that to some extent he cannot help himself.

What Are His Good Qualities?

Parents can gain a new appreciation of their child if they make themselves list his good qualities. It seems to be a part of human nature to take for granted the things we like in life and to focus our attention on the things we do not like—in our jobs, our marriages, our children. So parents who are distraught because of a child's behavior or school problems may be able to look at him in a new light if they stop to recognize that he is affectionate, compassionate, imaginative, fearless, and truly penitent for misdeeds. Is he a good athlete? Does he have a lively sense of humor, a gift for salesmanship, or a flair for some artistic endeavor? Every child has some endearing or admirable traits. If you sit down to make a list of your child's good qualities, you may be astonished at the number that he has—and that you take for granted.

Acceptance Is Never Total

Acceptance of a child does not mean that you ignore his undesirable behavior or that you praise him for poor work. It does mean that you take him the way he is and do your best with what you have. You do not say, "David will have to learn not to tear his clothes"; you buy David sturdier clothes. You do not say,

"Bruce should know how to carry a pitcher of milk without spilling it"; you fill the pitcher only half full. You recognize that your child came to you with certain inborn characteristics, and you meet him halfway.

"Okay," you say. "I know my child has some good qualities. And I can even accept some of the impossible things he does and realize it isn't his fault. But I can't do it all the time. There are times when I don't like this child at all, times when I think I can't face spending another day listening to his whining, watching him pick on his little sister, nagging him to hurry up to meet the school bus.

"It's pretty tough to tell myself how great Adam's artistic ability is when I go into his room and see he's drawn with Magic Marker all over those walls it took me two days to paint. At times like these, I don't accept him, I don't like him, I don't love him. I just wish he'd never been born."

Every parent has these feelings from time to time. And the parents of a hyperactive child would not be human if they did not have them more often than most. You do not have to feel guilty about not being a perpetual fountain of love. You are not a monster because you lose your temper occasionally or because at times you just want to be left alone. If you have had any of these feelings—or some others that you think are so horrible you cannot even admit them to yourself—you have a lot of company.

Instead of burdening yourself with guilt, accept yourself. Accept the fact that no one is perfect, including parents. And go on from your own *self*-acceptance to try to build your life so that you can bring out all the positive feelings that you have about your child—the warmth that comes when you tiptoe into his room and see him sleeping peacefully or those feelings of love and remorse that crop up after he has just left for school in tears following a violent argument and you wish you could wipe out that whole morning. You can build on these sympathies to deal with your child in a way that will allow your loving feelings to come out and strengthen the bond between you and your youngster.

Speak Openly and Honestly with Your Child

Once you have accepted the fact that your child has certain basic characteristics that cannot be easily changed, you can help him to accept himself. Children usually respond well to an approach that recognizes their problems but helps them realize that everyone else has problems. For example, you might point out that Sean, who lives down the block, has poor eyesight and has to wear glasses, that Molly is fat, that Nicholas is painfully shy. Or you might point out some of your own deficiencies. Maybe you have a lot of trouble controlling your temper, or maybe you are so poorly co-ordinated that you're a washout on the tennis court, or maybe you do not have enough will power to give up smoking or go on a diet.

Once you have made the point that your child is not alone in having problems, you might say something along these lines: "We know that you sometimes act before you think and you sometimes do or say something that you're sorry for afterward. But just because you make some mistakes, this doesn't mean that you are not a worthwhile person. It just means that while Amy has to concentrate on improving her reading and Dexter has to learn to stick up for himself, you have to work hard on controlling your impulses."

While it is healthy to acknowledge with your child what his problems are, it is even more therapeutic to accentuate the positive with him. Make a special point of emphasizing to him, as objectively as possible, some of his good qualities. "You really deserve a lot of credit for winning that radio for selling the most raffles of anyone on your Little League team!" "We were really proud when we saw you sticking up for your little sister yesterday at the park!" "Not many people have a sense of humor like yours—it's a real gift to be able to make others laugh." "You know, you're lucky to have so much energy—you've really got what it takes to succeed at a lot of things." Help your child to recognize that he is different in some ways from other children—as we are all unique in our own ways—but that he can make the most of his differences, build on his strengths, and channel his energies in a constructive way.

Do not confine your "pep talks" to those times when your youngster is really down in the dumps but try to be aware of the need for bolstering his morale on a day-in, day-out basis. Keep praising him for those things that he does well. Commend him when you catch him being good (or less bad than usual). And when things go right, say, when he has been on time for the school bus every day for a week without your nagging, let him know that you recognize the effort he is making. Give him some extra time and attention; take him out for a treat. When he remembers to bring his books home from school, do not take this achievement for granted; remark upon it. Let your child know that he has the right to feel good about himself. And even when he slips up now and then, emphasize the six days when he did well—and not the seventh day when he slipped back.

One of the most vital points to get across to your youngster is the reassurance that even though he may be having trouble in school—and may continue to have problems there—that this does not mean he will not do well in life. Even a young child can understand the uniqueness of the school situation compared with other real-life situations. You can underscore this, perhaps, by pointing out to him various life settings in which people are not required to sit still for long periods at a time, do not have to turn in quantities of written work, and are permitted to speak to their colleagues pretty much whenever they feel like it.

Listen to Your Child

Remember that communication is a two-way affair. Often it is more important for you to listen to your child than it is to talk to him. One of the ways in which you can show your child that you accept him and sympathize with him is through a technique devised by Carl Rogers, a truly original and creative psychotherapist. You can avoid confrontations with your children and at the same time encourage them to talk out their feelings by the "active listening" described by Dr. Rogers in his book, *Client-centered Psychotherapy*.

Parents tend to interrupt their children's conversation with well-meant reassurances or with arguments that are ultimately of the "I know best" type. Such responses come across to the child as rejections of his feelings. When Noah dashes into the house, slams the door, hurls his books down on the floor, and sputters, "I won't go back to that fruit school again," your first reaction is likely to be an angry "What do you mean—you *won't* go back to to school?"

In active listening, you would lead Noah into releasing his feelings by repeating the last thing he said, by making some gentle interpretation, or just by indicating that you are listening to what he is saying. You might say something like "You had a bad day today?" or "You don't feel like going back to school?" Or you can present some version of what William Page of the Nashville Learning Center has called the "sympathetic grunt," saying no more than "um hum" or "hmh." After you have made your simple statement (or grunt), you would wait for your child to expand upon his feelings. At this point, you are not concerned with dealing with your child's problem in a rational way, but in offering him a sympathetic ear. If you want your child to feel free to express his feelings to you, you *have* to fight the urge to argue with him. You have to avoid saying things like "But your teacher really likes you," or "The law says you have to go to school so that's that," or "What makes you so special that you need a special school all to yourself?"

By active listening, you are offering your child your acceptance of his feelings, an acceptance demonstrated by your willingness to listen to what he has to say.

Communicate Your Love Without Words, Too

You can communicate your love for your child in many ways besides direct conversation. Physical gestures of affection are especially important for hyperactive youngsters, who often seem to crave close contact with parents and teachers. A hug, a cuddle on the lap, a touch on the arm, or holding hands while walking down the street are all forms of communication. Compared with many other countries, our way of raising children is rather impersonal, deficient in spontaneous affection. This is particularly true in the relationships between fathers and sons, most especially by the time a boy reaches the age of about ten. Fathers are often afraid that it is "unmanly" to show physical affection toward their sons; they are afraid of turning the boys into "sissies." Yet in other cultures, as in the Mediterranean countries, embraces between grown men are quite common and reflect not at all on their virility. Perhaps the reason adult encounter groups that stress physical contact are so popular these days is because few people in our society have received a healthy amount of physical affection.

Parents show their love for their children in many other ways, too. They demonstrate their concern when they show an interest in their child's well-being, when they establish rules for his own good and enforce them fairly, when they look out for his health and general welfare, when they want to be assured of the safety of his activities, when they want to know where he is and whom he is with, when they make his friends welcome in the home—when, in short, they demonstrate their caring attitude without hemming a child in with overly rigid restrictions. They also show their love by being sensitive to a child's feelings and needs, by expressing interest in the things that interest him, by giving recognition to his efforts to do well (even though the efforts are not always successful), and by making a child feel that he can come to his parents with a problem, without being laughed at or put off or having his troubles dismissed as trivialities.

Spend Time with Your Child

In a healthy family parents earn their authority by proving that they care for their children. One way of doing this is to show your children that you enjoy their company. It is often difficult to find

activities that the entire family can enjoy together or even that one
parent can enjoy with one child. It is especially hard when the
family includes a hyperactive child. But the search is worth the
effort.

The essential yardstick here is the appropriateness of a particular activity for your family. You may enjoy the idea of dressing
up the entire family and going out to an elegant restaurant. But
if Marc cannot sit still at the table, cannot get through a meal
without spilling something, and cannot keep his voice down below
a bellow, the ideal picture in your mind will turn out to be a hor-
ror in the restaurant. It is far better, then, to reserve your fancier
outings for those times when you go out without the children and
to confine your eating out with the youngsters to drive-in stands,
where you are not under pressure to conform to accepted standards. Better yet, in good weather, are picnic outings, when children can eat with their hands, do not have to worry about spotting
their clothes, and can run around between courses.

Your vacations can be tailored to the needs of your family. One
family that includes two hyperactive boys finds a break from routine and a chance to appreciate each other more when they go
away to a dude ranch. Twelve-year-old Ernie is an expert horse-
man who spends his entire day at the stables, caring for the horses,
taking them out, even taking responsibility for taking guests out
wrangling. Ten-year-old Alan, for whom sitting still is normally an
exquisite agony, spends from four to six hours a day quietly fishing
alone at the edge of a clear stream.

Parents can enjoy doing things with their children without worry-
ing about the educational value of an activity. The best lesson a
child can learn from shared activities is that his family likes to be
with him.

Spend Time Away from Your Child

Parents and their hyperactive children also need regular periods
of time away from each other, so that everyone can come back

together feeling refreshed and able to start out again in good humor. This is particularly important with younger children so that the parent who is home most of the time with the child can avoid the feeling of being trapped. The siblings also benefit from a vacation apart from their hyperactive brother or sister.

It is a good idea to cultivate several neighborhood babysitters, who can take your child for a few hours during an afternoon or evening. You can use this time to go out—or just to get some peaceful moments in your own home. Sometimes it is possible to make a regular arrangement for a teen-ager, male or female, to come in several afternoons a week to take your child out or to stay with him while you go out. A call to the student placement office of your local high school may yield a rich return. Other sources of baby-sitting help are older men and women who have free time during the day, along with the patience and energy to keep up with your child, parents at home with their own children who are happy to earn a little extra money by taking in another child for a few hours a day, or another family who can exchange baby-sitting services with you.

After-school and Saturday recreation programs run by your local school or park district are other ways in which you and your hyperactive child can get a breather from each other, while allowing you to spend some uninterrupted time with your other children.

An occasional weekend apart for parents and children can be a wonderful tension releaser. If it is at all possible for you to find someone—a grandparent, perhaps, or some other relative or friend —who can take your child for a monthly weekend, both you and your youngster will benefit. If you have another child, maybe each child can get a regular turn at a "vacation," and you can have precious time alone with the stay-at-home.

Summer camp can be a boon for a hyperactive child and his family. When Tony has shown that he can be away from home for longer and longer periods—if he separates easily from you to go to school and if he enjoys sleeping out at the houses of friends and relatives—and when he himself wants to go to camp, he is ready to go. For most children, this happens somewhere between the ages of seven and ten. Not all children, however, like camp. It is rarely a good idea to send a child to camp when he really does not want to go. The child's own attitude should be the barometer of his readiness to go. If he is fearful and anxious, he may not benefit from the experience. A child like this may do better at a day camp close to home or in a local playground program.

Many hyperactive children blossom at camp, where they can go from one vigorous activity to another, where they do not have to be neat and mannerly, and where they can learn new physical skills. They'll come home taller and tanner, to a family that is refreshed and eager to welcome them. For many families, a summer at camp bears out the adage "Absence makes the heart grow fonder" and is well worth the financial effort.

If you decide that your youngster is ready for camp, you have the problem of finding the right place. You can find out about camps from friends whose children have gone, from The American Camping Association (Bradford Woods, Martinsville, Ind.), and perhaps from your pediatrician or your school psychologist. Once you have received the names of one or two camps, you will want to find out as much as you can about them. Meet the camp director. Ask as many questions as you want. Find out how structured the camp program is, bearing in mind that your hyperactive child will probably do best in a camp that is fairly structured, without large blocks of free time, but that is not highly competitive. It is best to be honest with the camp director about your child's personality and to come right out and ask whether the counselors are likely to be mature and understanding enough to help your child have a good summer.

Life with Father

A father's participation in the life of his family is especially influential. Dr. Stanley Coopersmith found that boys with high self-esteem were likely to have close relationships with their fathers, and other studies have brought out the significance of the relationship between a girl and her father. The more time and interest a father lavishes on his children, the more worthwhile they will feel. (In those families without a father in the home, the mother carries a double burden. Some of the special concerns of the single parent are explored in Chapter 10.)

We are emphasizing the father's role, not because he is more important than the mother, but because in our society a mother usually spends far more time with her children. Too many fathers are so busy advancing their careers (partly for the sake of their children) that they give short shrift to their families in terms of time. It is a sign of robust health in a family when the father takes an active role with the children, sharing both the pleasures and the challenges of child rearing. The mother is relieved of the burden of feeling that whatever happens with the children is her sole responsibility. And the children thrive on the awareness that both their parents take a deep interest in them.

It has been said that "togetherness" is the most under-used word in parenting. It is important to find activities that a father can enjoy with his child. The choice of these activities is a wide one, depending on the interests of the particular individuals. Helen's father, for example, enjoys doing woodworking with his daughter, teaching her how to use real tools; Doug's father likes to play ball with his son; Carl and his father spend many happy hours playing together on their recorders. Cooking, hiking, fishing, bicycling, craft activities, swimming, or whatever—the specific activity matters far less than its capacity for allowing a child to experience success and allowing the child and his father to enjoy doing it together.

A Sense of Humor

The ability to see the humor lurking in the most unlikely situation is an invaluable asset in any home. The parent of one ten-year-old recently said, after watching a television series involving discussions with the parents of hyperactive children, "The parents' stories would have been hilarious if they hadn't been so true to life." If you can find some element of fun in some of the situations that are true to *your* life, and if you can deal with as many as possible with a light touch, you will be able to eliminate a lot of friction.

If a mother is asked, "Was that a take-apart toy?" and she can answer, "It wasn't, but it is now," she can deflect some of the hard feelings that come up in daily life. And your whole family will benefit if you try to devise humorous solutions to some of your problems. One father, for example, told Eddie, eight, and Gary, nine, to pound on each other's bed when they got angry, instead of on each other. As a result, Gary would often go into Eddie's room absolutely furious—and then come out laughing because he could suddenly see the ludicrousness of his hunching over and beating on his brother's bed.

The humorist Richard Armour has related an incident from his own family life. Furious with his son, Jeff, for having left his expensive new bicycle out in the rain, the father said bitterly, "Put it out in the driveway and let me run over it. We might as well finish it off." Despite the boy's contrite apologies, the father became more incensed, until Jeff's sister suggested, straight-faced, that they destroy the bike in a more interesting way—by dropping it from the roof. The children's mother caught the spirit and suggested putting the bike on the railroad tracks. At this point, the tension broke. An angry father was defused and able to laugh at his own overreaction.

In the excellent book, *Your Child Is a Person,** you can read about Larry. "Larry's parents labeled him 'the monster' very early in life. But this was really a term of endearment. They seemed to enjoy him even when they were holding their breath for his safety. They reported his extraordinary physical exploits good-humoredly and even with pride as he grew." If more parents could keep their

---

* Stella Chess, M.D., Alexander Thomas, M.D., Herbert G. Birch, M.D., Ph.D. (New York: Viking Compass Books, 1972, paperbound).

sense of humor about their "Larrys," more "Larrys" could learn to cope with the challenges of their personalities without developing feelings of rejection.

Of course, many of the problems centering around a hyperactive child are anything but funny. And even the ones that might be amusing to an outsider, who can chuckle over the exploits of a comic-strip "Dennis the Menace" do not tickle your funny bone at all. But you may be able to be amused through your consternation when Jonathan's teacher calls you up to tell you that Jon made a sound like a frog for half an hour straight during math. Hyperactive children are often daring, inventive, outrageous—and funny. It is a blessing to be able to enjoy these aspects of your child's personality.

Getting Along with Siblings

The way a child's brothers and sisters feel about him strongly influence the way he feels about himself. A certain amount of rivalry, jealousy, and fighting is expected in every family. But if Kenny believes that his brothers and sisters hate or despise him, he will reflect his view of their opinions in his own low regard for himself. For this reason, as well as for the self-esteem of your other children, who are all too likely to feel that you favor your hyperactive child, it behooves parents to pay attention to sibling problems.

Knowing your own ambivalence toward hyperactive Johnny, it may seem preposterous to you that well-behaved, achieving Jimmy may feel that you love Johnny more. Yet Jimmy is keenly aware that you spend more time with Johnny, are always on the phone with Johnny's teacher, and let Johnny "get away with more." *You* realize that you treat your two children differently because their needs are different. Yet if you put yourself in Jimmy's place, you can understand his point of view.

Here again, communication may be the key to understanding. Children can sometimes be very understanding and compassionate toward other people's problems, even when those other people are their own brothers and sisters. Your other children may respond to an honest discussion of the problems of your hyperactive child. You may be able to help them understand why Luke, who seems perfectly normal in every respect, is just not able to perform the same number of chores or maintain the same level of personal tidiness or the same degree of self-control that his brothers and sisters are capable of.

You can point out to your other children that what you are doing is asking for and rewarding a certain level of effort on everyone's part, rather than a particular standard of performance. You can make the analogy with grades in school. Children easily see the unfairness in Susan's getting A's with a modicum of effort, while Donald works much harder and gets only C's. If these two were being rewarded for their efforts rather than their performances, the grades might be reversed. You may not be able to change the grading system in your children's school, but within the family you can apply the axiom: "To each according to his need; from each according to his ability." Emphasize to your children that each person has to be judged individually and try to help them appreciate the fact that just as you expect more from an older child than a younger one, so you expect more from a child without major problems than you do from a hyperactive youngster. Be sure to remember to point out your hyperactive child's good qualities to his siblings and not dwell on the bad.

This kind of rational approach works in some families, especially those in which the siblings are at least of junior high school age. Too often, however, you can reason until you are blue in the face, and the siblings will stubbornly insist, "Nothing is wrong except that you have spoiled him rotten! You never let *me* get away with any of that stuff!" You may never be able to get your other children to shake this opinion entirely, but you can try to dislodge it in a number of ways.

You can, first of all, provide the same type of "active listening" that you offer your hyperactive child. You can allow the other children to express their jealous feelings to you and let them know that you understand their resentment. You can boost their self-esteem. Take them off on their own for a shared good time. Show them how much they matter to you. The more secure they are in your love and in their own worth, the more understanding they will be of the special problems of their hyperactive sibling.

There are also a number of practical ways you can work at diminishing the amount of friction among your children. You can enlist your other children as your allies by schooling them not to respond to the hyperactive child's irritability and teasing. Let them know that you realize how difficult this is and how grateful you are when they manage to keep the peace in the face of strong provocation. Give them a stake in their sibling's good behavior by rewarding them for not egging him on. If you establish a reward system for your hyperactive child, you can occasionally reward his brothers and sisters for his good behavior as well as their own. These rewards can take the form of family outings that all will enjoy or some other shared treat.

If at all possible, give each child his own bedroom. One parent recently lamented, "If you have money, so many of these problems are solved. The kids can go away to camp, they can live in the country and have room to roam, and they can each have their own bedrooms." Even families with modest incomes can arrange some privacy for each child. Partitions can be built to divide a room in two; rooms can be built over a garage; a den or a dining room can be converted into a bedroom. It can be a terrible affliction for an older brother to have to put up with a young hyperactive child in the same room, and so a less than ideal solution may still be an improvement over putting the two boys together.

One bane of an older sibling's existence may be the impossibility of being able to entertain his or her friends in peace. A hyperactive child can be a pest, coming in to bother his siblings and their friends; if the hyperactive child is the elder, he can be a bully, as well. Parents must establish strict rules forbidding the hyperactive child from going into their siblings' rooms without being invited. It is sometimes helpful to allow the hyperactive child to invite a friend (particularly a friend who seems to have a calming influence) whenever a sister or brother is also entertaining.

Making and Keeping Friends

Some hyperactive children are popular with other children, who enjoy their active, energetic, amusing, and adventurous personalities. But many hyperactive youngsters sadly lack friends. Given to incessant fighting and silly, show-off behavior and unable to follow the rules of a game or to see it through to completion, Glenn is likely to run into the house sobbing, "Why don't any of the kids like me?" What can you do? You cannot assure him that they do like him but cannot show it; you cannot say they are not worth having as friends; nor can you say that it does not matter. It matters dreadfully.

You *can* encourage Glenn to express his feelings about his lack of friends and let him know that you understand how he feels and that you sympathize with him. Meantime, from what he says and from your own observations, try to analyze the root of his problems with peer relationships. Then at some neutral time—*not* at the moment when he is most unhappy—sit down to talk with him about the situation. Perhaps you can tactfully point out some of the things he does that antagonize the other children. Maybe he can make special efforts, say, to listen hard to the rules of a game and adhere to them, to control his silly face-making or to "take the chip off his shoulder" before he leaves the house to play.

You can also make practical suggestions that take into account the special demands of his temperament. Encourage him to plan his social life so that he is usually with just one child at a time. Teach him how to recognize when tension is building up within him to such a point that a fight is bound to follow—and to extricate himself from such a difficult situation before the fighting and the tears and the angry words.

Encourage your child to bring his friends home to play at times when you or another adult can be home and alert to what is going on. Try to provide a place for the children to play where they will not have to worry about making too much noise or too much mess. At relatively frequent intervals, wander "casually" into the room. If the children are showing signs of restlessness or trouble, suggest a change of pace—cookies and milk or a switch from indoor to outdoor play or a brief session in front of the television set. If things get too wild, pleasantly tell the playmate that it is time for him to go home, but urge him to come back another day.

When your child is invited to another youngster's house, speak to the other parent ahead of time. Explain briefly that he sometimes get overexcited when playing and ask the other parent to send him home if things get out of hand. Forewarning the other parent may prevent an unhappy outcome.

One way of helping your child expand his social life may be to encourage him to take part in some structured group activity. Scout and YMCA leaders enjoy being with children and may be very skillful in working with them. If you are lucky enough to have someone like this in your community, your child can derive great benefit from being in such a program. If not, look around for other activities, possibly those built around a particular interest—classes, for example, in art or music or judo. It is often difficult to involve a hyperactive child in outside activities, because he may equate them with school and expect to experience failure and rejection again, as he has so often in the past. One way to get around this reluctance is to choose an activity that can include a parent as well. Some community centers offer father-and-son Indian Guide programs; others provide mother-and-child art classes. Eventually, you can encourage your youngster to participate in outside activities on his own.

Self-esteem and having friends are inextricably bound up together. A child who does not have friends is bound to think poorly of himself. And the child who thinks poorly of himself usually has trouble making and keeping friends. He may be too preoccupied with himself to be friendly to other children or want so badly to have friends that he overdoes it. He becomes so silly or aggressive that he repels the very children he would like to attract. The more you build up your child's self-esteem in other areas of his life, the more able he will be to make and keep friends.

Pets

An animal does wonders for a child's self-image. It never talks back, scolds, or criticizes. When you have flunked a test at school, been scolded at home or fought with your best friend, what comfort it can be to run with your dog or play with your kitten or let your guinea pig climb up your arm. Many children who have trouble getting along with people have a real feeling for animals. A child's self-esteem can get a boost from the knowledge that no matter how bad things may get, his pet is still his loyal friend.

If you do let your hyperactive child get a pet, you have to have a clear understanding ahead of time about how much responsibility the child himself will assume for the pet's care. And you have to be realistic about how much you can expect him to assume. Very few children can take on much of an ongoing responsibility, without reminders, before the age of about ten or eleven. If your child is younger than that, you will have to be prepared to remind him to feed and exercise his pet—and sometimes to do the job yourself. You also have to remember that an impulsive child will probably not treat his pet too gently, so it is best to choose one that doesn't mind some rough handling—a good-natured, sturdy dog, perhaps.

Other Adults

Your hyperactive child will be coming into contact with many other adults from early childhood—grandparents, aunts and uncles, baby-sitters, neighbors, your friends, his friends' parents, and then teachers, bus drivers, scout leaders, camp counselors, and so forth. Some of these persons may be very understanding of his personality, but many others will wound him—and you—time and time again.

One father grows purple with rage, remembering the time that eight-year-old Joey thoughtlessly swung a broom around in the air and hit the little boy next door. The younger child's father grabbed Joey by the scruff of the neck, stormed up to the boy's front door, and said to Joey's parents, "Here—now put this kid in a cage!"

A mother was faced with problems presented by her own mother. "Every time we went to visit my parents, my mother would give me a 'lesson' in child rearing and would hurt Warren's feelings at the same time. She made a special point of leaving dishes of candy all over the house, and then when Warren went to take some, she would say, 'No, no' and add, to me, 'You left the *good* Warren home today and you brought the *bad* Warren with you.' "

There is no way you can shield your child from all the cruel, unthinking things other adults will say. You can help him to recognize the kinds of behavior that are particularly likely to enrage adults and to turn them against him. And when a situation arises when he is the butt of some thoughtless words or actions of an adult, you can take some of the sting out by supporting him, at least in front of the abusive adult.

Tell anyone who comes complaining to you that you will deal with the situation privately with your child. Do not make excuses for his behavior; do not apologize for him; do not promise to punish him. Instead, listen to the complaint. Then, in private, ask your child for his version. Act accordingly. Do not be too ready to believe everything you hear. Sometimes your child may, indeed, have been the culprit, but at other times he may be blamed for another's misdeeds or be picked upon by an adult in a grouchy mood. One mother has said, "Once the die is cast and he gets a reputation for being the 'terror' of the neighborhood, people lie in wait for him."

Sometimes you should speak to another adult about your child. This need not mean apologizing in advance for the child's behavior. It might be wise, however, to tell the parent of a child having a birthday party what to do if your child starts to get overexcited or in trouble: this may involve sending him home or calling you or putting him in a separate room for a few minutes to cool off. *Never* talk about your child in front of him, however, either to criticize him to another adult or to make excuses for him.

Sometimes you can change the people in your child's life. If Colleen ends up in tears after every piano lesson, try another music teacher before you think of giving up the music. If Matthew has received three bus citations by the end of kindergarten, see whether he or the driver can be transferred to a different route. If Laurie is in a classroom with an extremely rigid, humorless teacher, see whether she can move to another class. If a friend of yours is highly critical of the way your Sam plays with her Todd, see your friend when the children are not along. Go out of your way to look for sympathetic baby-sitters, Scout leaders, and other adults in whose company your child will be.

Competence

In 1890, the pioneering psychologist William James expressed his conviction that one of the major determinants of self-esteem is how we measure up to the aspirations we set for ourselves. In *Principles of Psychology* James wrote, "I, who for the time have staked my all on being a psychologist, am mortified if others know much more psychology than I. But I am contented to wallow in the grossest ignorance of Greek. My deficiencies there give me no sense of personal humiliation at all."

You can talk to your child about how great he is till you are blue in the face and he is squirming in his seat. But if he does not have a sense of his own competence in some area that holds significance for him, he will not be able to base a sense of self-esteem upon his own demonstrated abilities. Sometimes you have to take active steps to help him improve his abilities in the areas where he

Barkley, Russell A

Attention - deficit Hyperactivity disorder: a handbook
for diagnosis and treatment. NY: Guilford,
c1990.   # 618.928589 B2 3rd Floor

"Attention-Deficit/Hyperactivity disorder in the
classroom: a practical guide for teachers".
Austin: Pro-Ed, c1998.

Breggin, Peter Roger. Talking back to
Ritalin: what doctors aren't telling you
about stimulants and ADHD. Cambridge,
Mass.: Perseus, c2001

Feingold, Ben F. Why your child is hyperactive
NY: Random House, 1975

Hunter, Diana. The ritalin-free child:
managing hyperactivity & attention deficits
without drugs. Ft. Lauderdale, Fla.: Consumer,
1995

is deficient, such as school or sports, so that he can *feel* more adequate by actually *becoming* more adequate.

Academic Competence

The importance of a child's performance in school for measuring himself against his peers cannot be overestimated. Children are very shrewd in this respect. If you ask Alex to tell you the names of the "smartest" and the "dumbest" children in his class, he will immediately be able to name them. No matter how teachers play this down, as the most sensitive ones usually try to do, the children are keenly aware of a pecking order in the classroom. And whether reading groups are divided into "Mets" and "Jets" or "bluebirds" and "robins," children are sensitive to the implications of their own placement in these groups and to their own accomplishments compared with those of the other children.

A child who is not doing well in school, who is called "dummy" or "retard" by the other children, begins to think of himself in those terms. Surprisingly, even a youngster who knows that his tested I.Q. is well above average still considers himself a "dumbbell" if he is behind most of his classmates in day-to-day work. The question of how best to deal with poor performance in school is a complicated one, which will be dealt with more fully later in this book.

A crucial factor in how a child feels about his schoolwork is the attitude of his teacher. The teacher's attitude also influences the other children. Unless she conveys a child's inadequacies to them by her scolding and irritation, they are not likely to care about his poor academic work. They will, however, react to Brad's showing off in class, to Cissy's giving silly answers off the top of her head, or to Sonny's bursting into tears over his inability to get his work right. Much of this behavior can be avoided by a skillful, compassionate teacher.

Two things are essential. First, a child having trouble with school should undergo testing that will indicate his real intellectual potential, so that neither too much nor too little will be expected of him. Second, it is important to speak to the teacher, and to have your doctor or psychotherapist speak to her, to help her understand the child's problems and to help her find ways of evaluating what he has learned, since he may not be able to demonstrate what he knows through the standard tests and written work.

You will also want to point out to your child that school is a unique experience in life, one that is particularly difficult for very active, impulsive, restless children and one that he may never shine in. In few other endeavors is one required to sit still for long periods of time and to work steadily without speaking or moving around, stopping only once a day for something to eat or drink. Many schools put children under more stress than adults face in their jobs.

Reassure your child that even though he has difficulties in school, this does not mean that he will not do well in life. Emphasize that some of the traits that make school so hard for him— his high energy level, his aggressiveness, his lack of inhibitions— may make him a dynamic leader of industry, a brilliant lawyer, a famous athlete, or a success in some other field.

Competence in Other Areas

Sports and games play a vital role in children's assessments of themselves, especially for boys, making life inordinately difficult for those children who are poorly co-ordinated and for those whose impulsivity and impatience work against them.

Most hyperactive children do not do well in team sports because of the rules, the relatively small proportion of time spent in action rather than waiting, and the need to function in a team. Individual and constant-action sports such as gymnastics, tumbling, wrestling, and swimming are the best. Iceless hockey is one team sport, however, that seems tailor-made for hyperactive children, because it allows them to release an enormous amount of energy, requires little discipline, and can be enjoyed by players of any size and athletic ability (or lack of it). It is a fast and ferocious game played with a plastic puck and plastic sticks, so the players can lash out without fear of anyone's getting hurt. After about fifteen minutes, the players all look as if they have just come out of a sauna bath.

If a child is reluctant to start out on one of these sports because he does not get along well with other children or because he is clumsy, it is helpful for his father or mother or older siblings to take part in the activity themselves, maybe in an informal way. Parents should insist that the child go regularly at the beginning so he can acquire the basic skills that will enable him to enjoy the activity.

If your child is clumsy, you may be able to help him improve his physical skills. But if you feel that he will never shine athletically, do not push him into something he is bound to fail at. Do not nag him to practice when all the practice in the world will still leave him a mediocre player. Try to teach him the basic skills of the popular neighborhood activities so that he can avoid complete ostracism but concentrate at the same time on finding some activity that your child can do well.

In one family, Howie is a sensational athlete whose Little League coach wants to skip him from the Bush League to the Major League, while Lee is a poor athlete but a good musician. He takes drum lessons in school, plays in the school band, and is now talking about starting his own band to play at the junior high school dances. Both boys, the athlete with the "tin ear" and the musician with the "two left feet," enjoy the gratification of success in their chosen areas.

Your child may be good at arts and crafts, amateur dramatics, handling a paper route, playing with a Yo-Yo, dancing the ballet, baby-sitting, or pumping gas at the neighborhood gas station. Explore many different avenues to find an activity in which your child can shine. You can then encourage him by providing lessons or equipment or your own time and by praising him generously but realistically when he experiences success.

A wonderful way to build up the self-esteem of a hyperactive child is to capitalize on his or her adventurous spirit. Anything that entails a certain element of risk—such as sailing, canoeing, wilderness or survival trips, riding, and commando-type courses— is great for building up a child's sense that he or she has a special reserve of courage and endurance to cope with difficult situations. Needless to say, any such activity should be very well supervised; the youngsters should get adequate training to prepare them to be on their own, and they should be given as much independence as they can handle, no more and no less.

As a child grows older, his morale and his bank account grow together as he performs neighborhood jobs like mowing lawns and doing other yard work, raking leaves, shoveling snow, baby-sitting, washing cars, collecting supermarket carts, and helping shoppers with their bundles. Another great avenue for older boys and girls is the junior leader program of the YMCA, which prepares them to be camp counselors. A young person often seems to grow ten feet tall when he is responsible for younger children.

Musical instruments can give an interested youngster a wonderful outlet. You have to remember, though, that the discipline of practice may be a hard one for the hyperactive child to follow. If your youngster does not practice as long as you or his teacher feels he should, you have to decide how much the child is getting from the pursuit of this particular instrument. If music is a shared family interest, the hyperactive child may do better by learning to play the drums, rather than the piano or violin. But we do know of one budding concert pianist at Juilliard who, as a child, used to be sent off to the piano to release his excess energy.

Training in self-reliance strengthens a child's ego enormously. A youngster's feeling about his own competence grows as he learns to cook for himself, wash, iron, and mend his own clothes, go to the store to shop for food, clothing, and school supplies, handle his own money, stay alone without baby-sitters, and use public transportation at the earliest possible age. Survival training programs that teach adolescents how to go out into the wilderness and challenge nature are ideal for adventurous hyperactive individuals.

In our efforts to help our children achieve success through competence, we should not feel that we have to try to shield them from any failure at all. John Holt, the perceptive writer on children and education, has said that we should help children to see "that failure is honorable and constructive, rather than humiliating." Holt also writes in *How Children Fail,* "We ought also to learn, beginning early, that we don't always succeed. A good batting average in baseball is .300; a good batting average in life is a great deal lower than that. Life holds many more defeats than victories for all of us. Shouldn't we get used to this early? . . . What we fail to do today, we, or someone, may do tomorrow."

Virtue

People like to feel that they are "good," that they adhere to their personal ethical and moral standards and that they are discharging their responsibilities to their families, to society, and to themselves. Parents can help a child achieve the satisfactions of meeting standards, since they instill in him many of the values that he will take as his own. Then, by their expectations of the child, his parents not only show him that they have confidence in his being able to meet high standards but also can actually help him to do so.

The best-adjusted children grow up in families where the most is expected of them. We all do our best when we are challenged. The child whose parents expect him to perform up to his capabilities in school, to fulfill his commitments, and to participate actively in family duties as well as in family fun, is learning to formulate goals and to know the satisfaction that comes from meeting responsibilities and achieving success.

Parents who run a "tight ship" help their children. The Coopersmith study found that children who grow up in homes that are fairly strict, where high standards of achievement are maintained and where limits to acceptable behavior are clearly defined and consistently enforced, are more likely to develop high self-esteem than are children from relatively permissive environments.

The child coming from a permissive environment has little guidance in making his choices about the way he is going to behave in the myriad situations of daily life, and he often becomes uncertain and anxious about whether he is doing the right thing. The youngster who has a clear picture of what is expected of him knows when he is meeting expectations and when he is not. He develops a sense of security from the knowledge of how he is performing. Because he knows that his parents care about the way he behaves and are ready to act upon their concerns, he gets the feeling that his parents really care about him—about what he does and about the way he will turn out in later life.

Parents who run a disciplined home generally have a sense of direction. Beyond their immediate expectations and standards of behavior, certain underlying values help the family to chart its course through life and to set goals. Some families' religious beliefs guide them. Other families substitute a body of ethical standards and commitments to social causes. In any case, a sense of purpose transmitted from parents to children can help the children guide their behavior and build on their sense of worth.

Discipline implies structure. And structure in a home environment implies that there is a certain shape within the home. Parental regulations have been formulated to cover basic living situations; children are expected to participate in the work of the family as soon as they are old enough to assume simple tasks; and there is a certain regularity of routine, which is particularly important for the hyperactive child.

In the next chapters we will discuss some of the factors that enter into the structured home, including the setting up of routines, the formulation of reasonable expectations, and the merits of rewards versus punishment in helping your child meet your expectations.

Power

The extent to which an individual can influence the world about him gives him a feeling about his own effectiveness. The baby who knows that when he cries his mother will come to nurse him is already learning a sense of his own power. If he were to cry when he was hungry and if no one came, he would feel that he had little power to make life better. Children who feel that they cannot influence their environments in any way, that no matter what they do, they will not be able to make their needs known and have them satisfied, often give up trying. They become resigned to taking life as it is, without trying to change their own lives for the better.

On the other hand, there is the phenomenon of the "omnipotent child," or the child who tries to control the behavior of the entire family. Such a child may manipulate his parents through temper tantrums, psychosomatic complaints, or some other mechanism. The parents give in, letting the child decide when the parents may go out, where the family should go for vacations, and even what television programs they should watch. Since his every wish is granted at home, such a youngster becomes extremely frustrated when this does not happen outside the home. He develops an unreal picture of what life is like and is unable to deal with the normal setbacks and frustrations experienced by everyone. The child who is permitted to "rule the roost" is apt to become fearful and asocial. It is children like this who are most likely to develop "school phobia," a morbid fear about going to school.

The healthiest kind of home atmosphere is one that provides certain limits, with plenty of freedom within those limits. This implies a democratic atmosphere within the family. This does not mean that the children's opinions are given equal weight with those of the parents or that important family matters are decided by vote. It does mean that everyone in the family is respected as a worthwhile person in his or her own right, that everyone's opinion is welcomed on issues of importance to the family, and that everyone's feelings are considered. The parents' decisions are not authoritarian; by open communication with the children they explain the reasoning behind their decisions. The parents are always willing to hear the child's side of an issue and are ready to compromise on some points. When appropriate, the children share in making decisions.

For example, parents will not ask their children to decide whether to move to another city to take advantage of a promising job offer. Once the parents have decided to do so, however, they will explain to their youngsters why they feel it is worth uprooting the family. They will appreciate the children's feelings about leaving their schools and their friends, and they will try to involve the youngsters as much as possible in making plans for the move. The children's opinions will be sought on the kind of neighborhood they want to live in, the kind of house, and so forth.

In a democratic home the children's opinions are sought and respected and often heeded on such matters as the choice of family outings, vacations, extracurricular activities, purchase of clothing, distribution of household chores, and resolution of conflicts within the family.

A good mechanism for conducting discussions on these issues is the family council. The Miller family, for example, holds weekly meetings involving both parents and all four children, including three-year-old Kim. Every Sunday after breakfast, the Millers allot an hour to the council meeting. A different family member moderates each week, asking everyone present whether he or she wants to bring up anything for discussion. As each issue is taken up, the opinions of all the family members are sought to try to find solutions acceptable to everyone, or at least to a majority. Decisions can always be re-evaluated, and special midweek councils can always be called to deal with pressing matters.

Freedom within structure also means that a child should be permitted to learn, as far as possible, through the consequences of his own actions. He should have the freedom to skin his knee—

but not to break his leg. In other words, you would not let two-year-old Jenny run into the street, because the natural consequences of that might well be fatal; you would let her run down a steep hill, however, since the natural consequences of that would, at the worst, probably involve no more than a few bruises and might, at the best, teach her how to balance herself on a steep incline.

Letting a child learn through the consequences of his own actions means that parents do not have to feel responsible for everything a child does and should not nag him over every trifling matter. Parents should, rather, analyze the points of issue between themselves and their child and ask whether the child can learn from his mistakes in a given area. If so, the parents should turn a deaf ear and an unseeing eye and let the child learn for himself. More about consequences on page 108.

As a child grows, he should have more and more freedom to make his own choices. For example, when Dora is in kindergarten, you might help her pick out her clothes for school. When she is in third grade, you would assume that she can pick out her own clothes. By sixth grade, you would allow her to purchase some of her own clothes. Or you might tell your kindergartner when it was time to go to sleep, tell your third-grader when to get into bed but allow him to read till he got sleepy, and let your sixth-grader set his own bedtime.

Parental Self-esteem

One other interesting finding of the Coopersmith study on self-esteem is that parents who have confidence in themselves are more likely to have children with a favorable self-image than are parents with low self-esteem. When you are unsure whether you are dealing with your child in the right way, your anxiety and doubt communicate themselves to your child and unsettle him. The more confident you are that you are doing the right thing, the more assured your child will be. Even when you do not feel terribly self-assured, it is important to put up a good front. Parents should muster up enough acting ability to convey a sense of self-confidence in their ability to manage their children.

If you show your self-doubt to your children, they will certainly capitalize on it. They will interpret any tentative statement that you might make (such as "Don't you think you ought to go to bed now?") as a chink in your armor for them to exploit. And they will learn to put up such a fuss that you will eventually give in. Be firm from the start; let them know that no matter how much of a fuss they put up, what you say is what must be done.

Parents who lack self-confidence and undervalue themselves become so resentful of their inability to control their child that they seethe with repressed anger. This anger makes them extremely critical of the child and unable to accept him as he is. As a result, the parents get caught up in a depressing cycle of feeling inadequate, resenting the child's dominance, feeling guilty about the resentment, hopelessness, and more feelings of inadequacy. (This specific aspect of parents' emotional life is an important one to bring up with a physician or psychiatrist, since chronic low self-esteem may lead to depression.)

One reason for reading this book is so that both parents can get together to agree on developing a definite and explicit program for managing their child. When you have agreed on a program, have put it into effect, and have begun to find out that it works, your self-confidence is bound to rise. Your child's is bound to follow.

One of the greatest weapons of all is laughter, a gift for fun, a sense of play which is sadly missing from the grown-up world.

—Madeleine L'Engle
A Circle of Quiet

6 ESTABLISHING A HEALTHY CLIMATE IN THE HOME

The previous chapter discussed one aspect of a healthy climate in the home—the parents' awareness of how they can raise their child's self-esteem. All the chapters in Part II, *How to Help Your Child at Home,* are relevant to self-esteem because a child's feelings about himself are likely to be more positive if he is brought up in a home that has a definite structure.

In a well-structured home, the underlying values that govern the family's behavior are clearly stated, relatively constant, and agreed upon by both parents. The rules set up to maintain these values are enforced consistently and equally firmly by both parents. The parents make a point of rewarding children for good behavior and try not to reward them, even unconsciously, for misbehaving. Activities in the household follow a relatively constant routine.

A firm foundation is important for all children. Children are happier when they know where they stand. They want to know what to expect of the world and what the world expects of them. They want to know what the rules are and when they are breaking those rules. They want to know what consequences to expect when they meet standards and what to expect when they do not. They need parents who will make decisions for them until they are ready to decide for themselves. They need an orderly routine as well as times to be free. It is healthier for a child to grow up in a home that provides goals and limits than in a permissive one that leaves the child to choose when he goes to bed or what the quality of his schoolwork will be. The child who is faced with too many choices feels insecure, and if his work is accepted, whether it is good or bad, he is deprived of a sense of achievement. In a permissive home a child may be so indulged that he has difficulty coping with the demands of school and neighborhood. Such a discrepancy between home and the outside world may make a child fearful and too dependent on his mother or father.

The hyperactive child depends more upon external structure than do other children, since it is harder for him to analyze the requirements of a given situation and to establish internal controls. An impulsive, restless, distractible child will find it hard to meet acceptable standards of behavior if he is not given firm guidance by the adults in his life. Because of his adventurous and aggressive temperament, he is more likely to test rules. Because of his impulsiveness, he is prone to get into physical dangers or to be involved in situations where he may get into trouble with the police.

When we recommend structure, we are not proposing an authoritarian way of raising children or an approach that will prevent children from developing responsibility for their own actions. We are, instead, recognizing parents' obligations to help their children formulate acceptable standards of behavior and to help them develop controls for meeting those standards. A key element in this is the need to set realistic and reasonable expectations for their behavior and then to consciously work out parenting techniques that will help the children meet these expectations.

Setting Reasonable Expectations

For their own sakes and their children's, the parents of hyperactive children have to learn to accept what they cannot change. They have to recognize that each child is born with a bundle of personality traits that he will carry with him all through life. The work of Thomas, Chess and Birch, and of other researchers suggests that certain aspects of temperament remain relatively stable throughout life. Your hyperactive child will probably have a high activity level for as long as he lives. He will also probably retain a certain degree of talkativeness, impulsiveness, impatience, and irritability. The more you try to cast him into the mold of a patient, tractable, affable child, the more heartache both you and he will experience. Instead, for the sake of your own sanity and your child's happiness, you must take a look at your child and tell yourself, "This is the way he is—and this is the way he will probably continue to be." Once you have accepted—*really* accepted—this truth, only then can you realistically help your child try to change those aspects of his behavior that adversely affect his life at home or in school.

Accepting your child's innate characteristics does not mean that you are willing to accept every manifestation of his temperament or that you adopt an "anything goes" attitude. It means that you view your child's basic temperament as the framework within which he will behave. You can influence that behavior up to a point if you set realistic goals and if you are willing to meet your child halfway to help him attain those goals.

We have all heard such aphorisms as "A man's reach should exceed his grasp." Certainly we should not take the easy way out and be content with the least we can do but strive for our best. But as we set goals for our children and ourselves, we have to be flexible enough to realize when our goals are too high. For example, if one of your children wore glasses, you would not take away his glasses and say, "You should be able to read without these." So, with your hyperactive child, you have to recognize that while he may be able, with much effort, to become an adequate student and to learn how to channel some of his excess energy, he will never be patient, deliberate, and studious.

You need to make allowances for temperamental differences between one child and another and tell yourself that what is easy for one of your other children may be out of the question for your hyperactive youngster. Just because your other children have been able to meet certain standards at the age of ten does not mean that your hyperactive child will be able to do so.

Establishing Priorities

The mother and the father of a hyperactive child have to ask themselves and each other, "What's really important?" They have to talk to each other and come to an agreement. They may decide, for example, that the two most crucial things to work on at the moment are an improvement in their child's school situation and a need for him to learn to curb his impulsive behavior so that he will not get into serious trouble. They may, for the moment, forget about his sloppiness and his bad table manners. Two of the ways in which parents can change the behavior of their child—the establishment and enforcement of rules and regulations, and the rewarding of desirable behavior and discouragement of undesirable behavior—are discussed extensively in Chapters 8 and 9. Parents also influence their children's behavior in other ways.

Supervision

One vital way by which parents can help their hyperactive child do the right thing is by carefully supervising his activities. As long as you or another responsible adult is with your child, either participating in an activity with him or staying close enough so that you know what he is doing practically every minute, he will not get into serious mischief.

It may seem unfair that your neighbor can stay in bed until ten o'clock on a Saturday morning, while her docile little boy gets his own cereal and watches television. It is too bad that the parents of a hyperactive child cannot know the luxury of sleeping late and leaving the child to his own devices, but this can be a dangerous form of parental self-indulgence. The fact of the matter is that your child is different from your neighbor's child. As a result, your parenting has to be different.

Household accidents commonly occur in the hours when a curious, inquisitive toddler is wandering around the house alone, while everyone else is asleep. The parents of three-year-old Teddy were awakened at nine o'clock one Sunday morning by a telephone call from the police, who reported that they had picked up a pajama-clad Teddy about a mile away from home. After this scare, Teddy's parents worked out a system for spelling each other, taking turns getting up early, with the early riser making up for lost sleep by taking a nap later in the day.

The need for extra supervision remains beyond the toddler stage. One father was upset after his nine-year-old son, Franklin, had been threatened by a neighbor for draping the neighbor's shrubs with toilet paper late at night. Franklin's father was justifiably worried, because the neighbor had been known to fire his gun at nighttime prowlers. It turned out that Franklin's parents had decided that the boy needed a letup during the summer vacation, and so they allowed him to watch the late movies on television. Meanwhile, the parents continued to go to bed at their usual time —about 10:30. After the movie, Franklin would get bored and go out of the house to look for fun. After the toilet-paper escapade, Franklin's parents established firm rules about the boy's bedtime, insisting that he stay in his room after ten o'clock at night.

Most parents of hyperactive children recognize by a very early age the need for close supervision of their children's activities. It may seem unreasonable that you have to be the only mother or father on the block watching your child at play, but if you know that your child is likely to get into trouble if left to his own devices, you have no choice. For this reason, it is particularly helpful—and worth some financial sacrifice—to find some sort of relief so that you do not have to be by your child's side all the time: a baby-sitter, a nursery school, a well-supervised after-school or summer program.

Preventing trouble by close supervision is much more effective—and easier on everyone—than punishment after the event.

Routine

Routine is an important part of structure. It is easier for a hyperactive youngster to conform to parental expectations if he knows that there are certain predetermined times for waking up, going to school, playing outside, doing chores, doing homework, watching television, eating meals, and going to bed.

Schedules will be different on weekends than during the week, during the summer than the winter, and different when a child is ten than it was when he was seven. We can help our children, however, and especially our hyperactive children, by keeping routines consistent. If, for example, you have finally got your child to conform to an eight o'clock bedtime, you should not keep him out later than this because you feel like going shopping one night or because you are having such a good time visiting friends that you hate to leave. You must respect his schedule if you expect him to respect it at those times when he does not feel like keeping to it. It should take a truly extraordinary reason to vary your routine.

Many hyperactive children find it difficult to adjust to changes in routine. When you know that there will be a change in your child's usual schedule, you should warn him of it ahead of time.

Meeting Your Child Halfway

Change in your own behavior or your child's environment can help him live up to your expectations. Your own actions—something as simple as an occasional calm reminder or as drastic as a change in family life style—can help your child attain goals. Your attitude is crucial. You meet your child halfway when you compromise, when you stretch your limits of toleration to accept conduct that was previously unacceptable, and when you forestall crises instead of insisting on facing them head-on.

The mother of one hyperactive boy, herself a psychiatrist, recalls, "When Greg was little and we would go to visit my mother-in-law, the first thing I would do would be to remove all the little knickknacks she insisted on keeping in vulnerable positions on low tables. Then, when I saw that Greg had played 'nicely' for as long as he was capable of doing at one stretch, I would take him for a walk. I always tried to do this *before* any signs of trouble erupted, and I was usually able to avoid an unpleasant scene."

The father of an eight-year-old girl says, "I used to be a real demon when we were going for a long car trip. I would set myself a goal of so many hundred miles in one day, and if we didn't make that, I'd feel I had fallen behind schedule. Now I have come to realize that the time we spend traveling is part of our vacation, too, and if that's miserable because Katie has to let out her energy by pinching the baby or picking a fight with her brother, then it takes away from the pleasure of our trip.

"Now we stop the car every couple of hours to let all of us stretch our legs and work off some energy. Sure, it's mostly for Katie's benefit, but we don't emphasize this. Actually, we all welcome the breaks. And we all benefit from the happier atmosphere inside the car."

Other parents change other aspects of their family life in recognition of the limitations of their children's personalities. One husband and wife, for example, who used to do a great deal of daytime socializing with their friends and the whole family, have resigned themselves to getting together with other adults in the evenings, when they do not have to worry about separating brawling children. Another family that used to go en masse on Saturday afternoon shopping trips now handles the shopping differently. One parent takes the child who needs something, or one stays home with all the children while the other parent does the shopping alone. Other families resign themselves to keeping their homes childproofed, with all valuables and dangerous items put away out of danger, far beyond the toddler stage—as long as there seems to be a need for such an arrangement.

Some families make more sweeping changes. One city-dwelling family, for example, moved to the suburbs to give their quick-moving athletic son more opportunities for physical outlet. Another family sold their suburban home to move to the country, where their daughter could keep and ride horses. While these two families feel they have done the right thing, such a drastic change in life style is not indicated unless it also fits in with the adults' inclinations. The parents of hyperactive children try hard to do right by their children and often inconvenience themselves tremendously. When a major sacrifice, like a family move, does not produce the hoped-for improvement in the child, the parents are likely to be bitterly disappointed and resentful toward their child.

Only you can decide at what point your compromise for the sake of your child becomes a demanding sacrifice—and whether it is worth the effort involved. One set of parents may balk at keeping their breakable vases put away at a time when their child "should know how to move around so he won't knock over everything in sight." They then have to decide which is more important—a beautifully appointed home or the elimination of one more source of friction in the home. Another family may continue to take the children out to restaurants, even though each meal is a torture, because "he has to learn how to eat in a public place." These parents have to ask themselves how important restaurant manners are for a six-year-old.

So often, we parents have strong feelings about ways of doing things because of our own upbringing and because of a style of living we have unconsciously absorbed. When we stop to re-examine our values and ask ourselves, "Is this really important enough to make an issue about?" we find that some of the ideas we have lived with for years do not stand up to this kind of questioning.

We also tend to feel that life has to be an "all or nothing" proposition. Either our child does all we expect him to do—or he is a total failure. Either we continue to do all the things we once expected to do—or we are total failures. We forget that so much of life involves compromises, compromises that are easy to carry out once we accept their necessity.

Think Positively

Once you have set your priorities, determined your expectations, and formulated a plan for helping your child to meet those expectations (see the next four chapters), keep telling yourself how important it is to display a positive mental attitude. If you appear confident that your child will go along with you and will improve his behavior, he is far more likely to do so than if you seem doubtful yourself. A fair amount of acting ability is helpful here, because, of course, you do not always feel so sure of success. It is hard to display anything resembling a positive mental attitude when your child wakes up crying, just as he has done every day for the past six months, when you know that the first row will be about whether he will go potty and the second about what he will wear to nursery school and the third about what he will eat for breakfast, and so on ad infinitum. However, the day you can greet your child with the attitude that you know he has been this way in the past but you know he wants to do better and you can help him do better may mark the start of a new phase in both your lives.

You must *act* decisively and surely, even though you may not feel this way. You must express yourself forcefully to your child. Instead of saying in a wishy-washy way, "I think you should go to bed now," you should simply announce, "It is eight o'clock—bedtime." Instead of saying tentatively, "I don't think you should go outside today since you were sick yesterday," you should firmly tell your child that he is not to go out. The more definite you are, the less likely your child will be to make a fuss.

If you are to seem confident, you must avoid nagging, cajoling, screaming, and threatening. Once the rules are stated and the consequences—either positive ones for adherence or negative ones for disobedience—are stated and understood, there should be a minimum of discussion. You should not toss out numerous reminders of rules and conditions. You should, rather, show a matter-of-fact acceptance of the situation with an equally matter-of-fact readiness to enforce the rules as required.

Many times, the methods we have been using to help our children develop acceptable patterns of behavior seem to run aground. These methods are usually an extension of the child-rearing methods our parents used with us, combined with miscellaneous insights we have picked up through the years. For some families these intuitive methods seem to work fine. For others, including most families with hyperactive children, they do not.

The parents of hyperactive children have to plan their parenting to a much greater degree than do other parents. They have to be much more conscious of the goals they want to achieve and the ways to achieve these goals. The following two chapters discuss two different ways of helping children improve their day-to-day functioning. The two basic approaches—that of setting up and enforcing rules and regulations and that of helping a child develop good habits and discard bad ones—can be used at the same time in different areas of the child's life.

If you fault and blame your children, show yourself displeased and discontent when they do their best to please you, this is the way to provoke them to wrath and anger, and to discourage them.

—Benjamin Wadsworth
The Well-Ordered Family, 1719

7   HOW CHILDREN LEARN TO BEHAVE

Through work in experimental psychology, we have learned a great deal about how animals and people learn. An individual will acquire a habit that is rewarded, and learn not to do something that is never rewarded or that is punished. A pigeon, for example, will learn to peck at a green light if he receives a kernel of corn every time he does so. He will unlearn this habit if the corn stops coming and if he receives an electric shock every time he pecks at the light. If nothing happens when the pigeon pecks at a light, there will be "nothing in it" for him, and so he will not go on pecking at it. Psychologists have concluded that people learn in basically the same way as animals in the laboratory.

Parents are constantly arranging situations in which learning takes place. Although not always aware of it, we often unwittingly reward undesirable behavior. A mother may never notice her child when he is good but be quick to scold him when he is bad. The child, preferring negative attention to no attention at all, continues his bad behavior so that he will get his reward—attention from his mother. When the mother begins to notice her child's good behavior and ignore the bad, the child will adapt his behavior accordingly. The learning situation has thus been changed to reward desirable behavior.

Most acts in life carry some sort of natural consequence, either positive or negative. Doing satisfactory schoolwork carries the positive consequence of satisfaction with a job well done, plus the approval of parents, teachers, and classmates. Lack of attention to schoolwork carries the negative consequence of a feeling of failure, plus parents' disappointment, teacher's anger, and perhaps classmates' scorn. Playing games according to the rules carries the positive consequence of being asked to play again. An inability to play the game right carries the negative consequence of failure, as well as subsequent ostracism and loneliness.

Children learn through the natural activity of such positive and negative consequences, with some additional artificial consequences —rewards and punishments—imposed by parents and teachers. Let us discuss these aids to learning as they apply to the improvement of a child's conduct.

Rewards

One important principle that has emerged from work in motivational psychology is that the carrot is better than the stick. Children learn more by praise than by criticism, more when they are rewarded for good behavior than when they are punished for bad.

For most children, the normal social rewards are effective for reinforcing good behavior. A smile, a word of praise, or a special treat let a child know that his efforts to do the right thing "pay off" in terms of parental approval. Too few parents make full use of these social rewards in motivating their children. Too often, parents take a child's good behavior for granted and make no special efforts to commend him for keeping out of mischief. "Why should I make a big deal out of praising him for doing what he's supposed to do, anyway?" they ask. When people think in these terms, they are not taking into account the basic principles governing the way people learn.

Most children, for example, have been taught that they should try to find the owner of any valuable property they may find in the street. In fact, the laws of our land generally prohibit a person from keeping property that is not rightfully his. Yet when children do find large sums of money and turn it in to the police, a laudatory newspaper story usually appears, commending the children and reporting some financial reward for them from the owner of the recovered property. In recognition that it is often difficult to do the right thing, it is perfectly appropriate to reward children when they do "what they are supposed to do." Another example of this principle would be the lowered insurance rates offered to drivers with no traffic violations. Motorists are not supposed to violate the vehicle code; those who do are punished; those who accumulate no violations are only "doing what they are supposed to do." Yet it is only fitting that those people who do make special efforts should reap some benefits for doing so, aside from staying out of trouble.

In some families, rewarding children for good behavior comes naturally to parents. These parents are generous with their praise, their affection, and their attention. Other parents are chary of showing too much approval of a child for fear of spoiling him. Parents have to question their own attitudes and behavior. Do the parents welcome a child's periods of good behavior so they can get their work done or snatch a few moments of quiet relaxation? Do they quietly ignore their child when he is good, feeling that if they pay him too much attention, he will start acting up? On the other hand, do they stop what they are doing when the child becomes rowdy, thereby teaching him that to get Mother's or Father's attention, he has to make a pest of himself?

When this is happening in a home, the parents have to consciously change their own style of acting toward the child. They have to make a deliberate effort to reward a child when he is good. Parents are often thrilled to find a miraculous change in their child's behavior in response to the child's realization that being good brings good results, that virtue may be not only its own reward, but the spur to other rewards as well. Of course, you do not want to shower a child with lavish praise for small achievements or you will be debasing the coinage. Be generous with your approval, but be realistic.

For some children normal social rewards are not sufficiently motivating. Tangible rewards, such as food, toys, or money, sometimes help to bridge the gap between a situation where nothing motivates a child to do better and the point at which the social rewards of approval can take over. Eventually, the aim is for the inner rewards of achievement for its own sake. Tangible rewards have been used from time immemorial to influence children's behavior at home and at school. Remember Tom Sawyer's collection of tickets that led to his claiming a Bible from the Sunday school teacher? Schoolchildren have long been rewarded by stars on a chart (leading to a lollipop or a book), by certificates for being on time every day of the term, and by being made classroom monitors. Today we have lower automobile insurance rates for high school students who do well in driver education courses and free ball games for straight "A" students.

The object of using such material rewards is to get a child's attention, to begin to motivate him toward improving his behavior. At the first sign of beginning improvement, the person gives the reward and an accompanying social reinforcement, that is, a smile and words of approval. By a process of conditioning through association, the approval and the smile become as effective in motivating the child as the concrete items. The tangible rewards also serve as aids to the adult, reminding him or her to notice a child's good behavior and to reward it. Gradually, the parent becomes more used to giving approval and praise, the tangible items are phased out of the picture, and the social rewards become the prime motivators and reinforcers of desired behavior. The standards are also steadily raised so that the child has to reach a higher level of performance for a given reward.

A program of habit training that includes the granting of specific rewards for specific behaviors seeks to motivate a child by "priming the pump"—by offering special inducements until the parent and the child get used to giving and receiving the ordinary social rewards. Once a child has known the satisfaction of earning rewards, of reaping approval and of doing a job well, he is more likely to do the right thing for the "right" reasons, first the social rewards and eventually the inner rewards.

Putting a Reward System into Practice

Before you institute a reward system you have to decide on the reward. First, try social rewards. Make special efforts to praise your child for a job well done, to commend him for improvement, to recognize his efforts in living up to a family rule. If, after about a month of conscious effort, you feel you are not making enough progress, you may want to grant tangible rewards. A reward must be important to a child to motivate him, but it need not be material in nature. An effective reward could be an opportunity to be alone with a parent and to do something together like playing checkers.

Some families have found a token system to be most effective. Under this program, a child gets a token after exhibiting a specified type of desirable behavior. When he accumulates a certain number of tokens, he can exchange them for a specified reward. The token can be a check in a notebook or a gold star on a chart, or it can be an actual material item. One family, for example, went on the "bean standard." Each child received a kidney bean for certain types of good behavior; when a child accumulated ten beans, he could choose a fifty-cent item at the local dime store. When using a tangible item as a token, you have to be sure that this is something the child can obtain only from you. For example, paper clips would not be a good kind of token if your child could easily buy a box and keep them in his room.

The token system of rewards offers a great deal of flexibility. If your employer paid you in scrip that could be used only to buy food and clothing at the company store, your salary would not be nearly so valuable as if he paid you in legal tender that you could use to buy a car, take a vacation, or shop around for various purchases. So it is with tokens: if your child has some choice over what he can use his tokens for, he will be more highly motivated to earn them than if his reward always takes the same form.

Another advantage to rewarding small bits of behavior with tokens is that it avoids an "all or nothing" proposition. Ten-year-old Pam was yearning for a rod and reel, which her parents promised her if she could get through an entire month without being sent to the principal's office. Pam held out for three weeks without being sent from the classroom, but one day she came home sobbing uncontrollably and saying over and over again, "I blew it!" She was inconsolable because she had been sent to the principal and so had lost hope of getting her fishing rod. If Pam had been working on the token system, her three weeks of mighty effort would not have gone unrewarded. Had she been rewarded with a point for every day she managed to avoid being sent to the principal's office, she would have received recognition for her effort and she would have retained the points she did earn. Her eventual visit to the principal would have slowed her progress toward getting the fishing rod, but it would not have prevented it entirely.

Another problem with Pam and her fishing rod is that by setting the condition of not being sent to the principal's office as the basis for her reward, her parents were forced to take the teacher's word for Pam's behavior. It is possible that Pam's trips to the front office depended as much on the teacher's mood of the day as they did on the child's own deportment. This same principle operates when a youngster is rewarded for good grades on a report card; while good marks are often related to a child's efforts, they are not always so. Some children get high grades with little effort; some cheat; some have stricter teachers than others. It is always better, when possible, to reward a child for his efforts rather than the results. For example, it would be better to reward a youngster for doing one hour of homework each day than for getting all A's on his report card. And it would be better to reward Pam for the kind of behavior that can be observed at home than for that for which her parents have to accept outside testimony.

When instituting a token system, be sure your child understands the principle behind it—that tokens can be exchanged for something he wants. You can make this point with a very young child by giving the child a token and then, almost immediately, offering to trade the token for a little trinket, a cookie, or a hug.

In Chapter 9 we will talk about setting up a program that uses rewards to change aspects of your child's behavior, based on a contract agreed upon by you and your child. Rewards can also be extremely beneficial even when used outside any contract system. You can accomplish a great deal by rewarding your child when you catch him being good. If he does anything you approve of— holds a door open for you instead of dashing out and letting it slam in your face as usual, sits down to do his homework without being reminded, plays nicely with his sister—you can encourage him in these actions by rewarding him. The simplest kind of reward is some gesture of approval—a hug or a statement of your pleasure at his behavior. Or you could occasionally award a token or a special treat. Rewarding your child spontaneously in this way demonstrates to him that he is noticed when he is good.

Whenever you reward your child—whether on a contract basis for a previously agreed-upon type of behavior or on a spontaneous basis—your reward will do its work better if it follows within seconds after the desired behavior takes place. This is particularly important with hyperactive children, who seem to need quick gratification more than other children.

You should reward the first steps toward a goal. Suppose your eventual goal is for your child to get dressed, eat breakfast, make his bed, and be out of the house by 8:30 A.M. You can start by asking him to get out of bed at 7:00 A.M., telling him to come to you as soon as he gets up. When he does, you should reward him for this, even if his behavior runs downhill from that point on. In other words, you should reward the beginnings of change, instead of waiting for the child to reach an absolute standard of behavior.

One sure way to make a reward system fail is to set up a standard of behavior that is out of the child's immediate reach. (This is what happened to Pam, when she failed to earn her fishing rod.) Rewards have to be for small steps in the right direction, steps that the parent or teacher is virtually certain the child is able to take. If the steps are so large that the child cannot manage them, he will seldom, if ever, receive a reward. "What's the use of trying?" he will ask himself, and, discouraged, he will soon stop trying. Very soon the entire system will collapse in failure. It is not the system itself that is no good in such cases; it is a mistaken application of the system.

Punishment

A program of child raising that emphasizes rewards for good behavior and for efforts to achieve good behavior holds the most promise for achieving your goals. There are times, however, when punishment seems essential to stop some form of disagreeable behavior. Some acts carry their own natural consequences, which act as a form of punishment. For example, after Mickey has run into the sharp corner of a desk while tearing wildly around the house, he is more likely to be careful in the future than if he is merely told that he *might* hurt himself. And Heidi will be more inclined to dress realistically for the weather after she has gone out in the rain wearing a thin dress and torn sneakers than she would if her mother told her what to wear every morning.

Punishment influences behavior best when children can learn to avoid it, just as a rat learns to avoid an electric shock by remembering to run into another compartment of his cage. When rules are laid down, the consequences of not obeying them should be clearly stated and, if necessary, a child's memory should be refreshed from time to time. The child then has a clear choice. It is his responsibility if he ends up getting punished.

For example, Alvin knows that if he rides his bicycle without regard to traffic laws, he will be forbidden to ride the bicycle for several days. Annie knows that if she stays up half an hour past her bedtime on Wednesday, she will have to go to bed half an hour early on Thursday. The three children in the Green family know that when they leave shoes, books, toys, or other paraphernalia in the living room overnight, their possessions will go into a special box, not to reappear until the following week. When Ellen is having a temper tantrum, her father does not tell her to go to the "time-out place" right away. Instead, he says, "You must stop this or go to the time-out room." The choice is Ellen's.

Parents cannot and should not even attempt to draw up lists of all kinds of possible punishments for all different types of misbehaviors. This would put an undue emphasis on negative behavior and would also indicate to a child that you expect him to misbehave. We want our children to feel that we expect the best of them, not the worst. Also, children often do things that are quite unexpected, for which there are, therefore, no preordained punishments. When this happens, and when the offense is one that you feel is serious enough to be punishable, the ideal punishment should follow naturally from the disapproved behavior. For example, when eight-year-old Nicky wrote curse words on the sidewalk in front of a neighbor's house, he had to hose the neighbor's walk. When nine-year-old Priscilla took some candy from a local store, her mother accompanied her back to the store while Priscilla admitted what she had done and paid the shopkeeper with her own money. When four-year-old Timothy threw his blocks at a playmate, the blocks were taken away and locked up.

Withdrawal of Privileges

Many times, the behavior you want to stop is not the kind that has any logical negative consequence. In such cases, the best form of punishment is the withdrawal of privileges. Television viewing is often revoked for misdeeds, and this is probably a good choice, since most children today watch too much television, anyway. (Punishing a child by restricting his televiewing may have other benefits, like forcing him to use his time more creatively.) Other privileges that might be subject to withdrawal would include going to the Saturday movie matinee, staying up late on weekends, riding his bicycle, and having the freedom to go outside the yard.

Isolation

Isolation can be a useful negative consequence, with positive benefits as well, if handled properly. It serves the dual purpose of withdrawing from a child the privilege of being in company, and it also provides him with a period of quiet, which he may be able to use to "pull himself together."

One perceptive mother has made good use of isolation to help her child develop controls over his own behavior. "When Peter would invite friends over," she recalls, "the activity would keep building up, and the running and the noise would get worse and worse. When I felt it had gone beyond the normal limits for healthy seven-year-old boys, I would reach in and pluck Peter out of the group for a while.

"At first, he became angry at me for doing this, but after a while he realized why I was doing it, and he appreciated it. I was trying to help him to recognize at what point he was becoming impossible and to make it easier for him to be 'possible' again. As he grew older, he would often isolate himself voluntarily when he sensed he had had enough of being with a group of people."

Isolation is, of course, a kind of punishment, but it is a mild kind, with the potential for the benefits described by this mother. When you are using isolation more as a punishment than as a chance for a child to catch his breath and pull himself together, it is important to decide on a place where the child should go. It is best not to send the child to his own bedroom. His room should be a pleasant place, a refuge from the world and a spot where he can keep his favorite toys and books. Being in attractive surroundings like this is not a negative experience. On the other hand, turning the room into a place where a child is sent for punishment robs it of the cheerfulness it should have at other times. The right place for isolation is a small room or corner, with virtually no stimulation. This can be a corner of the basement, an unused room, a stool in the corner of the kitchen or utility room, or any other place that is not very interesting. It should not be a frightening place like a dark closet or cellar.

An isolation spot, or time-out place, is ideal for those times when a child is destructive or fighting with his siblings. When you realize that things have reached such a pitch that isolation is necessary, you should walk in calmly and tell the child that it is time for him to take time out for a brief period, like five or ten minutes. The child may not come willingly, of course. If he refuses to go of his own volition, it is up to you to exercise your physical strength to get him to the time-out place—even if you have to pick him up or drag him, kicking and screaming, all the way. Once you have done this once or twice, firmly but not hurtfully, your child will realize that you mean business. From then on, he will be more likely to go of his own accord.

You can set a kitchen timer so that the child will know when he may come out, or you can go in yourself to tell him when his time is up. He should not stay "in solitary" too long, only enough to get a grip on himself. He should understand that if he reverts to his former behavior, he will have to go right back into "solitary."

Limitations to Punishment

Though there is a place for punishment in bringing up children, its use should be limited. For some reason, it is much easier for many parents to accept the idea of punishing a child for bad behavior than rewarding him for good behavior. Yet the principle here is the reverse of the same coin—artificial negative consequences, just as rewards are artificial positive consequences. It is a mystery why so many parents think it better and more natural to try to motivate a child by making him fear the consequences of doing the wrong thing than it is to motivate him by rewarding his doing the right thing.

Children who are raised with rewards, praise, and support from their parents grow up to be more adequate socially than those whose parents punish a great deal. According to Dr. Stanley Coopersmith's studies, children with high self-esteem were more likely to have parents who favored the use of positive techniques in influencing their children's behavior than did children with a poorer self-image.

Punishment has many drawbacks. The most important is probably its general lack of effectiveness. When resorted to regularly, punishment tends to aggravate a child's behavior problem rather than solve it. One problem is that punishment, which is essentially a negative act, cannot teach positive values. It can only be a temporary way to stop a negative behavior. Yet it does not even do this consistently.

Another problem is that, for reasons that we do not completely understand, punishment may actually reinforce a child's bad behavior. Many children get unconscious satisfaction from seeing their parents "lose their cool"; a few provoke them deliberately. Children sometimes invite a spanking as a way of being helped out of a tantrum or a "wound-up" state, and it may be easier to have this done for them by the spanking than to do it themselves. Other children with very low self-esteem find it easier to be at the bottom of the heap than to try to struggle back up. Punishment can be a kind of martyrdom for them, showing them that they really are as low as they think they are. Other children use their parents' punishments as an excuse for feeling sorry for themselves. In addition, punishment gives attention to the very behavior that you are trying to eliminate. Since for some children any notice of their activities is welcome, punishing them may amount to recognizing and rewarding their behavior.

Punishment arouses anger and hostility in the child against whoever doles it out, making the child far less likely to want to adopt the standards of the angry, punitive adult. No matter how much you say that you are castigating the sin and not the sinner, it is the unhappy "sinner" who goes to bed hungry or watches the other children going off to the circus or has a tender behind. The child's *behavior* is not being punished; the *child* is being punished.

All too often, parents seeking to find a punishment that will really mean something to their child strip him of things he sorely needs for his physical or psychological health. Depriving a child of his dinner, for example, or of opportunities for fresh air and exercise is physically undesirable. Or punishing a child whose biggest problem is difficulty in making friends by making him cancel a date to sleep at another child's house strikes him at a particularly vulnerable place. In the same vein, you would not want to punish a virtually friendless child by forbidding him any contact with his beloved dog.

When we get into the two most popular types of punishments—physical punishment and verbal harangues—we find serious drawbacks in both of them.

Spanking

When you strike your child in the heat of the moment, your child sees that you have lost control of yourself, and the satisfaction this gives him can reinforce his bad behavior. A child may especially enjoy the undignified spectacle of his mother's chasing him around the house, trying to get hold of him. When a mother feels unable to administer physical punishment to a big boy and defers his spanking "till father comes home," the punishment will be ineffective simply because it follows so long after the original misdeed. Spanking insults a child's dignity, making him think less of himself. Furthermore, it is confusing for a child to find that the hand that strokes and cuddles also inflicts pain.

Another extremely important deterrent to hitting a child is the tendency of this sort of parental action to encourage aggressiveness on the child's part. Children who have been punished physically are more likely to have trouble later with aggressive behavior. One reason for this is that the parent serves as a role model for his children. Children do as we do, not as we say. You may caution your children to act calmly and reasonably, but when they see you lose your temper, act impulsively, and strike out when you become angry, they will automatically tend to act this way themselves.

Finally, physical punishment makes parents feel guilty. They feel like bullies, and this, of course, makes them think poorly of themselves. One walloping can strike a serious blow at the self-esteem of both parent and child. Corporal punishment administered on a regular basis insures two generations with poor self-images.

A common argument in favor of spanking is that it makes the parents feel better. But parents have to realize how much bigger they are than their children and what bullies they seem when they hit a child just for their own satisfaction. It is unfair to the child and an indulgence on the part of the parent to retain the privilege for this reason. The parent who feels this way should ask himself how he would feel if his child's teacher or older brother or the man next door chose to reserve such a right.

The one exception to this rule would be the occasional swat on the fanny for a toddler who runs into the street or does something else carrying the potential for real danger. But spanking should not be resorted to often and not at all with older children. If your child seems to be getting spanked fairly regularly, you have to conclude that your punishments are ineffectual. The child who is getting six spankings a day every day for months certainly is not showing any signs of learning from these measures.

Scolding

The most usual way that middle-class parents deal with their children's bad behavior these days is not through spanking but through a lot of reasoning and scolding. This sort of "verbal abuse" is often more difficult for children to cope with than physical punishment. They cannot fight back at this level, since they do not have the verbal skills that their parents have. The children are often overwhelmed by their parents' verbal virtuosity and, as a result, come to resent their parents.

Withdrawal of love is just as implicit in a severe scolding as in a spanking, since it is virtually impossible to be loving at the same time you are scolding or spanking a child. All children, especially the hyperactive, whose sense of self is likely to be quite shaky, need to feel secure in their parents' love. Since acceptance is such a basic factor in a child's feelings about himself, we would not want our children to be in doubt about our love for them. The kind of punishment in which an angry parent screams, "I don't want you near me! I don't want to have anything to do with you!" cannot help chipping away at a child's self-esteem and sense of security.

Helping Your Child—Reward or Punishment?

As we said earlier, to reward good behavior or the avoidance of bad behavior is far more effective than to punish bad behavior. Instead of taking good behavior for granted, as we often do, we should reward it with attention.

Hyperactive children present a special challenge in terms of behavior. Their distractibility, their impulsiveness, and their level of drive are much stronger than the forces on the side of control. As a result, many of them do not respond as favorably as the average child to the usual kinds of social rewards, the praise and smiles and approval. Nor are they as easily deterred by punishment, either the kind that follows as a natural consequence or the kind imposed by parents and teachers. Some hyperactive children will get burned repeatedly by matches and yet continue to fool around with them. Some are so resistant to the ordinary methods of discipline that their day seems to be one continual round of punishments. The parents of such a child are likely to throw up their hands in despair and say, "We've tried *everything* and *nothing* works!" When they say this, they are sincere. They have tried all kinds of disciplinary approaches, but it is likely that they have not truly analyzed their child's behavior as well as their own, to see how their attention reinforces his misbehavior.

Most people have trouble bringing up their children, because none of us have ever been trained to be a parent. Some of us can get by with a sort of inspired amateurism. But not the parents of a hyperactive child. You have to be much more aware of what you are doing with your child and why you are doing it than does the average set of parents.

You have a choice. You can say, "But my child *should* want to do well at school; he *should* want to play by the rules; he *should* want to do the right thing for its own sake." You can brood about the unfairness of your having to take more pains with your parenting than do your neighbors and friends. Or you can actively help your child to want to do the right thing. After reading the next three chapters, you can draw up a plan for helping your child behave better. You can develop a workable set of rules and regulations. You can attack your child's bad habits without attacking the child. You can change the entire direction of your child's life by helping him to develop and to work toward a set of goals that will guide him in a happy, productive life.

Let therefore your Rules to your son be as few as possible, and rather fewer than more than seem absolutely necessary. For if you burden him with many Rules, one of these two Things must necessarily follow; that either he must be very often punish'd, which will be of ill Consequence, by making Punishment too frequent and familiar; or else you must let the Transgressions of some of your Rules go unpunish'd, whereby they will of course grow contemptible, and your Authority cheap to him.

—John Locke
Some Thoughts Concerning Education, 1693

8   RULES AND REGULATIONS

What John Locke said three hundred years ago is just as true today. A child who is faced with too many rules learns that many of them can be broken with impunity and ends by losing respect for all of them. Rules seem to proliferate in the typical household, because they are provoked by specific situations, instead of being planned in advance. Before the parents know it, they are announcing new rules left and right, even as the old ones are being ignored.

When a child is hemmed in by too many rules or is out of control by reason of too few, he will constantly get into trouble. His parents will nag, scold, punish, and feel more and more frustrated. They will feel inadequate because they cannot make their child mind. They will resent his lack of obedience, and they will come to dislike the child. The child, of course, will realize his parents' anger and dislike, and his self-esteem will plummet. The worse he feels about himself, the worse he will behave, and the angrier his parents will continue to become.

This cycle is painfully evident in the families of many hyperactive children. These youngsters are constantly breaking rules of the household, the classroom, or the playground. Because of their short span of attention, their minds wander even as they are being told what to do or not do, so that they often never even hear the rule. Because of their impulsivity, they act before they think, and the rule they are breaking remains buried in the back of their minds without entering their conscious awareness. Because of their spirited, adventurous natures, they test the rules more than other children. It is especially important for the parents of a hyperactive child to think about the rules for their child. They must consider the importance, the reasonableness, and the enforceability of any rule before establishing it.

What Rules Can Cover

Household rules can be applied to clear-cut situations when there is no doubt about whether a particular act has been done or not. Either Cathy runs into the street alone or she does not. Jack jumps on a trampoline either with adult supervision or without it. The child who breaks the rules in such clear situations will, if he gives any thought to the rule, know immediately that he is breaking it.

Rules are applicable when a definite time is involved. Either Victor turns his light out at eight o'clock or he does not. Either Judy reaches school before the tardy bell rings or she does not. Either Michael finishes his homework before the beginning of the TV show he wants to watch or he does not.

Rules are applicable to behavior that is under the child's control, as opposed to thumb-sucking or bed-wetting which are more or less involuntary.

Setting Up Rules

Before you set up new rules or evaluate the old ones, you have to ask yourself what a rule is and what makes a good rule. A rule is a statement of anything that you expect your child to do or not to do, any code of behavior he is expected to adhere to, any type of behavior that is expressly forbidden, any chore he is supposed to perform, any responsibility he must fulfill. A good rule is reasonable; it can be understood and followed by the child; and it is enforceable.

A Good Rule Is Reasonable

A reasonable rule serves a useful purpose. Some of the useful purposes a rule can serve are maintaining safety (not playing in the street, not playing with matches, coming home right after school); sound hygiene (brushing teeth after meals, washing hands before dinner, not eating sweets); helping a child learn the skills he will need in life (doing homework, getting to school on time, taking care of his own personal needs); sharing the work of the family (setting the table, raking leaves, emptying wastebaskets); respecting the rights of others (not going into his brothers' and sisters' rooms without permission, not taking others' belongings, not hitting smaller children, not being cruel to animals); and convenience for family (conforming to schedules, getting to dinner and to the school bus stop on time).

On the other hand, parents sometimes box themselves in by enunciating rules that really do not serve a useful purpose but are presented to the child to "teach him self-discipline" or to "show him who's boss." Such rules are difficult to justify and even more difficult to enforce. To judge the rules you are laying down in your own family, ask yourself, "What useful purpose does this rule serve?" If you cannot think of any, throw it out.

Whenever possible, especially with an older child, parents should discuss the rule with the child and allow him to react to it. The child will be better able to understand the purpose for a rule. If he objects to it as unreasonable, the parents should re-evaluate the rule. For example, Mrs. Brown is a "night person" who has trouble getting up in the morning and likes to stay up until midnight. Yet she has insisted that her twelve-year-old daughter, Cassie, who is basically the same way, go to bed at nine o'clock. When Cassie pointed out to her mother that she cannot fall asleep before eleven anyway, Mrs. Brown extended Cassie's bedtime to ten o'clock, contingent on Cassie's continuing to get up and be out of the house on time in the morning. Other times, a child may object strenuously to a rule, saying, "It's not fair. None of the other kids on the block have to do it!" If the parents feel that their rule *is* fair, they should let their child know why they think so and what the purpose of the rule is. They should then stick to their guns, making the point that they have certain standards that other families may not have. The point of discussing rules is not to abdicate control of the household to the children but to demonstrate respect for their opinions and to encourage them to assume more responsibility for setting their own standards.

A Child Understands a Good Rule

To help your child understand a rule, you should phrase it simply; if necessary, have your youngster repeat it back to you. You should clearly define the behavior you expect of your child. In other words, you would not say, "Be good." You would say, "Don't hit the baby. Brush your teeth. Do what the baby-sitter tells you to do." You would not say, "Clean up that sloppy room." You would say, "Put away the clothes on the floor. Pick up all those little pieces of paper. Make your bed. Put your shoes in the closet."

A rule should not be expressed in the form of a question unless the child actually has a choice. Asking a child, "Do you want to go to bed now?" invites the inevitable answer, "No." It also muddies the fact that you think you are stating a rule and your child thinks you are asking a question.

A Child Can Follow a Good Rule

There is no point in setting up a rule that your child is unable to adhere to. You cannot tell a child not to have mean thoughts; none of us can control our thoughts, only our behavior. So you cannot tell Angela not to hate her baby brother, but you can tell her not to bite him. You cannot insist that Brad go to sleep at a certain time, but you can insist that he be in bed with the lights out.

Before you ask a child to perform any activity, you have to be sure that he knows how to do it. This may mean that you will have to invest some time in teaching him all the steps involved in making his bed, cleaning up the kitchen, or getting ready to do his homework. You may feel that he should already know everything that is required. Whether he should or should not know is irrelevant. What does matter is whether he does or does not know. When you know that your child can perform a task because you have taught him or you have observed that he is capable, then and only then can you ask him to do it.

You Can Consistently Enforce a Good Rule

There is no point to setting up a rule that you cannot enforce. If you will not know when the rule is adhered to or when it is ignored, you cannot possibly enforce it. You should be able to observe either the behavior itself or its results without having to depend on your child's honor or the word of other people. For example, you can set up a rule that no food is to be thrown at your dinner table, but you cannot set up a rule forbidding the throwing of food at school. That is up to school authorities to forbid and to enforce. You can restrict television viewing when you are home, but you cannot say, "Don't watch TV while I'm gone." You can forbid a child to smoke in the house, but you cannot say, "You are never to smoke." You can set up a rule, then, only if you can be present and are willing to make the effort to enforce the rule absolutely. Otherwise, you cannot be consistent about enforcing the rule.

Consistency in enforcement is extremely important. It is important even when such consistency conflicts with the interests of the parents. If Freddy is not permitted to watch television during the day, his mother cannot sit him in front of the TV set on days when he is particularly difficult and she is harassed, just to get him out of her hair. This does not mean that rules can never be relaxed in extraordinary circumstances. It does mean that parents have the obligation to respect the rules they establish for their children, if they expect their children to respect them. Exceptions should be made only for reasons that serve everyone's best interests, and only for exceptional reasons.

"Never," "Time," and "Before" Rules

A "never" rule forbids a certain type of behavior absolutely and at all times. Examples are "Never play with matches," "Never go swimming alone," "Never take money that does not belong to you," and "Never toss your coat on the couch."

A "time" rule specifies a time of day when an activity must be performed. Examples are "Dishes are to be washed by 7:30," "Snacks are not to be eaten after four o'clock," "Be home from school by 3:30," and "Be home for dinner at 5:30."

"Before" rules state that a child must do one thing before engaging in some other activity. Examples would be "Make your bed before you come down to breakfast," "Do your homework before you watch television," "Wash your hands before eating dinner," and "Clean your room before you go out to play."

Enforcing Rules

Rules are mainly enforced by the parents' attitudes. They can also be reinforced by rewards and punishment.

Punishment

You should punish your child when he violates a rule by enforcing a consequence that has already been stated. If he is to be rewarded for following the rule, the fact that he does not receive his reward is in itself a kind of punishment.

Parents' Determination

The parents' will power is the main factor in whether or not children observe rules. If they confidently expect their children to obey, if they consistently act as they say they will, and if they keep a close eye on the children, the chances are good that the rules will be followed.

This determination is illustrated by a mother who told her little girl to hang up her coat. "I got the standard answer, 'Don't want to.' So I said, 'Come, Mommy will help you.' I went over and took Crissy's hand. Still holding her hand, we picked up the coat and put it on the hook. Of course, I practically did it for her, but I did include her in the act, and she did realize that I am going to follow through on the demands I make of her."

A father whose ten-year-old son was habitually late coming home for dinner decided one evening to go out in the neighborhood to find him instead of waiting at home, getting angry, and then punishing the boy. When he located Eddie in a friend's yard, he said, "Come on, Eddie, time to go home," and backed up his words by taking the boy by the elbow and practically dragging him home. A couple of these instances were enough to impress upon the youngster that his parents meant business and that he would save himself trouble and embarrassment if he got home in time under his own steam.

Many situations lend themselves to such direct action. Those that do should be handled as simply, calmly, and expeditiously as possible, without scolding or other punishment.

Reward

You can reward your child when he follows the rule if it is one embodying a positive action (like making his bed) and when he refrains from a forbidden activity (like screaming in your ear when you are on the telephone). Rewards can be social ones like praise and commendation, or tokens like checks or stars, or tangible items like small toys. Such rewards should be given only every time you begin to apply a rule. When your child observes the rule fairly regularly, you should reward him only occasionally.

Testing of the Rules

Whenever you expect some new type of behavior from your child, you can expect him to get worse before he gets better. Every child has to test the authorities in his life to find out whether they truly mean what they say. Once he discovers that you do mean what you say and you do live up to your word, his testing will become less frequent.

Suppose Mary is supposed to make her bed before she goes to school. On this particular Monday she is out the door to catch the bus by the time you realize that the bed is still unmade. You know that if you call her back to make her bed, she will miss the bus. What should you do?

The following courses of action are open to you:
- You can call Mary back, have her miss the bus and walk to school. She makes her bed, but she gets no reward because she did not follow the rule.
- You can let her take the bus and be sure that she makes her bed as soon as she gets home—before homework, play, or snack. She gets no reward.
- You can make the bed yourself and, in consideration of the time you had to spend on it, institute some type of negative consequence. Mary gets no reward.
- You can make the bed yourself, say, "She's only a child," and give her her reward for the day because she did everything else that she was supposed to do.

The alternatives are listed here in a descending order of preference, with the first by far the best, the last definitely to be avoided, and the two middle ones as possibilities. You have to use your own judgment in these situations.

Taking a Look at the Rules in Your House

If you want to make a fresh start with the rules in your household, evaluate the present situation. Which rules seem to be causing the most trouble? Are they reasonable? Does your child understand them? Is he capable of following them? Does he know the consequences of not following them? Can you enforce them?

Both parents should sit down together with pencil and paper to make a check list of rules. Jot down all the rules you expect your children to follow and evaluate them according to these criteria. If you conclude that your rules are being blithely disregarded, it is time to act.

Remember, though, that you cannot change everything at once. You will be overwhelmed, and your child will be bewildered. You should change things one rule at a time.

To begin, follow these guidelines:

1. Husband and wife together should agree on one rule to be enforced absolutely.

2. Discuss the rule with your child. Tell him why this rule is important. Encourage him to voice his feelings; if you think it appropriate, modify the rule accordingly. Explain to him how you are going to help him to remember the rule, either by rewarding him when he follows it or by punishing him when he violates it.

3. Be consistent about recognizing your child's efforts to adhere to the rule. When you catch him being better than usual, commend him.

4. Be firm about following through on punishment when necessary. Once a consequence has been agreed upon, put it into effect when it is called for.

5. Ignore irrelevant behavior on your child's part when you enforce the rule. This step requires herculean efforts from most par-

ents. It is extremely hard for us to avoid rising to the bait of a child's militant sullenness; or his calling us names and accusing us of being mean, unfair, and a host of other things we do not like to be called; or his pitching an elaborate and embarrassing temper tantrum. It is hard to ignore a five-year-old screaming at the top of his lungs while both his hands are clutched tightly around your ankles. But in this step lies the crux of rule enforcement. If you can force yourself to ignore any behavior not relevant to the behavior you are trying to obtain, you will be removing from your child the joy of distracting you from your planned program, as well as the gratification of being noticed for the wrong thing.

Once you realize that you do have the power to enforce a rule and that your child can improve his behavior with your help, your self-confidence will return. The more self-assured you are, the more you will be able to enjoy your child and have good times with him.

The first and most important step in management is, that
whatever a mother says, always must be done. For this
reason, do not require too much; and on no account allow
your child to do at one time, what you have forbidden him
at another.

—Lydia Maria Child
The Mother's Book, 1831

9 HELPING CHILDREN TO ACQUIRE
GOOD HABITS AND LOSE BAD ONES

Some of the changes you want in your child's behavior are improvements rather than cases of doing or not doing something.
Grades in school, table manners, tidiness, promptness in doing
chores, taking part in family conversation, and reading books are
all examples of things you would like improved or done more
often. But they are not the kinds of behavior that you can affect
by rules. Partly involuntary behaviors such as thumb sucking, bed
wetting, soiling, masturbating in public, and temper tantrums also
need a different approach.

If you are troubled by some behavior on your child's part that
fits into this category, use the guidelines in this chapter to bring
about change. These guidelines are not a prescription, of course.
Each family is unique; each child is unique; each problem is
unique. But, taking this uniqueness into consideration, you should
be able to construct your own program by building upon the structure set out here. The following guidelines apply the principles,
discussed in Chapter 7, that determine the way children develop
their behavior. When you apply these guidelines, you are simply
following common-sense principles in a systematic way.

Guidelines for Habit Training

1. Define the problem. What are the kinds of behavior that are most distressing to you and to your child? Make a list of everything your child does or does not do that you do not like, ranging from the mild to the severe items. Do not be alarmed if you end up with a long list. Of all these things you would like to change, pick one. Your habit-training program will work only if you concentrate on one problem at a time. You may want to pick the problem that bothers you the most or the one that seems the easiest to solve. In any case, you will have a starting point.

2. Analyze the problem. Suppose you have picked being late for the school bus. How many minutes is your child late on an average day? How many days a week? Does the getting-ready process break down at the dressing stage or the breakfast stage? Or does it never get started in the first place? What happens when you are not there? Does he get off to school all right on his own? Is the problem really yours, in the sense that you are assuming responsibilities that he can handle himself? Are you unwilling to let him face the consequences of being late?

3. Explore your child's motivation. What factors are operating to reward his behavior? Do you pay extra attention to your child by nagging him every morning to get ready? Do you drive him to school, thereby giving him more of your time? Do the teacher and other children notice his coming in late? Does he avoid a bully at the bus stop by missing the bus? Does he hate what he has to do in school first thing in the morning? Does he want to drag out his time at home because this is one of the few times he gets the chance to talk with his father? In other words, what is in it for him to miss the bus?

4. Think what you can do to change the external aspects of the situation. Would it help if you woke him up fifteen minutes earlier? Can you have his bus stop changed if he is regularly being beaten up by a gang of older children? Can you give him extra attention

at other times of the day, so he will not crave your attention in the morning? Whatever you can do to make the situation easier for your child to handle is worthwhile. Remember, you want some change in behavior but you are not going to expect the impossible. And you are going to meet him halfway as much as possible.

5. Set aside a time for both parents to talk to the child when you all have time to discuss the problem and its possible solutions. If you plan to institute a reward system for all the children in the family—which usually works better than focusing on only one child—a family meeting is a good forum for proposing the program.

Tell your child or children that you want to help them learn behaviors that will help them get along better at home, in school, and with other people. Describe high levels of performance to them, expressing confidence that they will be able to meet these standards. Reassure your children that you do not expect them to climb the mountain all at once, only one foothold at a time, and that you will help them make a start. At first, you will reward them for modest improvements, since it is hardest to begin to change. Then, as they demonstrate their ability to make changes in their behavior, the standards will become higher, although they will continue to earn rewards.

This discussion with the children directs the child's own attention to the problem and makes him want to change.

6. Contracts. Sometimes, in a program like this, it is helpful to draw up a contract between parent and child. (See sample contract on page 213.) The contract would stipulate what the child promises to do and what the parents promise to grant him. The contract makes explicit what parents have usually done implicitly.

Some parents feel uneasy about setting up a contract with a child, feeling that it is a form of bribery. But, apart from the semantics of the issue, one can justify a contract system on three bases:

- It is a way of getting the child's attention to begin working toward the development of more positive behavior patterns. Since the child helps to set his own goals, he may set higher goals for himself than he would have reached if you had set the goals.

- It works, when more conventional approaches do not.
- It has built-in obsolescence. You continually raise the amount of work that has to be done for a given reward; the reward changes from material rewards to intangible social rewards; and eventually the behavior becomes self-reinforcing.

If you do decide to draw up a contract, you would discuss with your child the type of behavior you are interested in improving and ask him how he thinks he can improve. Discuss the type of reward that he is interested in earning and the system for earning it (the use of points, stars, tokens, and so forth). After both you and your child have signed the contract, post it where you can all see it.

7. Aim to change behavior bit by bit. Start with something you know your child can do and then reward him when he does that. For example, set a loud alarm to wake him up at seven o'clock—and then reward him for getting out of bed immediately. After a couple of days of prompt arising, raise the ante. Tell him that he will now have to be washed by 7:10 to get the same reward. Then work up to his being dressed by a certain time, eating breakfast, making his bed, and finally being at the bus stop in time to catch the bus. Keep expecting more and more for the same reward. Reward him as he improves; do not wait for perfection.

Always give your child a social reward as you award him his point or token. By a smile or a comment, show your pleasure at his achievements. Your approval is an important reward in its own right that will eventually become a prime motivator. You are pleased when you see your child's behavior improve, so let him see your pleasure and enjoy his part in having contributed to it.

8. Allow your child to experience the natural consequences of his behavior as much as possible. Do not bail him out. The natural consequence of missing the school bus should mean that your child has to walk to school, provided the distance is reasonable. When you experience the consequences of his misbehavior, you can some-

times pass this on to your child. For example, if you live too far from school for him to walk, and your driving him there makes you late for work, you can say to your child that because you were half an hour late for work, you will have to bring some work home. As a result, you will not be able to go to the store to get him new sneakers.

9. Do not nag. When your child does not perform the agreed-upon behavior and therefore does not earn his reward, he does not need a long lecture from you. The most effective way of handling times like this is to point out briefly and calmly that you are sorry he did not earn his reward today, but that you are sure he will (do whatever he is supposed to do) tomorrow to earn tomorrow's reward.

10. Be consistent. The more reliable you can be in your expectations and in your follow-through, the better your program will work. You can undo a great deal of work by letting things slide. When you are tempted to take a holiday from your program because Johnny looks so tired that you cannot bear to wake him up or because you are not feeling your best and do not want to make an issue of his getting up, remember that taking the easy way out by slipping back into old habits will in the long run make it much harder for you to accomplish your goals.

11. Reward your other children when the hyperactive child behaves well. If they egg him on to undesirable behavior and constantly reinforce misconduct, their influence will counteract your efforts. You can stop this by giving them a stake in your hyperactive child's good behavior—for example, by rewarding all the children for not fighting or for being on time and by making the reward contingent on the behavior of all the children.

12. When you have attained success, change to intermittent reinforcement. Once Johnny is catching the bus regularly, let him know how proud you are of his achievement.

After a certain amount of time has gone by during which he catches the bus every single day—say, a period of two weeks—tell him that he no longer needs to be rewarded every time he catches the bus, as he has been, but that you will still reward him periodically, as long as he continues to catch it regularly. To anyone unfamiliar with behavior-shaping programs, it seems incredible that a child should be willing to give up getting rewarded for an activity. But this happens, time and time again. The inner rewards do take over; the sense of accomplishment in living up to a high expectation becomes a powerful reward itself, and the reward that you have been giving diminishes in importance.

How One Family Instituted a Token Reward System

While the guidelines above seem to ensure success for most families, you do not have to follow them slavishly. You can work out a plan that seems better for your own family. To illustrate the flexibility in this type of system, we will quote, below, from Mrs. Black, who decided to try a point system with her family. The Blacks did some things we do not generally recommend and did not do others that we do, but their system seems to be working well for them, which is the ultimate measure of success.

Mrs. Black says, "I was opposed at first to a reward system. I thought it was just bribery, paying kids to do what they ought to be doing anyway, but I finally decided that anything was better than the way we were living. I was always screaming at the boys and nagging them to do this and do that. My husband would walk in the door and within five minutes explode because of all the tension in the house. So then I talked him into trying the point system. He hated the idea at first, too, but he finally agreed to go along with it.

"Steve is nine—he's the hyperactive one—and Brian is seven. We decided to start with Steve's lying, which was driving me crazy. He was making up such fantastic stories that I was afraid he didn't know the difference between reality and fantasy. And I could never believe what he said. He told me some story about the school nurse and what she did and said, and so I got on the phone and laid into her—and then had to call back to apologize because Steve admitted that he had made up the whole thing.

"Brian is pretty good, but he does get sassy sometimes, so we figured while we were rewarding Steve for not lying, we'd reward Brian for not talking back. This would include him in the program, give him a chance to earn points and, we hoped, eliminate some of his freshness. Then both the boys got so enthusiastic that they kept coming up with other things to get points for. We finally decided to reward five kinds of behaviors. If, in an entire day, a boy does not lie, doesn't argue with me when I tell him to do something, isn't fresh, obeys within a reasonable time, and doesn't fight with his brother, he can earn a total of five points.

"I record the points every day on a calendar in the kitchen, and I use a special green Magic Marker that I bought just for this purpose.

"I keep the whole thing positive. I never give demerits or take points away. Maybe I'll tell one of the kids at the end of the day, 'You didn't get your point for minding, but you still got your four other points.' I'm a little stricter in grading Brian, so that Steve won't fall too far behind, but so far the boys don't seem to notice this.

"Then, when either of the boys earns twenty-five points, he gets a quarter. When he has accumulated one hundred points, he gets a meal out with one parent at a place of his choice—within limits. We usually stick to the pizza parlor, MacDonald's, or the local Chinese restaurant.

"We have been using the point system for about five months now, and it's been terrific. The fighting has been cut down at least 90 per cent, and all the other behaviors we've worked on have improved. If I want the boys to fall in line, I just say, 'Watch out or you won't earn your points,' and this is all they usually need. In fact, they keep coming to me with new things I should give points for, and I am planning to take a couple of items off the list and substitute other things, like making their beds and doing their homework.

"Apart from the general improvement in behavior—mostly for Steve—the system has a lot of other benefits. The climate in our home is much more peaceful now. And my husband is really enjoying those lunches out with the boys. He says he gets to know each one of them in a way that just hadn't seemed possible in the hurly-burly of family life.

"Most of all, I justify the point system because I think a lot of the things the boys were doing were just bad habits and not basic character traits. I think if we can change these habits now when the boys are young, we'll really be doing them a big favor."

As we said, this program does not conform to all the guidelines set out earlier. It does not work on one problem at a time, nor does it use intermittent rewards. But the Black family is happy with it. And, in the end, that is what it's all about—what's right for your family.

Grant unto us men, O Lord, to perceive in little things the indications, common seeming though they be, of things both small and great.

—St. Augustine
Confessions

10 SOME SPECIAL PROBLEMS AND WHAT TO DO ABOUT THEM

The problems of raising hyperactive children are like those with other children, only "more so." The solutions we offer in this chapter will be helpful to many parents, but we hope they will be particularly helpful to parents of hyperactive children. In this chapter we also write about the special problems of single parents and families in which both parents work outside the home.

Distractibility, Short Attention Span, Inability to Persevere

You can help your child to combat his distractibility by teaching him how to divide work into small units and by training him to ignore distractions.

When your child is working on any task requiring concentrated effort, such as doing a homework assignment or cleaning up his room, or building a model, he will do much better if his work is divided into small units and if he gets immediate feedback for completing one unit at a time. Set him a limited goal: have him do two math problems out of a page of ten, or glue only one wing on an airplane, or straighten out the clothes in one drawer. As soon as he has accomplished this first unit, he should show you what he has done. Now praise him for completing the task. Intersperse his work with periods of going outside, or taking a snack break. Then check his work and send him back to do another limited job. Gradually, your child will learn to work a little longer at a time. Meanwhile, he will be learning that he can accomplish things in short spurts and that he can budget his time in this way.

If your child is easily distracted by sounds, put a loud ticking clock in his room. Call his attention to its presence and then tell him to perform some task, maybe homework or a puzzle. Tell him that you will reward him when he finishes the unit of work. When he finishes, praise him and, if you wish, give him some token or small reward. Gradually extend the length of time that he has to attend to his lessons, until he is able to concentrate on his work for anywhere from fifteen to thirty minutes, depending on his age. During the daily training times, occasionally substitute other distractions like a softly playing radio, or a music box, or a sound-effects record, or footsteps outside his door. Using the same principles, you can accustom your child to visual distractions like a TV set with test patterns, or a picture and no sound, or a flashing light, or some other stimulus.

Even if it takes your child many sessions over a period of several days to complete a simple project, you should insist that he see it through and not abandon the activity in the middle. If he never finishes anything, he will never experience the reward of fulfilling a specific aim. Since the gratification of completing a job is an important reward for persistence, *you* should persist to help your child achieve this end.

Nine-year-old Andrea's schedule after school might go something like this:

3:00	milk and cookies
3:15	homework
3:30	go outside to play ball
4:00	homework
4:15	practice clarinet
4:30	go outside to play
5:30	read

5:45   work on craft project
6:00   set table
6:15   eat dinner

Excitability

The emotional swings of a hyperactive child are hard on the whole family and call for prevention rather than scolding after the event. The keys to prevention are *avoidance* of situations that produce excitement, *preparation* for situations that cannot be avoided, and *recognition* of an impending emotional upset.

Analyze the times when your child is most likely to get upset and think of ways to forestall this. If he often gets into trouble just before dinner, maybe he should eat earlier or have a more substantial after-school snack. If it is usually late in the evening, maybe be should go to bed earlier.

Hyperactive children tend to get wound up with a group of other children. Whenever possible, encourage your child to play with only one or two friends at a time. Hold birthday parties on a small scale and out of doors, where it will not matter so much if things get out of hand. Do not take this child on a long shopping trip with the whole family, because he is bound to get bored and start stirring up the other children.

Try to avoid direct confrontations, especially about trivial things. Hyperactive children often get up in the morning in a bad mood and make provocative remarks about the clothes they want to wear being dirty or impossible to find. Parents should stay cool and avoid getting involved in arguments over this kind of thing.

Many hyperactive children fall apart over an unexpected change of plans. You can prevent disaster by the way you discuss future plans with your child. Try not to tell him about upcoming events too far ahead of time or he will pester you unmercifully in his impatience. When you do tell him, hedge the plan about with eventualities. Instead of saying on Monday, "We're going to drive into the country on Saturday to pick apples," tell him on Friday, *"If* the weather is nice tomorrow and *if* everything is okay in the family, *maybe* we'll drive into the country to pick apples. If we can't, we'll do something else." If an unexpected thunderstorm makes its appearance Saturday morning or you wake up with the flu, you will have helped your child anticipate the possibility of a disappointment. Adults generally realize that the best-laid plans are subject to all sorts of if's and maybe's, but children—and especially impatient, excitable children—tend to be more demanding.

You can also prepare your child for those situations when he is not sure what to expect. By telling him, step by step, what is going to happen, you will provide some measure of security. Suppose he is going to a strange doctor to be tested for allergies. You can explain that you will go with him to the doctor's office, that you both may have to stay in the waiting room for a while, that the doctor or nurse will take him into another room, where they will make little pin pricks to find out why he has been coughing and wheezing so much, that he will have to wait there for a few minutes so the doctor can look at him, and that he will have to wait while the doctor talks to you to tell you the results of the tests. He may not look forward to going to the allergist's, but knowing what to expect, he will probably face the prospect more calmly than if it were a complete unknown.

Learn to recognize the signs of an imminent explosion and take immediate steps to prevent it. Take the child out of the situation— away from the children he is arguing with or away from the homework that is frustrating him—and into a neutral quiet room. Once there, try to get him to explain his problem, try to understand how he feels, and try to see how you can help. Leaving him to go on trying to handle the situation on his own will only result in his getting more and more frustrated. He has already demonstrated that he cannot handle the problem. Telling him to shape up or calm down is meaningless and ineffective.

If your child is so upset that he is simply falling apart, dissolving in tears, and unable to think or talk rationally, the last thing in the world he needs is for you to lose your temper and scold him. One youngster may respond to being cuddled in his mother's lap, another to being alone in his room listening to the radio, another to pouring his heart out to his father, and another to hugging his dog. Try to help your child find techniques that will help to calm him, and help him learn how to use them.

We have been talking here about a more or less involuntary collapse. A temper tantrum used by a child as a calculated effort to get his own way is another story altogether. A child who expresses his anger by throwing tantrums should also be removed from the situation, or he should have his audience removed. Even though it may take a superhuman effort, you should remain calm yourself. Tell him gently but definitely that you will not be able to talk with him until he can act in an acceptable way. You may have to pick him up bodily and take him to a place where he can be alone. No matter how mortified you are by his tantrum, you must *never* buy peace by giving in to him. Every time he gets his way by throwing a tantrum, he will be encouraged to use this method again. Even if you ignore his tantrums most of the time but give in once in a while, you will be reinforcing this behavior. A child will stop throwing tantrums only when he comes to the conclusion that they will not get him anything at any time.

One way to get rid of tantrums is to tell your child that you are going to ignore him while he is throwing the tantrum—and then do exactly that. Or, when your child starts to pitch a tantrum, you may give him alternatives. Tell him calmly that the choice is up to him: either he stops this carrying on immediately or he will have to go to the time-out place. If he does not stop immediately, you have to get him to the time-out place. If you prefer and if it would cause you no great inconvenience, you can go out of the room, leaving the child alone. If the child's brothers and sisters react to his tantrums by egging him on or by excitedly running to tell you about them, you can enlist their help by rewarding them for ignoring the tantrums or for leaving the room as soon as one begins.

Day-by-day adherence to routines and limits for acceptable behavior will tend to flatten out the peaks and valleys in a child's emotional life. For a schoolchild, a regression to earlier levels of excitability and irritability may reflect a school problem that should be investigated, or an undue amount of pressure being applied at home. Finally, the higher a child's self-esteem, the less likely he is to be upset by every little thing. The child who feels insecure about his own ability will be threatened by any mistake he makes or any minor setback. When parents help a child value himself more highly, they will observe fewer tantrums.

Impatience

A hyperactive child finds waiting the hardest thing in the world. When he wants to go to the show, he wants to go right away—not next week, not tomorrow, not in half an hour. When he goes to the doctor, he cannot understand why he has to stay in the waiting room instead of going right in. He fights with everyone in his class because he must always be first in line. He may have such a need to be first that he cuts short his activities in order to get to the door before anyone else.

Parents can help an impatient child in several ways. First, they can minimize the strains on his limited reserves of patience as much as possible. They should not tell him of an impending treat until the last minute. They should carefully hide any special gifts or foods until the moment they are to be enjoyed. They should make special efforts to be prompt in calling for him. They should get him into the habit of taking a book or a game to places like doctors' waiting rooms, where he will have time on his hands.

Some children are inordinately impatient because they have trouble grasping the concept of time. Parents should provide as many tools as possible that measure and mark off time and should encourage the child to use them. For example, Ronnie's father gave him an hourglass-type egg timer, showed him how it worked, and told him not to speak until the sands ran through. After all the sand reached the bottom half, Ronnie showed his father, who congratulated the boy for having waited three minutes and gave him a penny. Dougie, who wanted to tell his father about a fight at school, burst into tears when he found out that his father would be coming home half an hour late. Dougie's mother gave the boy a kitchen timer, showed him how to set it for thirty minutes, and then showed him how he could tell how long he had to wait till his father would be home.

Parents can also help an impatient child learn to accept delay by playing games that call for taking turns. The parent should say aloud, "Now it's your turn, so I will have to wait for mine." When the child becomes impatient, the parent can use techniques similar to those used in helping a child be less impulsive (see next section). The child should learn to say to himself, "Stop, think, wait."

When a child does wait patiently, he should be praised. Parents should at first reward very short waits and then expect more and more patience for the same amount of approval. When a child behaves badly, he should be denied the treat he is whining or screaming for. He should learn that waiting patiently will get him what he wants, but that kicking up a ruckus will not.

Impulsiveness

Much of the trouble the hyperactive child gets into can be traced to his tendency to act or talk before he thinks. To train your child to delay his responses, you will have to teach him a whole new way of approaching life. You have to teach him to consider the consequences of his actions—not right after he has done something—but on an ongoing, day-in and day-out basis. Riding a bicycle recklessly in the streets is a good example of impulsive behavior. You might try to prevent this by supervising your child closely in his first trips around the neighborhood, instructing him in the rules of traffic, and going over the natural consequences of ignoring these rules. When your child is first riding his bicycle, you should ride with him and see that he stops properly at stop signs, stays on the right-hand side of the road, gives signals, and so forth. Whenever the child fails to observe these rules, you should make him stop. Patiently point out the likely consequences of his ignoring the rules if a car should happen to come along. The first few times your child is about to set out to ride his bicycle on his own, have him recite the most important things he has to remember: what to do when he comes to a stop sign, what to do when he wants to turn a corner, what to do if a car door is opening in front of him. The idea behind this is to get him to instruct himself about the rules, to be prepared for unexpected eventualities, and to *think* about what he is doing. Observe him occasionally to see whether he is putting this training into practice; if so, he should be rewarded; if not, his bicycle should be taken away from him for a day or two, an appropriate consequence of his failing to use it properly.

Whenever physical danger is not involved, your child should be allowed to face the consequences of his impulsive behavior. If he dashes out to school without a coat, he should be left to face the consequences of feeling cold. He may learn something from this experience, but he will not learn anything from having you chase after him with his coat. If he tears up his schoolbook in a fit of frustration, he should be made to face the teacher and to pay for the book himself, either out of his allowance or by giving up some treat. If he taunts older or bigger boys, he should have to "face the music," as long as he is not in real physical danger.

You can play problem-solving games with your child to practice delaying his responses. Encourage him to count to ten before making a move. The card game, Concentration, is a good impulse-control teaching tool. In this game you spread the shuffled cards face down on a table. At each turn a player turns up two cards. The object of the game is to pick two matching cards—two deuces, two sevens, or two jacks, say. When a player turns up two different cards, he has to turn them back over, and the next player takes his turn. The first few turns are trial and error, since neither player knows where any of the cards are. The winner of the game is the player who can best remember the locations of the cards from having seen them turned up in previous turns. As you take your own turn, talk out loud, musing, "Well, I've turned up a four here—and I'm sure I remember that on your last turn you turned one up over there—so I'll try to find that one." Again, you are trying to get your child to think instead of turning up any two cards, willy-nilly.

You can probably think of other ways you can teach your child that it pays to take time to think instead of guessing wildly. Marion Blank, Ph.D., a psychologist at Albert Einstein College of Medicine in New York City, tells of an experience with four-year-old Peter, a hyperactive boy who was eager to blow out the candles on a cake. She used Peter's interest in doing this as his reward for exerting unaccustomed effort to listen to instructions, control himself, and delay his responses. Dr. Blank told Peter that he could blow out the candles if he said, "One, two, three, blow." Peter happily said, "One, two, three," then looked abashed and said, "I forgot the other thing." Dr. Blank blew out the candles herself and explained to Peter that because he did not complete the task correctly, he could not do it "this time." In order to make him feel that it was worthwhile making an effort, however, Dr. Blank immediately said, "I'll give you another chance." She re-lighted the candles and repeated the instructions. Peter listened carefully, followed directions, and blew out the candles.

An experiment that we conducted at Washington University showed that a group of hyperactive boys who usually gave heedless, slapdash performances could learn to control impulsive behavior. We asked twenty boys to do a paper-and-pencil maze, a test often used to judge impulsiveness. After each boy had done the maze once, half of the group were given training in saying to themselves a set of commands that emphasized the importance of listening to directions and thinking out the solution before trying to give the answer. The boys were given this training with the help of a set of cards similar to the drawings on pages 144 and 145 and were then asked to apply these principles to a series of other tests. The other ten boys, who were not given verbal training, were also

INSTRUCTIONS

1. THIS IS A

   STOP!

   LISTEN

   LOOK

   and

   THINK

EXPERIMENT

2. BEFORE I START ANY OF THE
   TASKS I AM GOING TO DO, I AM
   GOING TO SAY:

   STOP! STOP

   LISTEN

   LOOK

   and

   THINK! BEFORE! I

   ANSWER

LISTEN!
LISTEN
LISTEN
LISTEN
LISTEN

LOOK!

and

THINK!

BEFORE! I ANSWER

asked to do the other tests. The following day, all the boys were given another maze to do. The boys who had received the special training improved their maze performance, whereas the others did not. The trained group cut fewer corners, crossed over fewer lines, lifted their pencils less, and threaded the maze with fewer irregular lines than did the untrained group. It seems reasonable to conclude that their improvement was due to a more prudent approach to the solution of the problem.

You can apply the principles of this experiment to teaching your own child. Copy these figures, or ask your child to copy them, onto large pieces of paper that can be hung in your child's room. Point out to your child that he can do a better job at practically anything he tackles if he tells himself the reminders on the posters.

Stay with your child while he applies himself to a piece of work—solving a sheet of math problems, using a pancake mix, doing a puzzle, or putting together a model airplane kit—any task that involves a series of steps. Remind him to stop before each step, to listen to your instructions, or—even better—to look at the written instructions and then to think before he gives the answer or does the problem or performs the task. Have your child say the commands, "Stop," "Listen," "Look," and "Think" out loud.

Before your child does his first task, ask him, "Now before you start something new, what do you say?" He should eventually say something like "Before I do anything, I am going to say STOP! LISTEN! LOOK! and THINK! before I answer." Stay with your child and ask him to repeat these commands to himself before every problem or every step of his task. Every time he does say one out loud without being reminded, praise him. Every time he gets the right answer, praise him. Then tell him that you are going to leave the posters up in his room, where he can see them when he does his homework. Come in occasionally for a follow-up session.

You should attempt to work like this with your child *only* if you can be patient when things do not go as smoothly as you would like, when he does not get the idea, when he cannot remember the commands. If you have found from past experience that you get too emotional and too exasperated when you try to teach your child, you had better not try anything like this. Perhaps you could ask an older child or your youngster's teacher to try this approach with him.

In summary, everything we suggest here has to do with increasing a child's ability to label what he is doing or is about to do, or to dig out of his memory the appropriate self-instructions.

Overactivity

The incessant, restless motion of a hyperactive child makes parents nervous and irritable. A certain amount of this excessive activity can be eliminated, but it would be unrealistic to expect to get rid of all of it, no matter how hard you or your child tries. You will probably have to force yourself to tolerate your child's restlessness in front of the television set and his squirming while he is reading. One trick for achieving tolerance for such annoying habits as drumming the fingers or kicking the feet is to pretend that your child belongs to someone else. Would these same habits bother you so much if a neighbor's child was engaging in them? Probably not.

Your tolerance need not be boundless. You should certainly set limits on the amount of rough and loud behavior that you are prepared to accept. Make plain to your child what the rules are—for example, no jumping on people, no tearing around the house, no rambunctious behavior when out in public with the family. Provide alternatives when possible, such as a basement or back yard, where children can be as boisterous as they like, with equipment that can be jumped on to substitute for mother's back. Then make plain to the child what the consequences for violating the rules are—having his friends sent home, having to go to a quiet place to be alone for a while, or working off his energy at some vigorous task.

You can help your child to channel his energy constructively by encouraging him in such active pursuits as running with his dog, riding his bicycle, skating, jogging, wrestling, or playing iceless hockey. You can assign him household tasks that involve a lot of physical exertion, such as washing the car, shoveling snow, raking leaves, and chopping wood. You can teach him ways to occupy his hands purposefully by providing materials for and teaching him such simple hand activities as tying knots, modeling clay, and wood carving—all of which involve a minimum of mess and can be participated in for a few minutes at a time.

You can make a special effort to teach him control of his own actions. Hyperactive children are not necessarily more active than other children at all times; they are active at inappropriate times. Other children may be just as active on the playground, but when it is time to go in and sit still in the classroom, they can control their activity, whereas hyperactive children cannot. They need to learn how to exert control when it is called for.

A child can learn to master his movements by playing a game like "statues." In this game the child moves around till he gets the signal to stop, at which point he "freezes" into whatever position he was in when he heard the signal. Through playing a game like this, he learns that he is in control, that he can stop moving when he wants to badly enough.

A child can also be trained to sit still. Determine the longest period of time that your child can sit still. Then tell him that you will reward him if he can remain in his seat for thirty seconds longer, or one more minute or two more minutes, depending on his age and "sitability" quotient. Keep rewarding him for very small improvements and keep extending the time period until he is sitting still for, say, fifteen minutes for a four-year-old or half an hour for a grade-school child. (He should be able to engage in some activity while he is sitting—reading, coloring, or doing puzzles.)

Most people fidget when they are bored. One of the problems

of the hyperactive child is that he tends to have a low threshold of boredom. You can help him by exposing him as seldom as possible to situations that make too many demands on his ability to attend. You can also learn to intervene at the first signs of restlessness. This does not mean that you have to "bring on the dancing girls" or feel that you have to entertain him constantly. It does mean that you give extra thought to the places that you take this child. It can be sheer torture for a child like this to try to sit quietly through a choir recital, a long dinner with distant relatives, or a movie more suitable for adults.

You want your hyperactive child to feel that he is part of the family and to participate in shared family outings. But if he is going to get bored on these outings and become wild, no one will enjoy them, and "togetherness" will be a mockery. Include your child as often as possible, but always provide some sort of safety valve if the experience gets to be too much for him: another room where he can be alone for a while; the chance to go outside, even at someone else's house; some activity that will give him an excuse for getting up and moving around, like greeting late-comers and taking their coats. If you cannot allow for a release like this, you will be faced with a hard question that only you can answer: "Should we include Sam in this family activity, or would we all be happier if he stayed at home this time?"

Sometimes it is better to find a baby-sitter that your youngster likes, leaving him at home on those occasions when the family will be on an outing that you feel he will not be able to handle. You do not want to do this too often, or you will be making your child feel rejected and left out of all the fun. When you do decide not to take him with you, be sure the child knows that you are not leaving him home to punish him but to protect him from a boring and difficult experience. Compensate for these times by making a special effort to plan some outings around his special interests. Gradually expand his activities as he shows more ability to display acceptable behavior.

Accident-Proneness

You have to expect your child to acquire a certain number of minor bumps and bruises. These are part of a normal growing child's life. They are also the way he learns which activities are dangerous. A minor accident provides consequences that will teach a child how to avoid a major accident in the future. You certainly would not want to overprotect your child so that his normal, natural curiosity would be stifled and he would be afraid to try anything new. But you do want to exert as much influence as possible to help your hyperactive child avoid serious accidents.

Hyperactive children are prime prospects for accidents because of their high activity level, their impulsiveness, their lack of attentiveness, and their frequent emotional upsets, all of which have been shown in various studies to be strong factors in children's accidents.

Your hyperactive child requires closer supervision than the average child. A disproportionate number of childhood accidents occur in the early morning, when parents are asleep but children are very much awake, and in the late afternoon, when parents are busy and children are tired, hungry, and at loose ends. It is up to you to know where your child is, what he is doing, and, as far as possible and particularly with younger children, that he is doing it in a childproof environment.

Give your home and yard a careful check for things that might cause accidents. Put locks on every door and closet in the house. Eliminate furniture that can be easily tipped over. Put upper-story window fastenings out of reach or put bars on the windows. Lock your car, especially when it is parked on a slope. Replace wooden seats on swings with cloth or leather. Replace patio doors made of clear, easily shattered glass. Get rid of toys with sharp edges. Never leave a gun where a child could possibly get at it. Lock up all power tools when not in use. Do not get a trampoline; unsupervised, unskilled jumping can cause gruesome accidents, and an impulsive, impatient child will be too tempted to jump without proper knowledge and supervision. It is better to let him learn and practice this sport at school or camp or the "Y."

Lock up all potential poisons. The mother of two-year-old Aaron has said, "Poisoning has been impossible in our home, because all medicines, cleaning fluids, and insecticides—anything moveable including the dishrag—is removed to a storage room that is padlocked at night." Parents of a vigorous, superinquisitive toddler, who may get up at any hour of the night and can climb to any closet, have no choice but to lock away all dangerous substances if they want to avoid accidental poisoning. If these items are out of sight as well as out of reach, so much the better, since curious children will not even be tempted to try to get at them.

General education for safety has two facets. One involves teaching children how to do things the right way, and the other involves warning him what activities he should not engage in at all. We want children to know the safe ways of doing things. We want them to have fun sledding, so we teach them how to steer the sled and how to avoid getting the rope caught in the runners. We warn them of the dangers of steering into the path of another sledder. We show them where the sledding is fun and safe, and we teach them not to go in the streets. We want our children to enjoy water sports, so we teach them how to swim, to wear life jackets whenever they go boating, and what to do when a boat capsizes. We teach our children the rules of bicycle safety (see page 141). When we teach a child how to do something the right way, we prepare him for unforeseen circumstances, so that he will be able to handle himself in an emergency without panicking.

The other side of the safety education coin involves the "don'ts." Since children are often ignorant of the implications of their actions, they must be taught to anticipate consequences and to avoid completely doing many things. Parents should establish strict rules prohibiting certain kinds of behavior; they should carefully explain why these activities are dangerous; and they should scrupulously enforce the rules. Children should know exactly why they should never play with firecrackers, squirt lighter fluid on a barbecue grill, play inside cars, throw rocks and sand, fool around with power tools, play with matches, guns, and knives, or touch power lines.

Bed Wetting

Enuresis can be vexatious to parents, but it is best not to regard this as a problem until it becomes a social problem for the child. Some 15 per cent of all children—more boys than girls—continue to wet the bed regularly after their fourth birthday, but most of these children outgrow the habit without any special help from their parents. Some people believe that children wet the bed because they are insecure, emotionally disturbed, or under pressure. Yet this theory for bed wetting among preadolescents has been seriously questioned as the result of several studies. (It is true that a child who wets the bed periodically often does so after some emotionally charged episode.)

Less than 1 per cent of children who wet the bed do so because of some physical disorder. When a child has some malfunction of the kidneys or the bladder, or some other urinary ailment, he usually has trouble holding back his urine during the day, as well. You should take a bed-wetting child to the doctor to rule out any pathological basis for lack of urinary control.

Researchers are still trying to find out why the other 99 per cent wet the bed. There seems to be a wide range of possibilities, including genetic factors (adults who wet the bed as children are more likely to have enuretic children) and a lack of proper training (parents have never taken the trouble to discourage the bed wetting). In most cases, the origin of the problem is unknown.

If your child is not upset about his bed wetting, the best thing for you to do would be to get him some waterproof pants and matter-of-factly suggest that it would be a good idea for him to wear them until he is regularly waking up dry. That way, he will not have to sleep all night in a wet bed, and you will not have a daily laundry problem.

When the child himself is concerned about his bed wetting and wants help in stopping it—perhaps because he wants to be able to sleep at a friend's house or to go away to camp—you should try treatment. One approach that often helps a child who wants to stop wetting the bed is to reward him for staying dry. The child keeps a diary in which he records his dry nights; he gets a star for every dry night; when he has accumulated a certain number of stars, he gets a reward. This kind of procedure helps the child to focus his attention on the problem and gives him an added incentive to "kick the habit."

Another technique that works is the "bed buzzer." With the "bed buzzer," an electrical device sets off an alarm when the child begins to urinate. The child wakes up and goes to the bathroom. After a number of trials the child learns to wake and go to the bathroom when his bladder is full. Studies of relatively resistant enuretic children have shown that the bed buzzer is safe and effective. Its one drawback is that the treatment is not as easy to organize as the commercial companies that sell the apparatus say it is. Unless an experienced person supervises the treatment, it will probably not work.

Sometimes a doctor will prescribe antidepressant medicine to make a child sleep more lightly so that he will wake more easily when his bladder is full. Usually the drugs reduce the frequency of wetting, but this effect does not carry over to the time when the drug is stopped. The child has learned nothing. Occasionally, a month or so of not wetting the bed *can* break a child's habit patterns so that he can then go on to achieve bladder control on his own.

In general, parents should adopt a patient, conservative attitude toward bed wetting. If it is not a problem for the child, it should not be one for his parents.

Chip-on-the-Shoulder Attitude

Some children always seem to be "asking for it." They adopt such a bellicose manner that they virtually dare anyone to be pleasant to them. Anything that anyone says or does gives offense to such a child. When a child presents such a disagreeable face to the world, he is saying that he knows no one could possibly like him. Parents can deal with this attitude by treating the causes of the poor self-esteem. They should encourage the child to get rid of some of his resentment verbally; they should be willing to listen to him and should help him to recognize the sources of his discontent. At opportune times, they can gently lead him into an understanding of the ways his own attitude contributes to his problem.

Clumsiness

Some hyperactive children are well co-ordinated, but many others fit the description of "all thumbs" and "two left feet." An impatient, poorly co-ordinated child will probably never shake off his clumsiness completely, but, with help, he can overcome it somewhat.

Things should be as easy as possible for an awkward child. His clothes should be easy to manipulate. They should have zippers rather than buttons, snaps instead of hooks and eyes. Difficult fasteners should be replaced. Shoes should be easy to manage, too. It is better for a child who cannot tie his laces to run the risk of flat feet by wearing loafers than to have to face one more difficult and frustrating task. His toys should be substantial and simple rather than models of mechanical intricacy that require careful, skilled handling.

The cruelest problem facing an ungainly child is social failure. He is always the last to be chosen for a team, if he is chosen at all. His parents should make every effort to teach him the games played in his neighborhood. An excellent school for children with learning disabilities, the Gateway School, in New York City, has a fine physical-education program that places a great deal of emphasis on teaching street games to the children. One of the school's most successful techniques involves having the child break down the steps in a particular activity like turning a jump rope or throwing a ball, so that the child may teach the skill to someone else. The teacher will say, "Suppose, Karen, you had to teach Billy how to turn the rope. What would you tell him to do?" These children often have to be taught what other children grasp intuitively—how to stand when throwing a ball, what the arms should be doing while the legs are moving, and so forth.

Sometimes a clumsy child can benefit from a special physical-education program in the community—at the "Y" or Boys' Club. He will get some good out of the experience *only* if the adult leading the program is patient, understanding, and mindful of the needs of an unathletic child. If the instructor is overly concerned with his team's winning, or if he puts too much pressure on the youngsters to perform up to a certain standard, the program will harm the child further.

Unfortunately, too many school gym teachers fit this last description. They are athletes, rather than sensitive teachers. If a poorly co-ordinated child has the misfortune to be in the class of an overly demanding teacher, the parents should go to school to speak to him and, if necessary, to the principal. It may help to have the child's doctor contact the school.

Poorly co-ordinated children often have difficulty writing. Sometimes they benefit from special exercises or the use of special materials in brief practice sessions with a parent or a tutor. Children who have trouble writing should learn to type at an early age. Some school districts offer typing in summer school; other times, a parent or special teacher can help a child learn.

Centers connected with hospitals or universities often conduct good perceptual-motor programs directed by well-trained people. They use special equipment like balance beams, climbing apparatus, and balls to teach children specific motor skills and help them improve their motor abilities. A child enrolled in one of these programs derives benefits from his realization that he can improve certain physical skills and also from his appreciation of the special interest shown in him. There is no evidence, however, that these programs have a carry-over effect. Teaching a child how to walk a balance beam does not help him to write any better, and teaching him how to overcome physical obstacles on a course does not help him become a better baseball player.

Destructiveness

Hyperactive children destroy clothing, toys, and household furnishings at an alarming rate, partly because they are impulsive, partly because they give things hard use, and partly because they often let their tempers get the better of them. Teaching impulse control can decrease the amount of destruction from the first count, investing in the sturdiest goods can help out in the second, and being adamant about enforcing respect for property can help out in the third.

The child who pokes a tool into the air-conditioner or brushes black paint on a neighbor's garage or rides his bicycle over the flower gardens may not mean to be naughty. It may never have occurred to him that he might be doing something wrong. Constant teaching and constant pointing out the consequences of one's actions seem to be the only solution. You will never be able to eliminate every thoughtless act, but with luck and time you should be able to instill in a child some sense of responsibility for his own actions.

The clothes you buy for your hyperactive child should be the strongest available. They should also be easy to put on and take off. An impatient child who has poor fine-motor co-ordination will shred into rags clothing that is hard to button or unbutton. You will probably have to spend more for your hyperactive child's clothing; your only consolation will be that in the long run it will be worth it, because the better a garment is made, the longer it is likely to last.

The toys you buy should also be simple and sturdy. The mother of nine-year-old Richard bemoaned the fact that the only toy that lasted him more than a month was a $25 wooden tractor. Large wooden blocks are another good choice of toys; they last forever and can be used in a variety of ways. If you are handy at the tool bench, you can make simple toys like these at a fraction of their commercial cost. In addition, the toy you make will have more meaning for your child. Stay away from intricate mechanical toys, since it is a characteristic of curious, restless children to take apart toys like this—and the toys usually do not get put together again.

The third type of destructiveness, the deliberate and sometimes vengeful destruction of property to get even with a parent or a sibling, is another story altogether. Susan, who wrote all over her sister's bedspread with indelible lipstick because the sister would not let her play with a certain toy, or Alvin, who urinated against the walls of his bedroom when he was sent in there after a temper tantrum, have to learn that they cannot get away with this sort of behavior. When it is possible to repair such damage, a child should be made to do it. This may mean vacuuming a carpetful of shredded crayons instead of going to the movies, scrubbing crayoned walls on a sunny summer afternoon, or replanting a torn-up flower bed instead of playing baseball. When an item must be replaced, the child should be held responsible, either by giving up some allowance money, by working off the debt, or by giving up something that costs a comparable amount of money.

Doing Chores

Children should learn to live co-operatively with others, to contribute personal effort to the common good, and to develop a sense of responsibility. One excellent way to foster these aims is to expect a child to perform household chores as soon as he is able to carry out a simple task. Even a preschooler is capable of emptying all the wastebaskets every day and assuming this job as his own responsibility. As a child gets older, he should be expected to make his own bed, keep his own room tidy, and pick up after himself. If he has a pet, he should be responsible for feeding, walking, and cleaning up after the animal. He should also do things that benefit the whole family. Both boys and girls should assume responsibilities such as setting the table, cooking, washing dishes, doing laundry and ironing, and performing yard work. It is perfectly appropriate for a boy to cook, make his bed, and run the vacuum cleaner, and for a girl to mow the lawn, wash the car, and clean out the garage. A child of either sex will be better prepared for adult life if he or she develops competence in all facets of household work, not just those that are traditional for one sex or the other. By learning how to discharge these duties, a child will be acting as a responsible member of the family. He will also be learning skills that will help him to be self-reliant, give him a sense of competence, and stand him in good stead for the rest of his life.

In some families, the parents condition the children's allowance on their satisfactory performance of chores. This is wrong on two counts. First, it gives a child the feeling that he should be paid for every nice thing he does. Instead, he should feel that he is expected to contribute to family life. Payment is not out of order for a small number of special jobs—possibly those for which you would be willing to pay an outside worker, such as helping to serve at a party, doing the big spring cleanup in house or yard, painting the basement, or washing the car.

The other reason why a child's allowance should not depend on his chore performance is that this subverts the basic purposes of an allowance: to help children learn how to handle money and to give them some independence, so that they do not have to consult their parents about every little frivolity. Parents should not punish a child by withholding his allowance (except for incidents of deliberate destructiveness, when some financial recompense is indicated to repair or replace damaged items).

Another word here about allowances: the allowance of a young schoolchild should cover such items as presents for the family, comic books, little toys, and Saturday matinees. As a child comes toward the end of grade school and into junior high, his allowance should be increased to provide money for lunch, public transportation, school supplies, and admission to the swimming pool. At about junior high school age, it is appropriate for a child to have a yearly clothing allowance. This does away with hassling between parent and child over whether the youngster needs another dress or another pair of jeans, and it gives the child a chance to practice budgeting his money. (It also turns out to be an economical way to pay for children's clothing, since children tend to be stingy with their own money!)

Many families successfully use a combination of rule enforcement and habit training to motivate their children to do chores. For example, suppose ten-year-old Mary is supposed to dust the living room after school on Fridays. When she does it, her efforts will be recognized with praise and possibly with some token reward. Since the chore is done for the benefit of everyone in the family, it is best if Mary's eventual reward involves other family members. Maybe she could earn points toward a special treat with a parent, or a chance to choose a treat in which the whole family can share.

The problem comes when Mary does *not* do the dusting. It is important that she be made to do it as soon as possible. It is a basic part of rule enforcement that the child actually do the task concerned. If necessary, the parent should literally put Mary's hand on the dustcloth and then accompany her around the room. The child must go through the motions of the job. If Mary's parents do not discover the undone work until after she has dashed out to play, they should bring her home at once to do it. If that is impossible (not just inconvenient), they should see that she takes care of it as soon as she comes home. If the parents tidy up because they did not catch Mary in time, they will be showing her that not doing the job pays off.

It is best to concentrate on getting a child to do one chore at a time. As soon as he is regularly performing one ask, you can switch the emphasis to another.

Eating Problems

Many hyperactive children are picky eaters. They exist on minuscule amounts of food, a situation that worries parents—especially when the children are scrawny. This is in almost all cases a reflection of a child's own constitutional needs for small amounts of food, rather than a poor habit. Nothing is to be gained and much lost when parents nag a child to eat. Nagging does not improve a child's appetite. The tension it generates at mealtime only makes the parents lose theirs. The child who sees that he can upset his parents by not eating has a powerful weapon at his disposal. It is far better to develop sound nutritional policies and to carry them out calmly and consistently than it is to try to solve the problem by making scenes at the table.

A child with a small appetite should be given only small amounts of food on his plate, with the understanding that he can always ask for more. He should be given only token amounts of food he does not care for. He should *not* be offered special foods other than that served to the rest of the family. After a specified time limit, all plates should be cleared away, no matter how little a child may have eaten. Snacking on "empty calories" should be prohibited.

Other hyperactive children have good appetites but atrocious table manners. Always in a hurry, they eat with their fingers, shovel food into their mouths, and spill, splash, dribble, and drop their food all over the table, the floor, and themselves. These children may never be so neat as their brothers and sisters, but they can improve when sufficiently motivated.

The application of habit-training principles, as described in Chapter 9, can improve table manners. Parents should pick out one annoying habit, such a picking up food with the fingers. They should then reward the child for every meal that he gets through without using his fingers. If his habit is so ingrained that he is not able to get through the entire meal without resorting to the offending mannerism, improvement rather than complete success should be rewarded. Parents can count the number of times the child uses his fingers during a typical meal and then reward the child every time he improves upon his previous record, until he can get through the meal perfectly. When a child gets five points, he may earn the privilege of getting an ice cream bar. Or when he earns twenty points, he may be able to go out for a restaurant meal with a parent. Once one habit has been extinguished, the parents can switch to intermittent reinforcement for that one and begin to work on another. Habit training can also discourage a child from getting up and running around the house during mealtimes.

While table manners and activity during mealtimes can be improved, the parents of a hyperactive child have to make some compromises in their expectations. This child will probably never be able to exert the same degree of control at the table that other children do. Parents who can close their eyes to some of this behavior and be content with something short of perfection will suffer far less grief than if they insist only on an adherence to the same high standards their other children meet.

Fighting

Parents tend to get upset at the constant poking, pummeling, and wrestling that goes on among young boys—especially when the going gets wild and one of the boys ends up in tears. Most of the time, parents should not interfere with harmless tussling. Most fighting, especially among young boys of about the same size, is nothing but horseplay. It should be thought of as healthy and normal, like the romping of puppies. A youngster will not suffer as the result of a few bumps and bruises, and many children—especially hyperactive ones—seem to need this kind of vigorous play and body contact.

Normal aggressiveness and competitiveness, which often involves fighting in younger children, should be tolerated as long as no serious injury is likely to result. As long as children are not fighting

with weapons or throwing stones or clumps of mud, it is unlikely
that anyone will be seriously hurt. Too many parents and teachers—especially in suburban neighborhoods—have become so prissy
that they cannot accept the kind of rough and ready atmosphere
that used to be considered a normal part of growing up. We
should, of course, encourage our children to find more constructive ways of settling their differences, but we should not become
alarmed by an occasional fight among well-matched children.

The kind of fighting parents should be concerned about is that
in which a youngster frightens and picks on younger children, or
uses weapons or throws things, or is involved on practically a daily
basis in explosive fighting. They should look for underlying reasons. The child who resorts to belligerence is taking out his frustration and sense of failure. He may be subject to excessive criticism from parents or teacher and be driven to take out his anger
on someone else. Unfortunately, he is apt to take it out on someone who cannot give it back, a younger child or perhaps an animal. If a child sees a lot of physical aggression in the home, if he
is punished for misbehavior by impulsive hitting out (possibly at
the hands of a heavy-drinking father), he will naturally be inclined
to resort to the same kind of thing when things are not going well
for him. The child who does poorly in school may seek self-esteem
in the ability to beat up other children.

Parents should make serious efforts to discover the underlying
reasons for excessive aggression. Meanwhile, they have to put a
stop to the fighting itself. They must impress upon the youngster
the seriousness of such behavior, the physical danger to other children, and the legal and psychological risks for him. Parents should
make rules prohibiting any rough stuff with little children, throwing anything at all, the use of any weapon other than the bare
hand.

When a child does get into fights, he should be left to face the
consequences, whether this involves being beaten up by another
boy or being berated by the angry parent of a smaller child. His
own parents should not cover up for him, make excuses, or shield
him from the results of his own actions—except, of course, when

serious harm is likely to occur, such as being set upon by a gang of older boys.

To encourage positive behavior, parents should praise and reward a child for every peaceful day. After a certain number of such days, he should be able to cash in his tokens for a treat or a prize. His brothers and sisters should also be rewarded for not reponding to his provocations. Parents should also do what they can to encourage a child to find friends who are like him, who enjoy physical activity and competitiveness. The more he can romp vigorously, the less likely he will be to resent more quiet youngsters and to pick fights with them.

On the opposite side of the coin is the child who cannot stand up for himself, and gets picked on constantly by other children. He may be small or poorly co-ordinated, his physical limitations aggravating his lack of self-confidence. Unable in real life to do what he would dearly love to do—acquit himself favorably when challenged by other children—he may become preoccupied with violence. He wants to read the goriest comic books, watch the bloodiest television shows, and fill his drawing papers with scenes of war, fire, and murder. He may have violent daydreams or nightmares. This kind of preoccupation should be regarded by parents as a serious warning that the child needs help in learning how to stand up physically to other children. The best antidote to his feelings of powerlessness would be a planned program to give him real power—lessons in judo, karate, boxing, or wrestling, and a general body-building program of swimming or gymnastics. Meanwhile, he should be encouraged to express his anger, to voice what he would like to do to his tormentors, to admit to the rage that fills his mind. He should also be encouraged to value his competence in nonphysical endeavors so that his real or imagined physical inferiority will not crush his image of himself.

Fire Setting

Parents are justifiably frightened when they find their child playing with matches. Preventive measures that all parents should take involve proper supervision of children, education about the danger of fire, and proper storage of matches and other flammable materials.

Children have to learn the consequences of playing with matches. They will not know about the risks of extensive burns—the pain, the scarring, and the long hospitalization—unless they are told. They will not know how easy it is to set a house on fire unless they are told. Parents and teachers can sometimes reinforce their own teaching by making arrangements to take a child to talk with the local fire chief or a physician at a local hospital. You are not trying to give your child nightmares—but you certainly should teach him about fire and its tragic aftermath.

Matches, cigarette lighters, gasoline, and other flammable material must not be left lying around the house in the path of temptation. While a determined youngster can ferret out well-hidden matches or can find them on the street or in friends' homes, the likelihood of his igniting a bonfire in the living room is far slimmer if his parents take pains to keep as few matches as possible and to lock up those. There is a popular idea that allowing a child to strike a match or light fires under supervision will defuse his drive to play with matches. This does give a child experience in lighting matches, so that he is less likely to strike them impulsively and drop them out of fright. But there is no evidence that doing this with a child who is fascinated by fire diminishes his preoccupation and discourages him from playing with matches at unsupervised times.

When fire setting persists despite these cautions and despite ordinary methods of punishing fire setting and rewarding the avoidance of such behavior, the problem is serious, but it can be dealt with by using an approach reported by the psychologist Cornelius J. Holland.

Seven-year-old Robert was regularly setting one or two fires a week despite repeated punishment until—under Dr. Holland's guidance—his parents instituted several measures. First, Robert's father told him that if he set any more fires he would lose the new baseball glove that was the boy's favorite possession. The firmness with which the father threatened to give away the glove or destroy it in the child's presence was a strong enough inducement for Robert to co-operate with his parents' planned program.

Robert's father also told him that if he found any matches or matchbooks around the house, he was to bring them to his father right away. That evening the father left an empty matchbook in plain sight, reasoning that since the boy had no use for an empty pack, he would be sure to turn it in. Robert did pick up the pack and took it to his father, whereupon the father gave Robert five cents, for the boy to spend as he wished. For the next few evenings the father kept placing full packs of matches around the house. Robert kept bringing them to his father, who would give the boy varying amounts of money, ranging from a penny to ten cents. The father told the boy that he should not expect money every time. When Robert found matches out in the street, he brought them also to his father and sometimes received money.

About a week after the start of the program, Robert's father told the boy he could strike a full pack of matches if he wanted to, under the father's supervision. The father also placed twenty pennies beside the pack and told Robert that for every match unstruck he would receive one penny, but for every match used, one penny would be removed. The first time, Robert struck ten matches and received ten pennies. The following night he struck three matches and earned seventeen cents, and the night after that, he refrained from striking any matches at all and earned the full twenty cents. For the next few trials, Robert's father told the boy he would not receive the same amount of money every time, and sometimes he would not receive any money at all. The trials kept up, with Robert receiving anywhere from nothing to ten cents. He did not strike any more matches.

After three weeks of this program, a potentially disastrous habit had been completely eliminated. Over the next several months, Robert's father and mother continued to hold occasional trials, varying the amount of reward from nothing to a few cents. They always accompanied the monetary rewards with a word of praise, a smile, or some other type of social reward, to let Robert know his behavior pleased them. Robert set no more fires, either at home or in the neighborhood.

Getting Ready on Time

There are two kinds of situations when a child must be ready on time. The first involves only the child himself. He must be at a certain place at a certain time—the school bus stop, the Cub Scout meeting, a class at the "Y." The other type of situation involves others—going with the family to church, to visit friends, to a show.

A child should assume responsibility at a very early age for getting himself ready in time. He should have his own alarm clock and watch. While he may need help from his parents in learning how to gauge a reasonable length of time for getting ready, he should set his own alarm for the agreed-upon time, and he should keep his clock wound. He should be responsible for getting out of bed, dressing, making his bed, getting down for breakfast, and being out the door at the proper time. When the child is late, he must face the consequences with the teacher or the principal; his parents should not bail him out by driving him to school. If the child's teacher sloughs off the lateness and says or does nothing about it, call her to enlist her support in your promptness campaign.

If you are nervous about your child's walking to school alone, either because of the distance or the traffic or the temptation to play hooky, follow him to school in the car on those days when he misses the bus. Be completely aboveboard about the fact that you are following him to make sure he gets to school all right. Assure him matter-of-factly that you are not refusing to drive him just to be mean or to punish him, but simply to help him realize that it is his responsibility to get to school on time. Make him understand that he will never learn to act for himself if you keep bailing him out.

Drastic action is sometimes in order. One morning, after Glenn had been late every single day for a week, his father realized that it was time for Glenn to be leaving the house. The boy was still in his pajamas. Glenn's father said cheerfully, "Well, Glenn, it's time for you to go." He gathered up the boy's clothes, together with an orange and a slice of bread, pushed the bundle into the startled boy's arms, and firmly led Glenn out the door, locking the door behind him. Glenn dressed in the bushes, although he was too angry to eat the food his father had given him. From that day on, Glenn managed to be out the door in time.

When a child is consistently late for activities involving others in the family or when the measures described are ineffective, habit training should solve the problem. In Chapter 9, we used the situation of getting a child up and out to school to exemplify the principles of habit training (see page 130). You might want to add a negative consequence for being late to your positive ones for being on time. The simplest, of course, is just to leave the tardy one home, but this is not always feasible. You might stipulate that the longer the rest of the family has to wait for him, the earlier he will have to go to bed that night, the sooner he will have to come in from play the following day, or the longer he will have to spend at some uninteresting chore.

Lying

Parents have to distinguish between the fanciful tales told by an imaginative small child and the kind of lying that interferes with communication between parent and child. The first kind of tale telling is harmless and usually outgrown. Parents can help a child to appreciate his fantasies as the stories they are by commending him on his imagination and telling him what good stories he makes up. They should not pretend to believe them in an effort to enter into his make-believe world.

More often, parents are concerned with lies told by a child in his efforts to avoid punishment, to get someone else into trouble, or to bolster a weak ego. When parents realize that a child is a chronic liar, they should stop to ask why. Is he getting criticized and punished so much that he is willing to say anything to avoid more of the same? Is his self-esteem so low that he needs to embellish his own or his family's accomplishments to feel better about his own worth? Does he have so much trouble making friends that he feels he has to tell fantastic stories to attract the other children? Is he so jealous of his brothers and sisters that he lies about them in an effort to seem like the "good" one to his parents? Parents have to work more on the underlying causes than on the lying itself.

A child should not be mousetrapped into a lie. If his parents know that he has committed a misdeed, they should not ask him whether he did it and then punish him for lying when he impulsively denies the accusation. It is better to confront the youngster with your knowledge and to discuss the problem openly and honestly.

Much of the time parents are in doubt whether or not a child is telling the truth. If they do not know the whole story, they should neither punish the child nor keep insisting that he is lying; yet they should also avoid appearing too gullible. When a child has been caught in repeated lies, his parents should point out the "credibility gap" he creates and the difficulties he poses for his parents, who never know whether or not they can believe him. It goes without saying that parents should be scrupulously honest with their children and in front of their children if they want the children to be honest themselves. The parent who encourages a child to pretend he is younger than he is to get on the train for half fare, or the parent who denies a promise made to a child is setting the child a model for dishonesty.

The most helpful approach parents can take is to reward a child for his honesty. One reward should be the withholding, or at least the modifying, of a punishment for an offense the child has truthfully owned up to. Every time the child does tell the truth about a difficult matter, the parents should commend him for being honest and should acknowledge that it is often not easy.

Poor Sportsmanship

The saying is that there is no such thing as a good loser, but only a good actor. No one likes to lose. Still, a person who has enough ego strength will not be so devastated by losing a game as will a person whose self-image is so shaky that he has to seize upon every opportunity for proving himself. Unfortunately, when things do not go right—when he loses at a game, for example—he feels that he has failed. His loss of face makes him so unhappy with himself that he makes much more of losing than the occasion warrants. Poor sportsmanship can also arise from a high level of competitiveness. A child who needs to compete all the time should have the chance to fulfill his competitive urges by taking part in a lot of competitive sports. The more he wins and loses, the more gracious he will be about both.

Parents can do several things to get a child used to the idea that playing a game does not have to mean winning every time. They can see that the child plays many games. If a child seldom plays games, each time will be invested with much more emotional meaning, and winning will be more important than enjoying the game. If he plays games often, he will eventually absorb the idea that he can lose and still live with himself, and accept the fact that losing may not be as much fun as winning, but that it is no disgrace.

When a child begins to get worked up about losing or starts to cheat outrageously, his parents can good-humoredly point out to him that when a person wins *all* the time, that means he must be playing with people who are not his equals, so he is not in much of a contest. They can also help him to realize that the penalty of poor sportsmanship is that no one will want to play with him. They should put this penalty into practice when the child's be-

havior gets out of hand, telling him that he will have to get out of
the game until he is ready to play properly.

Sleep Problems

The family of a young hyperactive child is often in a constant
grouch because no one is getting a decent night's sleep. The youngster, at the age of two or three or four, wakes up in the middle of
every night. Curious and restless, he wants to play noisily around
the house or come and talk to his parents. Parents should make
and enforce firm rules about the child's staying in his own room.
He should not be allowed to get into bed with his parents. If he
has been sharing a room with a brother or sister, whom he wakes
up, it is better to improvise makeshift sleeping quarters for the
innocent sibling, with the aim of containing the "public nuisance."

The hyperactive child's room should be childproofed so that
there is nothing dangerous in it—no uncovered electric outlets,
no electric heaters or vaporizers, no adjoining bathroom. The
child should be told that when he wakes up, he is to play quietly
in his room until someone comes in to tell him he may come out.
Some parents have learned to go into the child's room just before
they go to bed themselves to leave a little snack for him. Another
diversion is to rotate his toys, bringing the old ones out from storage one at a time and leaving one in the child's room every night.
Some parents find it reassuring to rig up an intercom system between the child's room and theirs so that they will hear him if he
becomes ill during the night or has a frightening nightmare, or for
some other reason really needs his parents.

If the child cries during the night, the parents should go in to
be sure he is well and not in need of anything. They should then
leave the room. No matter how much noise the child makes, the
parents should not give in to him or they will be buying continual
trouble. After several nights of being studiously ignored, most children realize that crying will not get them anywhere and that they
might as well stay quiet.

As children get older, the biggest sleep problem is getting them to go to their own room, get into bed, and stay there. Parents can take the turmoil out of bedtime by several measures—some preventive and others corrective.

First, parents should spend time with their children in the evenings. Too often a family scatters after dinner, with everyone doing "his own thing." Mother is reading, Father is going over some papers he brought home from the office, Teen-ager is doing homework, Fourth-Grader is working on his model airplane, and Second-Grader is watching television. The family is all in the same house, but there is little if any communication until one of the parents goes around saying, "It's time for bed." At this time, a child is likely to remember the burning question he had to ask his mother or the story he wanted to tell his father. Realizing the morning will be too hectic for conversation, he wants to cram in everything now. It is useless to remonstrate, "Why didn't you think of all this earlier?"

In a family with several children it is difficult for each parent to spend time alone with each one, but it is worth making some efforts along these lines, even if the time amounts to only an average of fifteen minutes per child. In most cases, this is enough for a child's questions or recitations. Some parents make a practice of taking turns at going into each child's room for a few minutes every night for a brief bedtime chat.

The evening should be a pleasant family time, with some bedtime routine a child can look forward to. Aside from being a good part of family living, such a routine is a way to wind children down and help them get into the mood for sleep. This might involve reading aloud, telling stories, playing a card game, engaging in some mild exercise, and/or having a light snack. In a family with several children, when parents cannot spend much time with each one, records often help a younger child to drift off to sleep. There are some inexpensive children's records with nursery rhymes, songs, or stories. A small child usually forms a special attachment to one or two of these and looks forward to hearing it every night.

Older children should be actively encouraged to read in bed for twenty minutes or so before they turn out their lights.

Reasonable times for going to bed should be set for all the children, with due consideration to each one's age and needs for sleep. Chronological age aside, some children need less sleep than others and should not be made to go to bed at an arbitrarily early hour. Adults accept the idea that there are night people and day people. Yet even those parents who readily admit that they do not get going until about eight o'clock in the evening and that their hardest job all day is getting up in the morning rarely recognize and accept the same phenomenon in their own child.

Parents should discuss the hour of bedtime with children. If a child wakes up easily in the morning, he is probably getting enough sleep. This is one of the criteria that should enter into a discussion about bedtime. (Making this point sometimes has the added benefit of inspiring a child to bounce out of bed more eagerly in the morning!) If two children are about the same age and get along well, bedtime can be more fun if they both go up together. If, as is more likely, the hyperactive child is always fighting with the sibling next in line, it is better to send each child to bed at a different time. Sometimes a difference of only fifteen minutes will lend prestige to the older child and help to keep two scrappers out of each other's way.

Once bedtime has been set, parents should consider it a rule to be firmly enforced. If a child is old enough to tell time and if he wears a wrist watch, he should be responsible for getting himself to bed at the right time. Otherwise, the parents will have to assume the responsibility of letting him know when it is time to start getting ready for bed. If a child is absorbed in some activity—playing or doing a project—he should have some warning that bedtime is coming up so he will have a chance to finish whatever he is doing.

Parents should realize that they can enforce only that behavior over which the child has control. Rules can govern the time at which a child starts getting ready for bed, the time by which he is to be in his bed, and the fact of his staying quietly in bed from then on. Such behavior can be rewarded to help a child develop good going-to-bed habits. It is pointless to make a rule about the time a child must actually be asleep. Sleep cannot be summoned by force of will. As long as a child is lying quietly in bed at the proper time, he should be considered to be going by the rules.

Sloppiness

Hyperactive children usually seem to be "natural-born slobs." They couldn't care less what they look like or how many piles of dirty clothing and scattered toys they have to step over. It is unlikely that your hyperactive "slob" will ever become neat as a pin. The price you would have to pay for trying to make him that way would be continual discord over essentially trivial matters. You can help him develop a modicum of neatness—just enough so that the rest of the family is not offended.

Regular routines should be established for brushing teeth, washing hands, bathing, making beds, putting away clothing and toys. If none of these routines is operating smoothly, start with one at a time and enforce its fulfillment with both the carrot and the stick, as explained in Chapters 8 and 9, and in "Doing Chores" on page 157 of this chapter. As soon as one routine is fairly well established, you can start in on another—always asking yourself how important it really is.

Some families keep the house reasonably neat by confiscating for a few days all items left where they do not belong. If Elliott leaves his sneakers in the living room overnight, they will be taken away and not given back to him until the following week. Parents and children should agree on the specifics of this rule: Does it apply to toys, clothing, schoolbooks, homework? What is the time limit for rescuing one's belongings? What rooms in the house are "off limits"? For how long will an item be kept from the child? Does the rule apply to everyone in the family, including the parents? (It should. This seems much fairer to the children. Much good feeling is engendered on their part by the power they have to confiscate Mother's shoes or Dad's jacket. They will also turn a keener eye to the premises in looking out for parental items they can seize, and in the process they are likelier to do better in putting away their own things.) After the children have been inconvenienced a few times by having to do without a favorite sweater or a favorite toy, they will remember to put away their things. (So will Mother and Father.)

Children should always be rewarded for improvements in their "neatness quotient." If Sharon puts away all her things for one entire day, if Michael remembers to brush his teeth every morning and every night for a week, if Katie combs her hair every morning with no groans of protest, their efforts should be recognized and rewarded. Parents must recognize, though, that they cannot expect to impose adult standards of neatness and cleanliness on young children. They have to learn to turn an unseeing eye to a certain amount of messiness, in the interest of tending to more important matters.

Soiling

Soiling the underpants is a common problem among young schoolchildren. A child becomes very busy in his school and play life and does not take the time to go to the bathroom. He gets caught short while he is outside playing, and his bowels move involuntarily. Or he may regularly neglect going to the bathroom for a long time until the entire functioning of his bowel is affected. It begins to fill up with feces, which become dry and hard and difficult or painful to pass. He puts off defecating even more. After a while, the bowel ceases to function in the normal way. Instead of sending up messages that it needs to be emptied, it forms mucus around the hard stool. The mucus leaks out, soiling the child's clothing, causing a disagreeable odor, and subjecting him to social misery.

Parents should insist that the child go to the toilet at a specified time each day, to sit there for a specified length of time, with the aim of moving his bowels. This may have to be in the evening since there may not be enough time before school in the morning. The child should receive some reward every time he performs.

To make defecation more comfortable, the parents can give the child a daily tablespoonful of a pleasant-tasting mineral oil suspension. If the problem has become very severe, it may be necessary to give the child a fresh start by giving him enemas for a few days. Before administering either the medicine or the enema, you should check with your child's doctor. If this concerted attack on the problem does not work, the child's bowel should be thoroughly examined, since there is the possibility of a physical disorder.

Stealing

Since children who get into the habit of helping themselves to things that do not belong to them may be on the road to more serious trouble, parents should act immediately to put a stop to any stealing, no matter how petty. When a child steals, the parents should ask why he is doing it. Is he impulsively picking up something he wants but cannot afford? Is his allowance so much smaller than that of the other neighborhood children that he steals to keep up with them? Is he trying to buy the friendship of children? Is stealing the way the boys in the neighborhood prove their manhood? As with lying, stealing may be a symptom of an underlying lack of self-esteem. While parents should act promptly and decisively to put a stop to the thievery itself, they should also make efforts to discover and deal with its underlying causes.

Parents of children with a tendency toward "sticky fingers" should remove temptation as much as possible. Money should never be left lying around. Both parents should keep their wallets close to them and should know exactly how much money they have on hand. All the children in the family should have banks that cannot be broken into and should be encouraged to keep their money in a private place. As soon as a child has accumulated a few dollars, he should be encouraged to deposit it in the bank.

When parents know without any doubt that a child has taken things—from other family members, from friends, from a store— they must confront him with their knowledge. Parents must not turn a blind eye to a child's stealing, must not help a child make excuses, and must not wish the matter away by saying it was such a small item that it did not really matter. Each time a child steals and gets away with it, the habit is reinforced. The child has to understand that he is responsible for his own actions and that he must make restitution of stolen property. He must be made to return it to a store, a friend, or the teacher. When he does so, a parent can accompany him to help him get through the ordeal. If the child has already spent stolen money, he must relinquish his allowance or sell some possession or work to earn enough money to repay the theft.

Parents must impress upon a child the necessity of being able to trust one's own family members, one's friends, and the members of one's community. A child must appreciate the seriousness of stealing. Parents do not have to humiliate a child publicly to impress upon him the necessity of respecting other people's property. When possible, they should keep the matter within the family. But when outside persons are the victims of a child's pilfering, they have to be involved in the consequences—even if only to get their property back.

If a child has been involved in several incidents, the parents must be alert for more. They should make him turn out his pockets when he is about to leave a store. They should ask for satisfactory explanations of new possessions and confiscate those that cannot be accounted for. If a child has been known to steal from stores, his parents should encourage the neighborhood merchants to report to them any problems with their child. The parents should assure their child that they do not enjoy acting as policemen but that they must fulfill their parental obligations by helping him to break this antisocial habit.

Talking Too Much

Some hyperactive children are chatterboxes who talk incessantly about anything and everything. If he talks so much that it is difficult for other people to get a word in, his parents should step in. In a good-humored but firm way they should tell the child that he has had his turn and should now let someone else speak.

When the Donovan family decided that nine-year-old Dennis had been monopolizing conversations long enough, they turned to a novel approach. Everyone in the family received twenty poker chips at the beginning of dinner. Whenever anyone spoke out on a wider scale than "pass the butter, please," or interrupted someone, he had to turn in a chip. If he spoke more than a minute, he had to turn in a chip for every additional minute. Once a person's chips were all gone, he could not talk for the remainder of the meal. The children entered into the spirit of the game, with a stopwatch called into play and poker chips flying furiously back and forth. At first, Dennis gave up all his chips in the first ten minutes of dinner. But after a while he learned to control his tongue, and the Donovan family were finally able to hold a give-and-take conversation.

Talkativeness can create a problem in a family when the parents are quiet people who value solitude and privacy. Such people often find it a considerable effort to listen to a child talk on and on. Sometimes parents "turn off" their talkative child so that even when he does say something important, no one is listening. The child who realizes that whatever he says falls on deaf ears may talk more and more in a desperate effort to attract his parents' attention.

Parents need not feel as if they have to be willing listeners all the time. They should set aside certain times during the day when they agree to listen to their child on an uninterrupted basis. They should explain to the child that they can give their full attention for a limited amount of time but that during this time, he has them all to himself. One problem with listening to a hyperactive child is that his speech often pours out at such a rapid rate that it is hard to understand. The child has to be reminded to slow down so his words can come out clearly.

Unwillingness to Share

We parents expect so many contradictory things from our children. We want them to be generous with their possessions, and at the same time we want them to take good care of them. We want them to absorb our values. Yet while we rarely lend out our cars, our golf clubs, and our fur coats, we expect our children to treat their things as communal property, to be shared with brothers, sisters, friends, and any neighbor child who might happen to drop in. We expect too much sharing from children, or not enough from ourselves.

To the very young child, sharing is unnatural. The toddler is just developing a sense of property, of what is his and what is not. A natural corollary of getting him to leave someone else's things alone is that he have the right to hold onto his own things.

An older child often does not want to share his belongings because his low opinion of himself makes him feel insecure. The insecure child feels that by letting another child use something of his, he is symbolically surrendering a part of his own territory and, by extension, giving away a part of himself. When his parents force him to share his things, they compound his insecurity by overriding his feeble attempts to protect his own integrity. Parents should refrain from calling their children "selfish" and appealing to their consciences in an effort to make them more generous. It is all too easy for parents to assume a lofty moral position from which they force children to share their most treasured possessions. Instead, parents should try to understand why a child is so posessive, and they should aim to build him up until he feels secure enough to be generous.

It may be helpful for the parents of an older child, especially one who is particularly aggressive and acquisitive, to offer incentives for sharing, such as awarding a point every time the child lets another youngster play with one of his toys. There also is no harm in matter-of-factly pointing out that a child who will not share his things with others is not likely to be offered the use of his friends' things. Then the child should make his own choices. If holding on to his possessions means more to him at the moment than either his parents' rewards or his playmates' company, so be it. The refusal to let other children play with his things is usually a temporary phenomenon that dissolves when a child realizes that he has to give up something to get something.

Verbal Static: Shouting at Parents, Talking Back, and Interrupting

Some hyperactive children annoy their parents and other adults by talking back in a fresh way, by shouting, by complaining noisily from morning till night about anything and everything, and by interrupting adult conversations *ad nauseum*. While a child should be allowed to express his feelings and opinions, including his negative ones, and to have some rights of protest, his parents also have definite rights to a certain amount of respect and courtesy. Adults do not have to and should not put up with unlimited torrents of abuse from children for the sake of the children's "self-expression" or "ventilation of feelings."

Ignoring this sort of verbal annoyance rarely works. It is a rare mother who can ignore a child shouting in her ear and a rare father whose blood stays below the boiling point in the face of a child's sassiness. Ignoring this sort of behavior means that the parents have to listen to it; given the limits of parental tolerance, they are likely to explode when they have had all they can take. Even if, by dint of superhuman effort, parents *can* ignore a child's provocative talk, it is usually impossible to get relatives, neighbors, and teachers to go along with this technique, and so the child ends up getting attention from one source or another, the parent becomes angry and embarrassed because of the child's behavior, and the obnoxiousness persists.

The best way for parents to put a stop to this sort of thing is to lay down firm limits. Parents should tell their children that they absolutely will not accept being shouted or screamed at and that negative comments or arguments will be accepted only if they are presented in a conversational tone of voice. Obviously, this still provides plenty of room for a child to express himself forcefully. Implicit in this demand is the requirement that a child come into the same room as the parent to deliver his remarks, rather than shouting from another part of the house. While setting forth this rule, parents have to agree that they will not shout at the child. This is a great additional benefit: the child gets a *quid pro quo;* the parents demonstrate a more desirable model of behavior; and a powerful reinforcement for the child's original annoying behavior is removed, the evidence that the child has provoked his parents into losing their cool.

Once the rule about no shouting has been established, parents can remind the child of it by asking quietly, as soon as his voice starts to approach a bellow or a shriek, "What's the rule about shouting?" If this reminder does not work and the child persists in going beyond acceptable decibel limits, the rule should be enforced along the lines discussed in Chapter 8, possibly by having the child spend some time in the time-out place. When the child does speak in a normal tone of voice, his parents should commend him for it, thus demonstrating that he can get their attention by positive means.

A time limit can also be imposed for the child who sounds off all the time. Parents can say that they are perfectly willing to listen up to a point—say, five or ten minutes—to a child's gripes (including raw remarks about the parents themselves), but that once the time limit is up, the child has to stop the barrage, so that everyone can get on with his or her regular activities. If this is a persistent problem, say, with a child who tends to keep up a running fire of rebellious talk throughout the day, then the parents may have to handle things by scheduling one or two gripe sessions per day and making complaints and accusations out of order at all other times.

The problem of interrupting—either breaking in on adult conversations in the home or bothering a parent who is speaking on the telephone—can be handled similarly. Parents should tell a child that they are entitled to hold conversations without constant interruptions, that they will permit only interruptions of an urgent nature, and that any infractions of this rule will have consequences. On the parents' part, there is the obligation to devote a reasonable amount of time to talking with and listening to their children. They also have to keep their daytime telephone sessions to a minimum, so that this does not become a means for them to neglect their children.

In all these areas parents should reward their children's efforts to improve. They can tally up the number of times a child shouts or talks back or interrupts in a given day. As soon as there is any improvement at all, this should be recognized. If David has been interrupting conversations thirty times in one day and then the interruptions drop to twenty times, the temptation is to be annoyed about those twenty interruptions. Instead, the parents can help David do even better by recognizing that a start has been made and that he is making powerful efforts to control himself. Instead of waiting for absolute compliance with the ideal standard—no interruptions—they should commend David for his improvement, recognize the difficulty of change, and express confidence in his ability to continue to do better.

Troublesome Children Are Often Troubled Children

When a child suddenly seems to be having problems of a different kind or intensity than he used to, his parents should consider more than the outward behavior itself. The child may be reacting this way to ask for help. The parents have to evaluate the demands being made on the child. They have to check carefully into their own behavior toward him to see whether they are asking the impossible. They also have to look carefully into his situation at school. It is more likely that the trouble may be stemming from the school setting, for the simple reason that the atmosphere at home is relatively constant, while that at school changes considerably from year to year, if not more often.

Some of the signs of too much pressure on a child are easy to read. He may formerly have been difficult and irritable at times but was most often happy; now he is irritable most of the time. He is unable to accept any criticism, is negative and unco-operative, and frequently bursts into tears or tantrums. He accuses his parents or other people of not liking him, is wont to break down and say that he is a failure or that it would have been better if he had never been born. He withdraws from normal social contacts and finds consolation only in his dog. He becomes more dependent on his mother yet resentful of her at the same time. He cannot get along at all with his father. He regresses in some habits, going back to sucking his thumb or wetting the bed. He has nothing good to say about anything or anybody. He is particularly hard on his brothers and sisters, heaping scorn on them, tattling on them, and trying to tear them down in any way possible. He complains of headaches and stomach-aches. His appetite decreases. He has bad dreams, grinds his teeth during his sleep, and hates to get up in the morning.

As the child's behavior becomes worse, his parents, his siblings, his teacher, and his classmates react more negatively to him. If he is lucky, someone close to him will realize that there is no mileage in further scolding and criticism. There may be a major scene during which one of the child's brothers or sisters emerges as his defender. Or he may get into real trouble at school. Or some other crisis may shake the parents into looking at the situation in a new light.

Some of these same behavior patterns develop when a child is not being challenged enough. A bright child who is not developing new skills, not making much headway with learning (perhaps because he is held back by being with slower children), not enlarging his mind becomes demoralized. He realizes that he is not progressing the way he ought to, and he becomes unhappy with himself. The same type of picture sometimes emerges during the long summer vacation if a bright, restless child is not channeled into regular constructive activities.

Parents can often discern the deeper problems underlying surface symptoms. They can do a great deal in the home, and they can work with the school to lessen the pressures on a child or to stimulate him further. When they cannot seem to locate the source of the problem, or when nothing they do seems to help, they should seek professional advice.

When Both Parents Work

Over and over again, we have been making the point that hyperactive children need a great deal of individual attention. They need close supervision, a well-structured home environment, and a close relationship with their parents. How, then, can parents manage this when both the father and the mother of a hyperactive child work outside the home?

The question of whether both parents should work at paying jobs usually means in our society, "Should the mother work?" When the mother's income is needed for the essentials of daily living, there is no question; she *must* work. But if she works because she *wants* to work—if she has a fulfilling career, if she wants to raise the family's standard of living, or if she simply cannot bear staying home every day with small children—she may wonder whether she is doing the right thing. There is no easy answer to this question; each mother must find her own answer.

By and large, the quality of parenting counts for more than its quantity. It is not so much the number of hours per week that a mother spends with her child that matter but what those hours are like. A woman who wants to be out working but is home instead out of a sense of duty is likely to be unhappy; she will resent the child for whom she is making this sacrifice, especially since the child is not likely to show any signs of appreciating what she is doing for him. A child fares worse with a frustrated, bitter mother who is home all the time than with a fulfilled, happy mother whom he sees less often.

Yet there are difficulties that the working parents of a hyperactive child must recognize and deal with. This youngster cannot be a "latch-key" child, left to his own devices for long periods of time. He is unlikely to have the inner discipline to make constructive use of his after-school and vacation hours. He is not the kind of child who can be easily left with relatives or baby-sitters, unless they have a special understanding of his nature and his needs.

Another problem is one of parental attitude. The mother who works outside the home often feels guilty and neglectful. When she is home, she is apt to be too permissive in an attempt to make up to the child for her absence during the day. If a child's parents have made good substitute care arrangements for their child, they should feel confident that they are doing the right thing. The mother should not let her neighbors, her relatives, her pediatrician, or her child's teacher (who, more likely than not, is a working mother herself) make her feel guilty about working. This is her decision to make. Neither should she let herself be sucked into a permissive attitude by her child's playing on her own doubts. Letting a child get away with murder will not make him appreciate his mother any the more. It will only hold him back from maturing and developing his own controls.

When both parents work, both should devise imaginative and ingenious solutions that offer good care to their child. One possibility would be for each parent to cut back somewhat on working hours. The person who is self-employed or who works for a flexible-minded employer should weigh the benefits of spending more time with a child against the loss of a proportion of income. With an older child, there are times when an adult should be in the home to supervise and to lend a stabilizing influence but does not have to provide actual care. Perhaps the parents can take turns bringing work home for times like these.

If at all possible, one parent should be home just before the child goes to school and when he returns home. Children have a lot to say at these times about their problems and their successes, and it is hard for them if there is no one they can talk to. If it is absolutely impossible for either parent to be home, especially after school, some form of telephone communication should be available to the child. Many parents forgo their afternoon coffee break in favor of a brief after-school telephone chat with a child. The parent can call home at a specified time each afternoon, or the child can dial the parent at work.

If the parents are lucky enough to be able to afford and to find a sensitive, understanding, flexible, firm person to act as a parent substitute while they are at work, both they and the child will benefit. Winston Churchill, who was virtually ignored by his mother when he was a child, was raised by such a person, who remained his dearest friend all her life.

Sometimes a teen-age boy or girl can stay with a youngster after school and during vacations. A teen-age boy can be a particularly welcome companion for an active young boy: he can be an influential model, can teach athletic skills, and can help with homework. Organized activities can also help to fill the gap between school time and parent time. Some schools maintain after-school programs that allow children to take part in sports, arts and crafts, or tutoring programs. Community centers, boys' or girls' clubs, or "Y's" often conduct well-supervised interesting programs. In large cities private after-school and vacation programs are sometimes offered. If enough parents press for such a program, they may be able to spur the establishment of one in their community.

Both parents should spend as much time as possible with their children on off-duty hours. One professional woman, the mother of four children, was recently asked her formula for succeeding both in the business world and with her family. Her reply: "My husband and I both love what we do during the working day, and we wouldn't want to give that up. But we also love our children and want to spend time with them. So they are our social life. We never go out on week nights; we always spend at least one full day and evening over the weekend with the children; and we always go on vacations as a family. We'll have plenty of years after they're out of the house to be by ourselves and with other adults. Right now, we'd rather invest our time in our children."

The Single Parent

It is difficult for a father and mother working together to raise a hyperactive child. How much more difficult it is for a single parent! The parent whose marriage has been severed by divorce or death can get terribly discouraged by the total responsibility for a child, especially when the child is a difficult one to raise.

The divorced parent who has custody of the child—usually the mother—has special problems. If the child seems like the father, the mother will resent those characteristics of his that remind her of the man who failed her. She may also worry that the child may turn out to be like his father, whom she may consider shiftless, irresponsible, and a general failure in life. Beset by feelings of guilt about her broken marriage and its effects on the child, she may try to make it all up to him by becoming too permissive. If she loses her control and the child does not develop any of his own, the home situation steadily deteriorates.

Some of the problems faced by the single parent include a lack of time and energy to be both the head of the household and the family breadwinner, the prevailing cultural attitude that a single parent cannot adequately carry out the responsibilities of parenthood, the loss of self-confidence following the breakup of the marriage, and the difficulties of dealing with the absent parent, who may be a confused and irresponsible person.

The continual press of demands from the children, the home, and the job make it terribly difficult to deal with the other problems. The parent who is raising a child by herself (or himself) should, without shame or a feeling of failure, draw upon as many resources of the community as possible. She has to make the greatest effort to arrange regular periods of rest or change, so that she can keep her sanity and not be worn down to the point where she is doing a third-rate job in every sphere of her life. She should make a deliberate effort to cultivate her own social life and to get away from the household regularly, say, one evening a week, to do something she particularly enjoys with adults she likes.

If the mother has relatives living near her, she should try hard to set up regular visits, perhaps on a monthly basis, for the children to go to stay for a couple of days with family. If her family lives far away, she should seriously consider moving back to where they are. If she has strong reasons for not doing so or if she has no family who could help, she should try to arrange a swapping program with a friend in the same situation, so they can trade off their children at regular intervals. Or she may be able to find a good baby-sitter, perhaps a neighbor, who can care for the child in exchange for the mother's providing some other service for the neighbor.

The single parent should make full use of such resources as Boy and Girl Scouts, boys' and girls' clubs, and the "Y." Also, the Big Brothers and Big Sisters organizations, which enlist adult volunteers in the community to spend time on a regular basis with fatherless boys and motherless girls, are particularly valuable aids to single parents. On an informal basis, the single parent should be very open with neighbors, the family clergyman, the school principal, and the child's teacher about the needs of her hyperactive youngster. Often a relative, a teacher, a principal, a Scout leader, a clergyman, a neighborhood parent, or an older teen-ager will take a particular interest in a child and be an invaluable influence on him.

No matter how many outside resources the parent draws on, however, she should still realize that her relationship with her child is the most important one. She should be sure to see that she and her children get out sometimes to have fun together and that she is not just filling the roles of cook, cleaning woman, and chauffeur. She should economize as tightly as possible on clothes, food, household furnishings and toys, in order to have money to take the children out to shows, hamburger stands, camping weekends, and so forth.

If she can find a parents' group in which she can talk with other parents of hyperactive children, or other single parents, or other parents with troublesome adolescents, she should be able to find a great deal of reassurance and support. If she cannot find any such group, she may be able to get good advice from a clergyman or a professional counselor. She may need advice and support in order to deal effectively with her ex-husband. Mothers frequently continue to put up with a lot of nonsense from a man. They may need help in learning how to stand up for their own and their children's rights. The single parent, like other parents, needs to develop a deliberate, planned approach to her hyperactive child and to be a firm disciplinarian.

The emotional conflicts faced by a single mother or father can probably be best resolved by going ahead to be a competent parent. Above all, a mother should not berate herself for robbing the child of his father. A father who is not interested in a child or whose life with his wife is miserable can be far more destructive by his presence in the home than if he is not around at all. Many single parents—whether mothers or fathers—do a wonderful job of bringing up boys and girls. It is more difficult, but it can be done.

PART III

How to Help Your Child in School

The chief offenses committed by youth at school, arise from the liveliness of their active dispositions. Few youth do wrong for the *sake of doing so.*

—Joseph Lancaster
Improvements in Education, 1805

11   SCHOOL PROBLEMS

For the typical hyperactive child, school is the bane of his existence, since it requires those abilities in which he is most deficient. It is particularly important to catch school problems early, since academic performance is a crucial factor in a young child's self-image. When a child does poorly in school, he is likely to develop attitudes that will keep him from doing better. He accepts other people's estimate of him as a "dumbbell" or a "retardo," and a self-perpetuating cycle of failure begins. Furthermore, the record of his failures follows him through school and colors the expectations of every teacher he will ever have; he also gets a reputation among the other children.

An adult who is unhappy in his job may be able to switch to a more satisfying one, but a child who does poorly in school has to stay there. The alternatives of special classes and private schools are not always available or feasible. So even though he is doing miserably in school, he has to go back day after day to face his failures. No wonder a recent study showed that children who were rated as hyperactive by their teachers were likely to be absent from school more than the other children, even though they did not seem to suffer to any greater degree from illness. Hating school, these youngsters apparently developed enough psychosomatic symptoms to allow them to escape.

Nature of the Problems in School

The hyperactive child's troubles in school stem from the school and from his own personality.

The School

The school years constitute a unique period in life, a time when individuals are required to suppress physical activity for much of the time, to suppress deviations from a predetermined norm, and to put up with an often-boring atmosphere.

In most schools, by the time children reach the second grade, they are expected to sit still for long periods of time without talking or moving around. They may have to sit quietly and listen to the teacher almost all day long, except for recess, lunch, and a weekly gym period. At an age when most children—and especially the hyperactive—are blessed with large reserves of energy and small supplies of patience, they are given too few opportunities to discharge the former and too many demands to exercise the latter. They have neither the cookie-and-juice breaks of the nursery school years nor the coffee breaks of adulthood. How many adults would cope with the same situation?*

Success in school requires a high degree of conformity, both to other people's direction and to the norm. Teachers tend to fit their lessons to the average child and do little for the slower or faster learner, or any child who needs special attention. This is excused on the grounds that giving a child individual help is not fair to the rest of the class. However, there is a small but growing band

* Charles Silberman, author of *Crisis in the Classroom*, tells the story of the time he was asked to submit testimony about schools to a Congressional hearing. Mr. Silberman was cautioned ahead of time, "Make your written testimony as long as you like—but please don't take more than fifteen minutes to present your spoken testimony. The Senators get awfully restless and don't like to sit still too long." Should we be requiring more patience from our children than our legislators are able to display?

of teachers who give all their students individual attention and seldom address the class as a whole. Teachers who like and accept active children can have a wonderful effect on a hyperactive child, in part because they influence the other children to enjoy him too. Unfortunately, most teachers set more stock by controlling children than working with them as they are. Another common failing in the schools is that they try to make learning a passive process. All children, but especially the hyperactive, need to take a vigorous part in discussing and acting on lessons. Too much of the time, children are supposed to be passive in school, when they have important things to say and do.

Fortunately, some schools allow children a great deal of freedom of movement within an overall structure; some stress individualized learning programs that teach every pupil in terms of his own strengths and weaknesses; and some are radically changing the curriculum to make learning more interesting and more fun. A few schools even allow romping, horseplay, and snowball fights between classes.

The Child's Personality

Because of his constant activity, he may absorb less information, and he will certainly do less work. When he is rolling his pencil on the desk, fiddling around with his papers, getting up and walking around the room and bending down to see what is on the floor, he may not hear what the teacher is saying, and he will not get his assignment done.

His short attention span also interferes with his taking in information. His lack of perseverance and his distractibility make it unlikely that he will finish classroom or homework assignments. When he does turn in a completed assignment, it is likely to be messy, slapdash, and illegible. He guesses wildly at math problems and in reading new words because he is impulsive and impatient. He spins his wheels instead of figuring out a deliberate approach to a problem. He does not check his work though it is full of careless mistakes. He may destroy his work when he feels he has started off badly and end up turning in nothing at all. Despite these problems, the hyperactive child can learn when he receives the right sort of encouragement and help both at home and at school.

Some children have trouble learning because of problems in perception, language development, or physical co-ordination. Most hyperactive children have no specific learning disabilities, but parents should be alert to this possibility. Visual-perception problems, for example, cause a child to confuse up and down, and left and right, with the result that he has difficulty in learning how to read and how to work with numbers. Auditory-perception problems interfere with a child's understanding what the teacher is saying. Small-motor co-ordination difficulties cause trouble with handwriting, coloring, and drawing. Speech problems interfere with a child's ability to express himself and make him embarrassed to speak in class or to read aloud. If specific learning disabilities are identified, special teaching techniques can help the child to learn in spite of them.

Problems in Doing the Work

The main problem most hyperactive children have in school is the difficulty of demonstrating what they know. Somehow, despite all the wiggling around, despite the inattentiveness and the impatience and the excitability, these children do manage to learn how to read and calculate, and get the gist of scientific and historical concepts. What they cannot do is demonstrate to the teacher's satisfaction what they have learned. Written work is their nemesis. If they are permitted to give reports and answers orally, they can show they know the work. The teacher who provides alternative ways of taking tests and doing reports, such as letting a child talk into a tape recorder or granting him a private conference, is truly a good teacher.

Behavior Problems

The impulsiveness, impatience, excitability, overactivity, and short attention span that characterize the hyperactive child often make him the outcast of the classroom—particularly if the teacher has little tolerance for deviant behavior. A litany of some of the misbehaviors that exasperate teachers can be seen on page 196, which shows a copy of a memo sent by a boy's teacher to his doctor. It is not surprising that a child who does these things should irritate his teacher. The child may become the teacher's "hostility sponge," blamed for everything wrong, including things for which he is not responsible. Disliked by his teacher and classmates, a child develops other ways to get attention in class, such as clowning and disruption.

The teacher's attitude infects the other children in the class. Consciously or unconsciously, the teacher may influence the other children to reject the child. Philip came home to tell his mother how his first-grade teacher had rearranged all the seats in the room two by two, but left him sitting alone. The teacher told the little boy, "No one would want to sit with you." Philip tearfully told his mother, "I guess no one likes me."

Home and School Can Work Together

Problems with school may appear in nursery school, in kindergarten, or in the first grade, but the school people usually do not contact parents right away. Kindergarten and first-grade teachers are used to wide variations in the behavior and learning patterns of young childen, and they often expect a child to grow out of his problems. Sometimes, a teacher feels that a child's difficulty stems from her own failure, and naturally she does not want to admit defeat. Also, the hyperactive child's behavior and performance vary from day to day, and the teacher may feel, "He could if he only would!" She keeps trying to motivate him to do better with-

MEMO: To Dr. Stewart
ON: Arnold ————
FROM: Arnold's Teacher

Arnold does not listen or follow directions or do any work in class.
He throws chalk, crayons, plaster, etc.
He rolls pencils and crayons on desk.
He speaks out without permission.
He beats himself on head and chest (eyes closed, clenched fists).
He crawls on floor.
He marks on floor and desk with chalk or pencil.
He makes peculiar noises and sounds.
He answers back.
He sits and plays with crayons or other "toys."
He walks around room without permission, especially to closet and
    pencil sharpener.
He peels paper from crayons and throws it.
He constantly breaks lead in pencil.
He bothers other children by talking to them or hitting them.
He picks plaster off walls.
He makes "parrot" talk in class.
He rolls up paper and looks through it.
He tears paper.
He rolls crayons and pencils on floor behind his desk.
He beats and hits desk with fists.
He closes eyes and shakes head slowly at first, then violently.
He "walks" fingers on desk tops.
He marks on board when in line.
He is constantly finding straight pins and returning them to me—
    when he doesn't try to stick somebody.
He fiddles with pins and decorations on bulletin board.
He seldom puts name on paper.
He hits and talks to neighbors—several children around him.
He waves air with hands and head.
He just sits and stares while tapping a crayon or pencil.
He imitates cars and planes with small objects—pencils, crayons,
    chalk.
He sharpens pencils and then breaks lead and etc., etc., etc.!!
He resents criticism and always has an alibi.
He "finds" things all the time.

out truly understanding the source of his difficulties. For these reasons and others, a child may be left to drift until he reaches the fourth or fifth grade. By this time, his work and his behavior are intolerable.

Parents Can Take the First Step

Parents can help to prevent years of misery by acting early. A super-energetic, difficult child is a prime prospect for school problems. Therefore, the parents should take the initiative at the very beginning of his school career by speaking to the child's teacher and to the principal. The parents may have recognized the problems at home or they may have been informed by the child's nursery school teacher that he had a much shorter span of attention than the other children, was more impulsive in his behavior, and was constantly getting into trouble.

When the parents talk to the teacher, they should avoid labeling their child as "hyperactive" or as anything else he may have been termed by a physician, a psychologist, or some other professional consultant. Words such as these do not describe the child's specific problems, and they evoke stereotyped images in the mind of the teacher, offering her an excuse for not exerting herself on his behalf. "Oh, I can't do anything with Frank," she will think. "After all, he's hyperactive." It is wiser to give the teacher a problem-oriented description of those characteristics that need special attention. Is he active, restless, aggressive, distractible? On the other hand, what are his strengths? Is he compassionate toward smaller children, eager to help with little jobs, appreciative of special attention? Does he respond favorably to compliments, or do they make him fall apart? What other personality traits should his teacher know about?

By giving the teacher a full picture of the child, the parents will be helping her and their child. The teacher will be less likely to blame herself for his school difficulties if she knows that he behaves in the same way at home. She may be more willing to offer the flexibility he needs and to use his interests to involve him in work and give him chances for success and recognition.

It is helpful to ask the professional person who knows your child best to contact the school. A pediatrician, psychologist, or psychiatrist who knows your child's temperament and intellectual abilities can be objective about the child in a way parents can never be. School personnel may be influenced more by the opinions of a professional person.

Parents Should Be Assertive on Behalf of Their Child

Many parents do not realize how much they can do to bring about a favorable school environment for their child. By speaking to the principal, parents may arrange to have a particular teacher for their child, one who is best suited to teach hyperactive children. If you feel strongly that some aspect of your child's schooling should be changed, your responsibility toward your child gives you the right to express your concern and ask for what you want. This may be a transfer to another teacher's class, to another bus route, or to another school. Remember that "only the squeaking wheel gets the grease."

Moving a bright hyperactive child up to the next grade may be helpful. Parents are reluctant to ask for this, afraid of being thought "pushy" and of pressuring their child. Teachers and principals usually resist early entrance or skipping and stress the idea that a child is "socially immature," even though he is unquestionably bright. Very often, the "immature" behavior is simply a reflection of the child's boredom; it disappears when he is challenged at a level commensurate with his ability. Parents may need to be more determined about moving their child up a grade than about any other encounter with school administrators.

When a school will not skip a child to a higher grade and is not able to provide the intellectual stimulation that he needs, it is a good idea for parents who can afford it to enroll their child in a private school. Many hyperactive youngsters thrive in relatively structured, intellectually oriented private schools that have the personnel to provide more individualized attention than would be possible in the public schools. Structure is an important part of the school atmosphere; a free and easy "progressive" school can be absolutely disastrous for the hyperactive child who needs strong controls and a sense of discipline. (Later in the game, at the junior high and high school level, the reverse may be true. The youngster who has become alienated by regular school may do better in a freer school atmosphere than in a more conventional one.)

Lines of Communication Should Be Kept Open

Parents should confidently approach teachers and principals to talk about their child, to ask for advice, or to complain. Make an appointment to meet your child's teacher so that she can give you her full attention. Do not arrive without warning in the middle of the day.

Be sure to spend enough time with your child so that he can tell you about school. You can get across to him the difficulties inherent in the school situation and reassure him that just because he is doing poorly in school, he will not necessarily fail in life. Parents should also try to understand a child's feelings about his teacher. This is one place where good listening is especially important. Parents should not feel duty-bound to support the teacher's authority in every instance. Sometimes teachers are wrong and children are right. Without tearing her down, they can discuss the limitations of a teacher's personality in a way that may help the child to understand her and her treatment of him.

Parents should speak more often with other members of the school staff. For example, they can go directly to a child's physical-education teacher to talk about the child's need to let off some of his aggressiveness and excess energy in controlled competitive situations.

Your child's school may also have on its faculty a remedial-reading teacher, a psychologist, a social worker or a guidance counselor, any or all of whom may be in touch with you from time to time. If this individual is sensitive and knowledgeable, he or she can be extremely helpful to the hyperactive child and his parents. The "helping person" can often smooth a child's relationship with his teacher, make referrals to other professional consultants, and provide a source of understanding and compassion for both child and parents.

When you realize that your child is having trouble in school, you should contact one of these staff specialists if no one has contacted you. Let the specialist know that you are grateful for any help that he or she can give you. Impress upon the professional person your interest, your receptivity to any suggestions, and your willingness to follow through to help your child. Keep in mind that this person across the desk from you is probably there because he or she cares about children and wants to help them. Even if you do not agree with his or her interpretation of your child's problem, try to recognize the specialist's interest in your child.

Emphasize your desire to know as much as possible about the school's efforts regarding your child. Bring up the subject of psychological testing if the school specialist does not mention it. Ask whether he or she thinks testing would be a good idea, and ask for the reasons behind the opinions. Find out which tests would be administered to your child and what information these tests yield. Impress upon the school personnel your desire to be informed ahead of time about any testing to be done and ask for an appointment after the testing, so that both parents can come in for an explanation and interpretation of the test results.

Most schools used to follow the policy of keeping a child's test scores secret—at least outside the school. All the child's teachers, the secretaries in the office, and other school personnel could find out a child's test results. The parents rarely could. It was assumed that parents would not know how to interpret these scores and might "misuse" the information in some way to the detriment of the child. Some enlightened school administrators now recognize that the parents have a right to know as much as possible about their own children. If your school refuses to discuss your child's test scores with you, you may take your request all the way up to the State Commissioner of Education, if necessary.

Aside from the philosophical principle of the parents' right to information about their child's progress and activities in school, letting the parents know ahead of time about planned psychological testing makes sense from a practical viewpoint. The alerted parents can see that the child gets a good night's sleep the night before the test, can postpone the testing if the child is not feeling well, and can withhold any drugs the child may be taking, all in the interests of more meaningful test results.

How Parents Can Help Their Children Do Well in School

Parents exert great influence on their children's performance in school by the atmosphere in the home, the activities they encourage their children to pursue, and the activities they participate in themselves. The expectations they hold, the home structure they maintain, and the interest they show are all vital factors that contribute to a child's success in school.

Reasonable Expectations

As long as schools grade pupils on absolute performance rather than on how well they use their native ability, some children will not be A students, however highly motivated they are and no matter how much effort they put forth. If you expect A's from a child who has average ability, you will be disappointed, and your child will sense this.

Testing a child's intellectual aptitude and achievement helps parents and teachers to form realistic expectations for his performance in school. Parents and teachers often overestimate the potential of a talkative, curious, and unusually alert child, with the unfortunate result that they expect too much of him. The results of testing may well show that he is learning at a normal rate for his intellectual potential. Psychological testing can also help the child from whom too little is expected. A child who has a relatively high level of intelligence combined with a low threshold for boredom responds well to challenge. As we wrote earlier, a child like this may need to skip to a higher grade, where he will be stimulated by more challenging material and actually "pushed" to learn.

Well-Structured Home Environment

Parents should use their authority to see that their child stays as healthy as possible to ensure regular school attendance. They should see that the child gets enough rest, which may mean a concerted effort on their part to see that he gets to bed at a sensible hour. (See page 171 for bedtime suggestions.) They should be firm about insisting that the child go to school regularly and not be swayed by imaginary bellyaches, headaches, or sore throats. The thermometer provides the only worthwhile guide for judging a child's illness. Parents cannot judge whether a child is well enough to go to school on the basis of his subjective comments. The rule has to be that the child go to school unless he has more than one degree of fever. Once a child has fallen into the habit of avoiding school through early-morning symptoms, he may develop a school phobia that will be difficult to overcome.

Morning routines should be worked out so that the child goes to school on time every day. (See page 166 for suggestions.) A child's persistent lateness creates teacher antagonism, which rebounds against the child himself. He is starting off his day the wrong way.

Stimulating Academic Development

Parents can help their children develop language skills in a variety of ways. First of all, they can encourage conversation in the home about subjects of interest to the child, in an effort to get him to talk more and to get practice in expressing himself. Conversations can revolve around the football games after school, the family's vacation plans, how the class behaved when a substitute filled in for the regular teacher, and so forth. When parents and children share common interests like music, woodworking, tennis, camping, and so forth, these are good topics of conversation. Parents should feel free to use new and unfamiliar words in conversation and to explain their meanings when asked. (It is a good idea to keep a simple dictionary in the dining room. The child can be encouraged to look up words himself—and the parent will be spared the embarrassment of being unable to define the words he uses.)

Shared activities that encourage academic skills are great for family fun and painless learning. Keeping track of batting averages and other sports statistics is good practice in arithmetic. Cooking gives practice in reading, measuring, and following directions. A game like "Animal, Vegetable, or Mineral" can be played in the car; it encourages thinking, the ability to categorize objects, and the use of descriptive words. Scrabble is a good vocabulary builder; Monopoly encourages facility with counting and handling money; Simon Says encourages close attention to directions.

Television watching should be carefully restricted. The child who is sitting in front of the "boob tube" for three or four hours a day is not achieving anything he can be proud of and is not exercising body or mind. A schoolchild should watch no more than a total of four hours of television during the days Monday through Thursday, no more than an hour a day (except for special programs with an educational value, when he might watch for two hours one night and give up his hour on another night). On the weekends, he may be permitted to watch two hours a night. He should not be watching television at all during the day, unless it is right before dinner, when some children sag so much that they are incapable of constructive activity. Most daytime hours should be taken up with more worthwhile activities like going to the "Y," playing outdoors, doing chores and homework. Furthermore, a child should earn the right to watch television by doing his homework, his chores, and some reading every day.

If your child is watching more TV than this, he is not being challenged enough by home responsibilities, by school assignments, or by interesting extracurricular activities. Your job, then, is to implement your rule limiting televiewing by seeing that his time is taken up by so many other interests that he does not have enough time for excessive television viewing. Also, you have to examine the example you are setting. Are you watching three or four hours of television a day yourself? What interesting and worthwhile activities is this keeping you from pursuing? How can you discourage excessive viewing on your child's part if you do the very thing you do not want him to do?

Children should be expected to do some reading every day. If a youngster is not a great reader, one of his parents should plan a weekly trip to the library with him to help him pick out books that will be fun to read. Do not worry about his taking out books that you think are too easy. It is better to encourage a love of reading than to insist that he read material that may be too difficult for him and that may turn him off. There is a wealth of lively, funny, enjoyable easy reading material on the shelves of any good children's library. You can discreetly mention to the librarian out of your child's earshot what his reading level is and ask her to help him select books that he will enjoy.

A certain time each day should be set aside for reading, with some other activity like watching TV or playing a game depending on fifteen minutes or half an hour of reading. As a child gets older, say into junior high, and is so burdened with homework that it is difficult to require him to read a set amount each day, you may want to offer incentives for special efforts in reading by rewarding him for every book read.

Reading aloud is a wonderful activity for the entire family. Reading to a young child prepares him for appropriate behavior in the classroom, since there is a certain discipline in sitting still and listening. Reading aloud can give children a feel for language, expand their vocabulary, and provide an intimate time together for parent and child. Furthermore, enjoying funny, adventurous, sad, and exciting books as a family can inspire a love of books in children and establish a superiority of reading over television.

Since hyperactive children have so much difficulty with written work in school, parents should do as much as they can to see that the child does a certain amount of writing and gets some pleasure from it. Sarah is encouraged by her parents to write short letters to favorite relatives as well as to her pen pal in another country. Roger writes at least once a week for some catalogue, map, tourist guide, or cereal-box premium. When Julie's family goes to a museum or on a trip, she always gets postcards, which she sends to her grandmother and her best friend. David gets his own supply of Christmas cards and Valentines; he addresses the envelopes to friends and relatives. Tim helps to draw up shopping lists, Christmas lists, and party invitation lists.

Whatever writing the child does, whether it is part of his schoolwork or something he has done on his own, should be recognized and praised, not taken for granted. Parents should not fuss about spelling and neatness, but should be grateful that the child is writing anything at all. They should provide their hyperactive child with strong paper that will take a lot of erasing and with an eraser of the kind used by typists. They should try to stick close to him when he is doing his writing, since he is likely to try to do it in a great hurry, make loads of careless mistakes, and then get upset and want to throw the whole thing away. The parent can try to slow him down and encourage him. He should be urged to check words whose spelling he is unsure about before he writes them down. And he should be made to check his work at least once after he has finished. He will probably continue to make careless mistakes in arithmetic and writing all his life. So it is important for him to form the habit of checking his work.

Showing Interest in Schoolwork

When a child brings home a paper to show his parents, he will be encouraged by their interest in looking at it and in wanting to hear his explanation of the lesson involved. A child will be discouraged from talking about his schoolwork if his parents are always too busy to look at his work or if they cast a quick glance at it, say "Uh huh," and then turn to something else. Parents should exhibit less interest in the grades a child earns than in his actual learning and the effort he makes. Their interest in his work should be positive and encouraging, with the emphasis on the child's successes and improvements—no matter how small—rather than on his mistakes and failures.

When Alice shows her father a spelling test with five words wrong out of twenty, he has two possible responses. He can say, "You didn't study hard enough or you would have got all the words right." Or he can say, "I'm glad to see that you got more words right this week than you did last week. You really are improving in your spelling." The second response is the one that will boost Alice's self-esteem and inspire her to continue trying her hardest.

Homework

How much help should parents give their children? How much supervision should they provide? Ordinarily, homework is best left between a child and his teacher. Homework is the child's responsibility. It is not helpful to him if his parents assume responsibility for seeing that he does his homework, if they nag him to do it, insist on seeing it and so on. A child should be left to face the consequences of his not doing his homework.

With a hyperactive child, however, this "hands off" attitude rarely works. The child will not assume the responsibility for doing his homework. He will go to school day after day without his completed assignments. He will not enjoy his teacher's anger, but he will not be motivated strongly enough by it to mend his ways. This child needs some help to get on the right track.

Paul, in fourth grade, never did any homework. His parents had never become involved in any of their children's homework responsibilities. From what Paul said, they assumed he had a teacher who did not believe in assigning homework. Then Paul's teacher called them in for a conference, telling them that he assigned about thirty minutes' work every day and that for the first two months of school Paul had never turned in a completed assignment. Paul's parents resolved to see that their son did his work. They became "homework cops," reminding Paul to do his homework, nagging him while he put it off, going in to check on him when he finally sat down, and looking at the end result. Such a rift developed between Paul and his parents that they decided there must be a better way.

Paul's father said to the boy, "I realize that it is hard for you to tackle your homework assignments. Do you want some help in planning your time?" Paul did not answer. His father went on, "What time of day is best for doing your work?" Paul shrugged and said, "I like to play ball after school, so I don't want to do it then. And at night I'm too tired." Father and son finally agreed that Paul would come in from playing ball at five o'clock, that he would do some of his work before dinner and the rest afterward, and that he would alternate between working at his desk and being active. Paul would receive a point every time he came in on time, and when he earned twenty-five points he would get the new basketball he wanted.

The next day, Paul came home at 5:05. He showed his mother his assignment for the day, which she helped him break up into several small segments. She suggested that he do five math problems, half of the total math assignment, and then show them to her. When he showed her the math problems, which took him ten minutes to do, she praised him warmly for doing them all and told him he could have fifteen minutes to do whatever he wanted to do, before he tackled the rest of his assignment. Paul quickly ran out to practice throwing his old basketball.

Fifteen minutes later, his mother called him in. She set him to work doing the other half of his math assignment. When he brought these to her, he received more praise, especially since he had now completed his math assignment and had only his spelling homework to do. After dinner, Paul's father took over. He reminded Paul to write out ten of the twenty assigned spelling words and to show them to his father.

"Good, Paul," said his father. "Now you have only those other spelling words to do, and your work will be all finished. Then we can play a game of cards."

Paul's first day on the new schedule went like a fairy tale. Not every day was like this. Some days he forgot to come in on time, and his mother had to go out to find him. Some days he had trouble sticking to even the small segments of work he was supposed to do at one sitting. But, over the long haul, this type of schedule, which allowed him to break his work up into short stretches that he could handle, worked out well.

Tutoring

You will note that in the example above, Paul's parents did not actively help him with the actual work. Neither of them did any tutoring. Their contribution was in giving him a hand in organizing his time and sticking to his work.

Some parents can tutor their children with benefits for all, but we are often too involved emotionally with our children to make good teachers, and we strain the parent-child relationship when we take over the job of teaching, too. If you find that you and your child work well together, by all means give him a hand. But if every homework session ends up in tears, scoldings, impatient outbursts, and tension all about, you would do better to step out of the tutoring role.

Tutoring is helpful with hyperactive children only when it is very low key and when it is designed to help a child with a problem he knows he needs help with. Often a high school or college student can accomplish more than a youngster's parents. If the student is sympathetic and understanding, he or she can also become a friend and a "model" for the child.

One kind of tutoring that is helpful to the hyperactive child is the flash-card variety. Because of his impulsiveness and his difficulty in stopping to figure out answers, it is helpful for this child to memorize as much as possible. This is particularly helpful with simple arithmetic facts and common reading words. He should, for example, have a much larger repertory of "look-say" responses to words than does the average child, who can take the time to figure out a word phonetically.

Modern technology has come up with an alternative to tutoring: the teaching machine. A number of educational firms put out teaching machines that seem custom-made for the hyperactive child. One of these is the Cyclo-teacher (put out by World Book Encyclopedias and selling for about $60). This machine includes a kit with programs in all the grade school subjects, plus some in more interesting areas such as "how your car runs" and "referee signals in football." The machine is a simple gadget in which one puts a circular piece of paper, together with the "program." The machine has three windows, one showing the current question, one with the answer to the previous problem, and one providing space for the child to answer. When he pushes down a lever, he brings up the correct answer and the next question. The questions become progressively more difficult. The small amount of writing involved, the immediate feedback of the correct answer, and the fun of working the machine make this an ideal instrument for the hyperactive child. Of course, the machine does its work best when it is used systematically under the encouragement and exhortation of parents or teacher. A machine like this is, unfortunately, expensive for the average family, but it is a good investment for the family that can afford it. It is also an excellent item for a PTA to present to a school.

In most cases, special tutoring—even that done by qualified professional teachers—is limited in its effects. It is often a waste of time and money and an imposition of additional pressure on the child. A youngster's interest in school is much more important than his level of achievement at a given time. The curriculum in grade school is so modest that the average child can quickly catch up when he has dropped behind, provided that he is interested in doing so. On the other hand, a child who is forced to keep up may become convinced that school is just a punishing experience and will be a prime subject for dropping out later on.

Lowell V. Kingsley, director of a Boston school for children with learning difficulties, has said, "Experience in corrective and make-up work indicates that if a student is retarded in school progress, the amount of material covered or the amount of 'time put in' does not have nearly as much significance as the efficiency of daily performance. Any gains made by getting more work done at home are more than canceled if negative attitudes are developed toward books, teachers, a certain subject or *toward the parent* who is trying to help. The five-hour school day is quite enough to take care of 'catching up' for most children including those who have school difficulties."

This is not to say that special teaching techniques used by the child's own teacher or by a specially trained teacher in the child's school cannot often overcome specific problems. It means, rather, that the child with problems in school will rarely be helped by after-school or summer-school remediation programs. This is especially true of the children we are talking about, whose problems are not so much in learning, but in doing assigned work. *We have to be careful not to confuse learning with actual performance in school.*

Joining the PTA

Parents of hyperactive children have a special stake in becoming active in the school's Parent-Teacher Association. By their participation, they demonstrate to their child's teacher that they care about the school, as well as their child's progress in it. They are also in a stronger position to press for changes in the school that will benefit their own youngsters, such as an expanded physical-education program, a variety of special educational services, and more extensive psychological services to help children with troubles.

Parents who are active in school affairs have children who are more successful in school. The interest of parents in their child's school, as shown by their PTA involvement and the number of times that they meet with school personnel, is highly correlated with a child's success in school.

If all of you knew that, by any means possible, you had to move every child ahead in every subject, you would sharpen up your wits to find a way for all of them to function well.
—The Schoolboys of Barbiana
Letter to a Teacher, 1970

12   THE POWER OF POSITIVE TEACHING

To better understand a hyperactive child the teacher needs reports from the professional people who have examined the child's emotional and intellectual make-up. If the child has not been tested or examined, the teacher should recommend a psychological and educational evaluation within the school district. This testing is essential if the teacher is to form reasonable expectations of the child. These would be concerned with how much work he should do, how he should do it (in writing, by talking, or through construction projects), and how much time he should be allowed, as well as the amount of material the child should learn. The following policies should help the hyperactive child to improve his school performance.

Individualized Teaching

A teacher who practices individualized teaching understands that each child has his own style of learning, his own abilities and deficiencies and his own personality. She adapts her approach to suit each child.

Some teachers set up written contracts with all the children in their class. Under the terms of these contracts, a child agrees to perform a unit of work in a certain way; sometimes the contract provides for a reward for completed work; at other times, the completed work is its own reward. Children may develop more re-

SAMPLE CONTRACT

I, *George Washington* agree to abide by
the rules of this contract with my parents.

I promise to *set my alarm for 7 o'clock and to get up out of bed as soon as it goes off*

Every time I *get up on time*
I will earn *one point*

When I earn *five points*
I will be able to *go out for an ice cream cone with my father*

Date *June 9, 1972* *George Washington* child
Martha Washington mother
Abraham Washington father

Note: This contract is subject to renegotiation by any of
the signers.

sponsibility for doing this work since they take a part in drawing up the contracts. With their signature, they assume a greater commitment to do the job. (See sample contract on page 213.)

Contracts with a hyperactive child should be worked out day by day. The teacher should begin with a contract which provides that the child work for a length of time she is certain he can actually manage. He can then fulfill his contract and realize immediate success.

Such a contract might specify that a child finish a piece of work in fifteen minutes. At the end of this time, if the child had done the work satisfactorily, he would get a brief free period, during which he could do something he particularly liked. This might be drawing at a desk in the corridor, reading comics, playing with the classroom pets, or using a workbench in the back of the classroom. The day's routine would be a series of cycles in which work was followed by a free period. The periods of work and the standard of performance would gradually be increased, while the free periods would stay the same. Having the child complete short assignments and report back to the teacher frequently provides monitoring of his work, immediate feedback, breaks in his routine, and prompt reward for completed work. At the beginning of the program, the average hyperactive child requires firm supervision and private direction by the teacher during the assigned work period if he is to realize success.

A teacher may feel that she cannot afford to give this much attention to the one or two hyperactive children in her class, when she has twenty or thirty other pupils. Yet when she stops to think of the time now wasted by the disruptions of the one or two and her reprimands to them, she will recognize the soundness of investing extra time at the beginning of the term to establish such a program.

A teacher should be flexible in letting a child show what he knows, even if this must be done in slightly unorthodox ways. She may, for example, allow Mario to tape his social studies report on a cassette rather than make him write it out. She may hold individual conferences with Jeannie to find out what reading she is doing and what she is getting from her reading, rather than insisting on book reports from everyone in the class. She can announce amnesties on lost credit for messiness or spelling for certain assignments.

Motivating Children by Rewards

For many years teachers have awarded gold stars to good pupils, have held out such activities as being monitors, erasing blackboards, and running errands as prizes for good classwork and good behavior. In a book written in 1805, Joseph Lancaster, a London schoolmaster, told of the good results he had had by awarding to diligent scholars such prizes as tickets and pictures that a boy could wear on his shirt, toys, bats, balls, kites, books, and—for "superior merit"—more valuable prizes such as silver pens or silver medals. Awarding prizes to the students, said Lancaster, was "a stimulus to order and improvement, which children, taught only under the influence of the cane and the rod, never can enjoy."

The important thing is for the teacher to become aware of the need for rewarding children's good behavior. Teachers, like parents, are too likely to take a child's good behavior for granted and to ignore it, while noticing and giving attention to poor behavior. A conscious effort to recognize high achievement and good behavior rewards those children who do achieve and motivates the others to do better. Teachers should use rewards for effort put forth, not only for actual achievement, and for improvement, rather than absolute level of performance. Too often, when the social rewards of the classroom are used at all, they are reserved for the competent, achieving, well-behaved children who do not need to have their behavior influenced, because it is all right already. By spreading around the coveted classroom jobs and other signs of approval, teachers can shape the behavior of those children who need to improve their behavior and achievement.

A teacher can often deal with the problem of one or two disrup-

tive children in a class by not only rewarding the youngsters themselves for socially appropriate behavior but also by rewarding their
classmates for not paying attention to disruptive antics. Deprived
of his audience, the disruptive youngster has less motivation for
acting up. The other children can also be rewarded for genuine
efforts at making friends with an unpopular child in the class.

Seating Arrangements

The teacher who wants to help a hyperactive child perform to the
best of his ability will pay special attention to his seating assignment. If a child is highly distractible, the teacher will take pains
to avoid seating him near a window with a view, or any other
distraction. She may encourage him to work part of the day at a
study carrel (a desk enclosed by walls on three sides) or in a spot
where his back is to the other children—always emphasizing that
this is not a punishment but a way to help him concentrate. She
should usually seat him close to her so that she can keep track of
what he is doing, engage his attention more easily, contain his
tendency to clown, and be able to speak to him quietly, without
the rest of the class becoming aware of any reprimands he may
receive. The clumsy child or the child who has a compulsion to
touch everyone or everything in his way will do better seated near
an aisle, where he is less likely to annoy the other children.

Children need quiet at those times when they are engaged in
projects that require close concentration. Every classroom should
have one or more quiet areas—places where a child can work
undisturbed by the other children. Study carrels are ideal for this.
Some children discover their own private places by crawling under
the teacher's desk or going into a corner of the cloakroom to work.

Keeping Order

The classroom teacher who wants to exert a positive influence on
her pupils will avoid shouting at them. This is a sign of failure, a

sign that she has lost her self-control or that she has no confidence in her ability to control them. When a child must be reprimanded, he should be spoken to so quietly that only he can hear what the teacher is saying. He will thus not be singled out and humiliated, and he will not attract the attention of his classmates.

Incorporating Physical Activity in the Daily Schedule

A good teacher plans her programs to include as much activity as possible. Children learn best by doing, rather than by reading or listening. The more projects they become actively involved in, the more they will learn and the more they will enjoy school. Children of all ages need more opportunities to work with their hands in the classroom. This is particularly true of the child with a learning or behavior problem who finds a day of reading and writing as interesting as a day in the salt mine. We know an imaginative principal and teacher in Webster Groves, Missouri, who made better students out of a group of difficult fifth-grade boys by letting them use a workbench in the back of the classroom.

Children need opportunities during the school day to get up and walk around, or just to stretch. They should be allowed to talk quietly and to work together, as long as they do not disturb others. The hyperactive child needs extra opportunities to move and to talk. He should be asked to run errands, erase blackboards, empty wastebaskets, water plants, and move furniture. He may welcome extra helps to keep at his desk when he cannot be moving around —such as a lump of clay that he can squeeze unobtrusively when he simply *has* to do something with his hands.

All children benefit from a good physical-education program, hyperactive children more than most. They should have at least thirty minutes of vigorous physical exercise every day. Furthermore, children should get real instruction in gym class, not just the chance to play games under adult supervision or to square dance. In most schools the youngsters who need physical education the least get the most of it, and those who enter kindergarten poorly co-ordinated and uncomfortable in the use of their body usually leave high school in the same state.

Activities that used to be an accepted part of growing up, such as throwing snowballs in the playground, tussling between a couple of boys, and other harmless ways of exhibiting activity and a certain degree of aggression, are now *verboten*. Society's threshold of tolerance for children's boisterous behavior has become so low that many people feel that children who act this way are abnormal or diseased. Children should be allowed to let themselves go to a degree and to play rough as long as no one is in real danger of serious injury.

Doing the Work

Teachers who give regular brief homework assignments starting in the early grades help children to form the habit of completing routine tasks. Children gain satisfaction from the completion of such tasks. They also learn how to plan their time, to work independently, and to evaluate what they are learning in the classroom. Brevity is an asset, though. Lengthy written assignments are unnecessary. The five-hour school day is long enough to cover the basic material in the elementary school curriculum. Lengthy homework assignments are boring and relatively unproductive for most children, and almost impossible for hyperactive children to complete.

Reading

A child should read well enough to absorb written information and enjoy the process. There is no pressing reason for him to read well out loud. The child who neither reads well for comprehension nor articulation is exposed to ridicule in group reading sessions. A teacher can check a child's comprehension of reading matter by asking him questions about what he has read, either in writing or in an individual conference. To check a child's pronunciation, the teacher can see him privately and ask him to read aloud when only her ears will hear.

Reading should be taught as a way to accomplish practical projects and for its ability to entertain. Children learn when they are interested in the subjects they are studying, so every attempt should be made to give them reading matter that reflects their interests. They should be handed sheets of directions for putting together models or performing other interesting tasks and encouraged to come to the teacher for help with the hard words. They should be given racing-car magazines and camping manuals, rather than the traditional limited-vocabulary readers. Since children love adventure, they should have access to books about exploring, detective work, space travel, and the life stories of courageous individuals, both male and female.

"Curse of Writing"

Eight-year-old Jenny proudly showed her mother the two kinds of writing she had learned in school: printing, which Jenny had labeled "mannuscrip," and handwriting, which Jenny had labeled on her paper "curse of writing." Both cursive and manuscript styles carry the curse of writing for the many hyperactive children who cannot turn in a page free of mistakes and misspellings. When these children have points taken off their papers for misspelling and sloppiness, they will eventually give up the effort. Knowing that no matter what they write, it will be acceptable only if it is neat, they will be even more inclined to put off completing writing assignments altogether. Teachers who want to encourage all children, and especially hyperactive children, to be creative and interested in schoolwork have to avoid a fussy emphasis on spelling and neatness.

Pupils Are People

A teacher is in a key position to help a child in trouble. She usually wants to help, but often doubts her competence to do so.

Simple interest and affection can go a long way. A teacher can help a troubled child by taking extra time to talk with him. She can encourage him to tell how he feels about school, where he feels there are problems, and what sort of things he really likes to do. Quite commonly, the hyperactive child has problems at home and in his neighborhood that he would like to confide to an interested adult. A teacher who can listen to children's troubles will be loved.

Since the teacher's attitude toward a particular child sets the tone in the classroom and spills over to the attitudes of the other children, she should make a special effort to find something to like about every child in the class. She should search for an area in which he is interested and perhaps competent as well. Every child has some talent or grace that can be recognized publicly and appreciated by teacher and classmates. Even the child who disrupts the class by clowning around can have this kind of activity channeled into play-acting and skits.

A teacher can help a child in his relations with the other children by the way she handles the class. She can draw upon the other children to help a disruptive child improve his behavior. She can take advantage of a period when the child is out of the classroom to talk honestly to the other children in an effort to enlist their help. Usually children respond very well when a teacher asks them to help one of their peers who they know is having trouble. The teacher should not fall into the common trap of punishing the entire class for the misbehavior of one or two members. Aside from being unfair to those children who do behave well, such punitive actions arouse a great deal of hostility toward the disruptive child. It is better to reward the whole class when Henry is good than to punish it when he is bad. The other children, then, will have more of a positive stake in helping Henry to be good.

The ability and personality of a teacher are more important than that teacher's sex. Yet boys, and especially hyperactive boys, often respond better to men in the classroom. This is probably because, as our society exists today, men are often more likely to encourage self-assertion on the part of their students. As more women become freer to accept the normal boisterousness of childhood, this difference will no longer hold true.

A Note to Parents

Parents reading this chapter may wonder about its place in a book addressed primarily to parents, not educators. While this book is primarily for parents, we believe that much of it has relevance for teachers, as well as other professional persons who see and work with hyperactive children.

> Children had rather be making the tools and instruments of play, shaping, drawing, framing, and building, than getting some rules of propriety of speech by heart; and those, also, would follow with more judgment and less trouble in time.
> —William Penn
> *Reflections and Maxims,* 1682

13   SPECIAL EDUCATION

The hyperactive child is essentially a normal youngster, but he needs better teaching than does the average child. Whether he needs better teaching within the ordinary classroom or needs to be in a special class or school depends on the severity of his difficulties. A rule of thumb for parents and teachers is to give a child as much extra help as he needs, but to keep him as close to the usual situation as possible. If a child needs to be in a special situation, the goal should be to return him as soon as possible to the regular classroom.

Special Help Offered by the Neighborhood Public School

The Classroom Teacher

In Chapter 12 we discussed some of the special techniques and approaches that a sensitive teacher can use with the hyperactive children in her classroom. The teacher who would like to do more but does not know how to go about it should have access to special resources within the school. She should be able to consult with the school psychologist, the social worker, the guidance counselor, and the remedial-reading teacher. She should also be able to meet with a specialist in learning disabilities who serves several schools.

Some school districts and the Association for Children with Learning Disabilities offer in-service training courses to teachers.

Special-Resource Persons

Many a child can function better in his classroom with regular attention from a special-resource person, whom he might see for half an hour or up to two hours every day. Such a helper might be a speech therapist, a remedial-reading specialist, a teacher who works with perceptual-motor disabilities, or someone who knows how to teach control of distractibility and impulsiveness. The resource person might come to the classroom, or the child might go out to another room, either alone or as part of a small group of children with similar problems. The resource person may be part of the school faculty or an itinerant teacher who serves several schools in a district.

Special Class

If possible, it is better for a child to remain in his regular classroom and receive special help from his own teacher, older students, or resource persons within the school. If the child's performance is far below his ability, if he becomes more and more discouraged, or if his behavior is intolerable, a special class may be the answer.

Six or eight children who need special attention can work together in a special class with a specially trained teacher. Schools may arrange for all academic subjects to be covered in the special class, while the youngsters take music, art, physical education, recess, and lunch with their regular classmates.

By working with a small class, a teacher can invest more time in those areas with which each child needs additional help. She can more easily determine each one's level of achievement and can give each child assignments that fill his needs and yet are within his capabilities. Billy, for example, missed learning the basic arithmetic facts in first and second grade because of inattentiveness. In his special class his teacher helped him learn his numbers in a wide variety of ways—through touch, hearing, flash drill, and games—to an extent that would not be possible in the regular classroom.

After a child has lived with five or six or seven years of knowing that he has continually failed and disappointed his parents and teachers, he has no sense of his own worth. An experience in a special class geared to his needs and designed to help him experience success can help him to appreciate and value himself. Many children blossom in the protected setting of a small class with a compassionate teacher who has both the awareness of what they need and the time to see that they get it.

Children who attend a special class should not be stigmatized as "brain-injured children" or "slow learners." The Great Neck, New York, school system hit upon a happy solution by calling its special classes "Individual Development" classes.

Transitional Class for First- and Second-Graders

A youngster in kindergarten may show evidence of a major problem with behavior or learning. This child may find a transitional class helpful in bridging the gap between the freer atmosphere of nursery school and kindergarten and the more structured setting of the classroom. The class is designed to help children avoid school difficulties later on. Many children who attend transitional classes integrate well into the regular classroom at about the third-grade level.

Special Public School

Some districts operate their own special schools, and sometimes several school districts will join to support such a school. The school will be staffed by teachers with degrees in Special Education and by specialists in reading, speech, physical education, vocational activities, psychology, social work, and guidance. There will be a high proportion of teachers to students. Aides will be on hand to monitor hallways and lunchrooms, providing more supervision than in the average school. The classes will all be small and geared to the individual needs of the students. While the educational services offered by the special school are superior, parents and teachers have to weigh its social disadvantages. Aside from his being separated from other neighborhood children, the child is likely to suffer a social stigma for going to "that place." These are real considerations. It is sometimes better to let a child endure a less than ideal academic situation for the sake of his social milieu. But when a child's academic or social problems are so severe that he needs help his own school cannot provide, a special school is the answer. A year or two in this school sometimes enables a child to return to his own school. In other cases, an arrangement can be worked out by which a child attends the special school in the morning but comes back to his own neighborhood school for afternoon activities. This way he can get the academic help he needs while maintaining his relationships with the children and activities close to home.

Private Schools

You may be unhappy with your public school system. Maybe the teaching is too authoritarian. Maybe there is not enough concern for individual differences among children. Maybe the classes are too large and the specialist faculty too small. Or perhaps your child needs special teaching that is not offered by your local school, and yet he does not fit into any of the categories served by the district's special school. Or maybe your district has no access to a special public school. If so, you may want to investigate private schooling.

Financing Private Education

If you are considering private school for your child, you have to decide whether he would be best served by a standard independent school or by one that specializes in teaching children with behavior or learning difficulties. If you choose a standard private school, you will have to foot the entire bill yourselves unless the school offers your child a scholarship. If you choose a specialized school, you may be able to get financial help, according to the following suggestions:

- If school officials determine that your child needs special educational services that the local system cannot provide, they may recommend that the state Department of Education provide a certain measure of tuition assistance. (In New York, for example, the state will pay up to $2,000 a year directly to a state-approved private school that provides services not available in the child's own public school system.) For information, speak to a representative of your local public school—principal, psychologist, or guidance counselor, to the director of pupil personnel services in the district, or to the director of special education for the state in which you live.

- Some social agencies (such as Jewish Family Service, Catholic Charities, and so forth) help to support schools for children with special educational needs. These agencies often help to meet the costs of full tuition when parents can pay only part or none of the tuition themselves. Service organizations like the Junior Chamber of Commerce, the Junior League, Kiwanis, and Lions sometimes conduct programs to help meet special costs of educating children with certain handicaps.

- Some private schools offer full or partial scholarships for families who cannot afford the cost of tuition.

- Certain medical or hospital insurance policies provide some coverage for the care and education of children with special needs.

- Members of the armed services can obtain financial assistance to help defray the costs of special education for their children. Your local military community service organization can give you information about your eligibility.

- You may be eligible for income tax deductions for the special costs incurred in educating your child. Check with your local Internal Revenue Office.

Finding the Right School for Your Child

Financing private education is difficult for most families, but finding the right school is sometimes harder. The following sources may help parents to find out what schools exist in their areas, what services they offer, what their educational philosophies are, and whether they are right for a particular child.

- The psychologist, guidance counselor, or principal of your local public school, or the director of pupil personnel services for the school district.
- Local representatives of a parents' organization, such as the Association for Children with Learning Disabilities or the Council for Exceptional Children.
- A family service agency may know or even have ties with a school that offers special services.
- A child development center run by a hospital or university, or a child guidance clinic.
- The Federal Government operates a special service to disseminate information to parents on evaluative and educational facilities in the various states, as well as the names of state education officers in charge of particular programs. (Some of the suggestions on locating financial assistance came from this service.) For information, write to "A Closer Look," The Special Education Information Center, Bureau of Education for the Handicapped, Office of Education, United States Department of Health, Education and Welfare, Washington, D.C. 20202. (The Office of Education does not endorse the facilities it reports: it merely passes on information given by the individual institutions.)
- Several directories of private schools can be found either in your local library or in the library of the closest college that has a School of Education. Three that are particularly comprehensive are:

Private Independent Schools, The Bunting and Lyon Blue
Book, published by Bunting and Lyon, Inc., 238 North
Main Street, Wallingford, Conn. 06492

The Handbook of Private Schools, published by Porter Sargent, 11 Beacon Street, Boston, Mass. 02108

The Directory for Exceptional Children, published by Porter
Sargent, 11 Beacon Street, Boston, Mass. 02108

- Some parents are interested in finding out more about "free" or
"open" schools, which reject traditional structure and discipline
in favor of more child-directed education. ("Free" refers to
these schools' philosophy; almost all free schools charge tuition.) Such a school may provide a welcome alternative for the
adolescent who is "turned off" by traditional schooling. It is
rarely suitable for a young hyperactive child, who needs more
structure than these schools provide. The following are good
sources of information about free schools; they all publish newsletters and periodically updated directories of schools across the
country:

New Schools Exchange
   2840 Hidden Valley Lane
   Santa Barbara, Calif. 93103
Alternatives!
   1526 Gravenstein Highway North
   Sebastopol, Calif. 97452
Summerhill Society
   339 Lafayette Street
   New York, N.Y. 10012
        or
   6063 Harges Street
   Los Angeles, Calif. 90034

Evaluating a Private School

It is difficult for parents to know how to judge the quality of a
school. The following guidelines may be helpful.

As a minimum requirement, the private school should have state accreditation. The school must meet official fire, safety, health, and sanitation standards.

A good school should have small classes. If it offers special education, there should be no more than twelve pupils in a class and fewer in the early grades. Members of the professional staff should supervise nonprofessional teaching aides. Depending on your own child's particular needs, you should find out what specialists are on the regular faculty or available as consultants: psychologist, psychiatrist, speech and language specialist, remedial-reading teacher and physical-education teacher.

The school should have clear objectives for each child, and should be able and willing to discuss periodically with the parents the extent to which these objectives are being attained. Academic expectations should be realistic. The child's social life should also be considered, with opportunities provided for recreational activities and chances to get together at school with other students. If the school provides special education, it should aim to return the child to nonspecialized education as soon as possible.

The school should be structured but not rigid. It should place the emphasis on rewards for good behavior rather than punishment for bad. Corporal punishment should not be administered. Parents should be welcome to visit the school at reasonably frequent intervals.

The director of the school should be the kind of person who inspires your confidence. He sets the tone of the entire school, hires the teachers, chooses the student body. As you walk around the school with him, you should notice a friendly atmosphere between him and the children and between him and the members of the faculty.

You should be able to visualize your child's fitting into the life of the school. If your child is poorly co-ordinated, for example, and this school lays great stress on competitive sports, your child would be miserable. On the other hand, if your child can never seem to get enough vigorous activity, that might be the perfect setting for him. Give the school at least a year's trial. If, after several months, you feel that you may have made a mistake and that the school is not doing for your child what you hoped it would do, start shopping around again and be prepared to transfer your child after the school year is up. Be sure, though, that your expectations for the school are realistic.

The Residential School

While it is customary in some countries (England, for example) for quite young children to go away to school, few children in this country go to boarding schools. Because such schools are unusual in the United States, a child may interpret being sent away as a sign that his parents want to be rid of him. However, there are times when a boarding school is desirable for a child in grade school. If parents are unable to give a hyperactive child the supervision and companionship he needs, and if he is also having major difficulties in school, he may be much happier in a small boarding school. Occasionally parents in their fifties and sixties are unable to keep up with a hyperactive child or to cope with a messy school situation. Such parents would be wise to consider sending their child away, primarily for his sake.

For a child over the age of twelve a good boarding school may be a boon rather than a last resort. We discuss residential schooling for the adolescent in Chapter 16.

There are boarding schools that take average children and those that take children with learning or behavior problems. You would find and finance a residential school as you do a day school, but there are additional aspects to evaluate. You will want to see the children's living quarters, meet the house parents, know what activities are planned for after-school and weekends, and see what the outdoor facilities are like. How often will you be able to see your child, either by visiting the school or by having him come home?

While it is a wrench and perhaps an admission of defeat to send a child away to school, it may be the wisest step for the youngster and for the rest of the family. A school in which the staff are dedicated to understanding and guiding children in their everyday life, as well as teaching them academic subjects, may be far better for a hyperactive child than an indifferent home and the regular school.

Man was made for joy and woe;
And, when this we rightly know,
Safely through the world we go.
—William Blake
"Auguries of Innocence," 1789

14 DRUGS AND THE HYPERACTIVE CHILD

We are putting this chapter about drugs in the section of the book that is related to school problems, since the largest single benefit derived from "drug therapy" is generally the enhanced ability of a child to do his schoolwork. Occasionally, medicines should be prescribed to help a child function better in his home life; these instances also are discussed in this chapter.

The diabetic child takes insulin every day; the allergic child takes antihistamines. Should the hyperactive child take drugs continuously for months or years to tide him over the most troubling years of his childhood, or even as a lifelong treatment? These are difficult questions. It is hard to say when these children should be treated with drugs, because hyperactivity is not clearly a disease like diabetes or asthma. It is a collection of symptoms that probably should not be thought of as a medical disorder but rather as a variant of personality. Furthermore, the boundary between the "hyperactive" personality and the norm or average personality is defined by the child's social surroundings.

Ideally, we would first determine the reasonableness of what is expected of a hyperactive child at home and at school. If the expectations were unreasonable, we would want to change the attitudes of parents and teachers, rather than give the child something to change him. However, in the real world, it is often impossible to change a child's environment enough so that he can adjust happily to it. The question is then whether he should be left to handle this experience as best he can, and with all the support available, or whether he should be given a drug that may solve the problem. To answer this question, parents need to know as much as possible about what drugs can do for a hyperactive child, and what their disadvantages are.

Types of Drugs

Tranquilizers and Sedatives

Tranquilizers regulate activity within the brain in such a way that they calm the patient, sometimes relieving both anxiety and aggressive tendencies. Theoretically, they would seem to be ideal for hyperactive children, but in actual clinical practice they rarely bring about enough improvement to justify the risks of such side effects as obesity, drowsiness, or dizziness. A significant drawback of these drugs is their tendency to put children "in a fog" and make their school performance worse. Another difficulty is that children quickly develop tolerance to these drugs, so that within a month a child may have to take large doses to get a small effect.

Tranquilizers are indicated in the management of a severely affected, brain-injured child to slow him down enough so that he can attend school, or, rarely, for a preschooler who is up and about much of the night, getting little sleep himself and depriving the rest of the family of their sleep (and then only when psychological means fail).

Among the most commonly prescribed tranquilizers are thioridazine* (Mellaril), chlorpromazine (Thorazine) and hydroxyzine (Atarax). The first two are considered "major tranquilizers," and belong to the family of phenothiazines, which includes other drugs sometimes prescribed for hyperactive children: prochlorperazine (Compazine), perphenazine (Trilafon), and fluphenazine (Prolixin). Another major tranquilizer is chlorprothixene (Taractan). "Minor tranquilizers," which are related to sedatives, include meprobamate (Miltown), chlordiazepoxide (Librium), and

---

* The generic, or class, name of each drug is given first, followed by the most popular brand name of each.

diazepam (Valium). These are prescribed quite often, though their effectiveness is doubtful. Compazine and Prolixin should generally not be prescribed for children, because of the strong possibility of these drugs producing frightening muscle spasms. Diphenhydramine (Benadryl) is an antihistamine that in relatively small doses is sometimes given to children to alleviate sleep problems and in large doses can be a powerful tranquilizer.

The only sedative that is ordinarily prescribed for children is the barbiturate phenobarbital (Luminal). It usually intensifies the problems of a hyperactive child by increasing restlessness and excitement.

Anticonvulsants

If a child's electroencephalogram shows a "spiky" pattern similar to that seen in epilepsy, some doctors prescribe an anticonvulsant medication though the child may never have had an actual seizure. The most common anticonvulsant prescribed for children is diphenylhydantoin (Dilantin, Denly Sodium, Diphentoin, Diphenylan Sodium, Ekko, Danten). Also prescribed occasionally are primidone (Mysoline) and ethosuximide (Zarontin).

While these drugs are effective in controlling epilepsy, their usefulness with hyperactive children has not been proved. Side effects from Dilantin, the most commonly prescribed anticonvulsive, can be quite serious. It is easy to give too much Dilantin, with the result that patients walk unsteadily, show poor co-ordination, and talk in a slurred way. Other possible side effects are leukopenia (a reduction in the number of white blood cells), skin rash, excessive hair growth, and overgrowth of the gum margins. The careful physician watches closely for side effects, and when the use of a drug is indicated, weighs the chance of side effects against benefits.

Antidepressants

Recent studies have shown that antidepressant drugs may improve the behavior of hyperactive children. These drugs are imipramine (Tofranil), nortriptyline (Aventyl), and amitriptyline (Elavil). The same drugs are widely prescribed for bed wetting and for the uncommon problems of sleepwalking and night terrors. (These drugs do reduce the frequency of bed wetting as long as children are taking them, but there is no carry-over effect when the medicines are stopped.)

Antidepressants are most often prescribed to adult patients for depression. In medical use this term means a persistent state of low mood, loss of interest, lack of energy, feeling worthless, wanting to die, difficulty in sleeping, and other symptoms. Adult patients with this problem may have no special reason to be sad, but have close relatives who have also been depressed; evidence suggests that this disorder is related to an inherited predisposition. We do not know whether comparable states occur in children. A thorough study of 6,000 elementary school children identified only two who might have been "depressed," so that it is not common, if it happens at all. On the other hand, there are undoubtedly many children who are chronically unhappy or depressed in the ordinary sense. Hyperactive children, those with learning problems, those who are physically handicapped, or who have broken homes often feel worthless and sad. With the right psychological help such children can adjust to their misfortune and rebuild their self-esteem. It hardly seems appropriate to call this "depression" and to give the children antidepressant drugs, but many physicians do so today.

The antidepressants can produce a number of side effects, such as headaches, drowsiness, a "jazzed up" feeling, blurred vision, muscle tremors, constipation, dizziness, and palpitations.

Central Nervous System Stimulants

Drugs in this category are by far the most frequently prescribed medications for hyperactive children. Among these drugs are the amphetamines (Dexedrine, Benzedrine, Medex, D-Amphetasul), methylphenidate (Ritalin), magnesium pemoline (Cylert), and deanol (Deaner). Cylert is a new drug, which is currently being tested for use in children, and Deaner is one that has been tried but is generally not considered effective. Since the stimulant medications are the ones most commonly prescribed, the rest of this chapter will be devoted to a discussion of their use with hyperactive children.

The Use of Stimulant Medication for Hyperactive Children

In 1937, Dr. Charles Bradley published the first report on the effects of benzedrine on children with behavior problems. He was director of the Emma Pendleton Bradley Home in East Providence, Rhode Island, a residence for children suffering from severe behavior disorders. He had prescribed benzedrine to raise the blood pressure in certain children in an effort to rid them of headaches. The benzedrine did not seem to affect the headaches, but it did dramatically change the behavior and school performance of the children. It spurred interest in school, apparently improved ability to work, and calmed noisy, aggressive youngsters. The children themselves called the medicine "arithmetic pills," because they felt they could do their arithmetic more easily when they were taking the drug.

For the next twenty years, most physicians ignored Dr. Bradley's report, perhaps because it seemed ridiculous to prescribe stimulants for children who were too active already. During the 1950's, a general awakening of interest in psychotropic drugs led to widening use of amphetamines, and the newly developed Ritalin (methylphenidate), among children. Better-controlled studies were made of the drugs' effects on children's behavior and learning difficulties. Partly as the result of advertising by pharmaceutical companies and partly as the result of hard evidence that the behavior of difficult children was improved by stimulants, these drugs became the "treatment of choice" for hyperactive children by the 1970's.

How the Drugs Work

Some hyperactive children—the proportion ranges between 20 per cent to 88 per cent depending on which report you read—show dramatic responses to daily doses of amphetamines or methylphenidate, usually within a couple of days after receiving the first pill. The youngsters concentrate better and do more of their schoolwork; they are less restless, less likely to fly off the handle, more agreeable to have around the house or in the classroom. Their activity is not less, but it is directed along constructive, purposive lines. The child who used to be an outcast on the playground is popular all of a sudden; the teacher welcomes him, and the parents can enjoy him.

These drugs do not act like tranquilizers. They do not dull a child's senses; they may increase the child's activity, but it appears to be less because it has become focused and purposeful. Some of the effects on hyperactive children are exactly like those seen in adults. In experiments the administration of amphetamine has been shown to help adult subjects maintain their interest in a boring task, and thus to continue performing at a high level. This corresponds to the commonly noted effect of the stimulant drug on children, who often seem interested in and able to attend to their schoolwork for the first time in their lives.

It seems paradoxical that a child can take a dose of amphetamines that would produce excitability and euphoria in an adult and not experience these effects. Yet the change in a hyperactive child's mood may be a mild form of euphoria; he feels more confident and at ease with the world. He becomes much more pleasant to be with because he is in a happier frame of mind. In his early trials of benzedrine, Dr. Charles Bradley was struck by statements from the children such as "I have joy in my stomach" and "I feel fine and can't seem to do things fast enough today," which illustrated the children's happier mood.

Hyperactive children ordinarily seem miserable much of the time. For all we know, part of the irritability and the low self-esteem of the hyperactive child may be an essential part of being hyperactive, rather than a result of the child's experience of failure and social isolation. Were this so, stimulant drugs might actually improve the child's basic personality. Seven-year-old Jeff may have recognized this change in himself when he said to his mother, "I have friends when I'm on Ritalin."

Predictability

Many a doctor considers the pills diagnostic tools in themselves. He prescribes them for a child, and if they have the desired effect, the doctor feels he has proof that the child must be a "true" hyperactive child. This is an unwarranted conclusion, however, since these medicines are not specific in their action. They have similar effects on a wide range of patients: emotionally disturbed children, delinquent boys, and children with various learning problems.

Researchers have found some clues to predict which children will benefit most from taking stimulants. W. Glenn Conrad and Jonathan Insel have suggested that children whose medical histories contain several indications of organic involvement, whose relationships with their parents are positive, and whose parents do not have any severe psychiatric problems themselves, are more likely to respond to stimulant drugs. Dr. James H. Satterfield of Los Angeles has found that the child with both an abnormal neurological examination and abnormal EEG is most likely to respond favorably to stimulant drugs. From other tests he concludes that children with the least amount of electrical activity on the skin surface and the greatest brain-wave activity are most likely to respond favorably.

Unfortunately the average practitioner is still in the dark about whether a given child will respond well to drugs.

Side Effects

For those children who benefit from stimulants, there may be drawbacks in the form of side effects, but these can usually be eliminated by lowering the dose. The common ones are loss of appetite, difficulty getting to sleep at night, the wan, pinched face with sunken eyes known as the "amphetamine look," and sadness, with a tendency toward crying spells. Some children experience nausea, headaches, cramps, or jitters. Then there is the "rebound" effect, that period of time during the late afternoon and evening when the effects of the drug have worn off and the child is reported to be "climbing the walls" or "worse than ever."

Overdosage may result in sleepiness throughout the day, overactivity, irritability, or an undue fixation on tasks. The most frightening side effects are fortunately the rarest, with an occasional child having muscle spasms of the face, jaw, or tongue, hallucinating, or having ideas that people want to harm him. The unusual child who is peculiarly sensitive to the drugs may show any of these symptoms on relatively small doses. A child who develops any of these latter symptoms should stop receiving the drug immediately or at the very least receive a smaller dosage.

Developing Tolerance

Children frequently develop tolerance to methylphenidate (Ritalin). After a month or so of taking the drug, it no longer has much effect. Sometimes the doctor will increase the dose, and at the higher level the drug will continue to be effective. At other times the child may be switched to one of the amphetamines, either because he is already taking a large dose of Ritalin or because undesirable side effects have appeared. Tolerance to amphetamine is unusual.

Long-Term Effects

No harmful psychological effect of long-term use has been discovered, but it may be too soon to tell. These drugs have been widely used with children only in the past decade, and children who were treated with these drugs have not yet been followed to maturity. We do know that abrupt termination of these drugs even after years of use does not produce acute symptoms of withdrawal. Children may get into the habit of taking them, but addiction does not occur.

As drug abuse is a serious problem among young people, it is natural to worry about predisposing children to later drug abuse by prescribing stimulants for them. So far, there is no evidence that carefully prescribed and monitored regimens of stimulants will lead to drug abuse. But not all administration of these drugs to children is so carefully managed, and, on the other hand, there is no good evidence that these drugs do not lead to drug abuse.

One attempt to look into this question has led to the conclusion that "dire predictions as to the outcome of long-term use of medications" are not supported. Dr. Maurice Laufer reported that the parents of one hundred former hyperactive children who were between the ages of fifteen and twenty-six were contacted. As children, these young people had received amphetamines or methylphenidate for periods ranging from six months to five years. Sixty-six parents returned the questionnaires, but they did not answer all questions. Of the fifty-seven who answered the question about subsequent experimentation with drugs such as marijuana and LSD, fifty-two, or over 90 per cent, replied that their children had not experimented. No one reported that a child was "hooked." In response to specific questions about experimenting with drugs similar to those they had taken on prescription as children (*i.e.*, Dexedrine, Benzedrine, "speed"), only three of the young people had done so as far as the parents knew and fifty-three, or 94.6 per cent, had not.

The conclusions of this survey would be a lot more reassuring were it not for the fact that only half the parents answered the question about drug use. We agree with Dr. Laufer when he says, "Who knows how the nonrepliers might have altered the figures!" Knowing too that most young people do not confide in their parents when they experiment with drugs, we have to take the low figures for drug experimentation with more than a grain of salt.

A serious physical complication of drug treatment was reported in 1972 by Dr. Daniel Safer and his colleagues from the Baltimore County Department of Health. They found that Ritalin and amphetamine treatment reduced the monthly weight gain of children to less than two-thirds of what would be expected in a normal child, and also reduced growth in height. The effects were found in children who took the drugs in relatively high doses (30 to 40 mg. of Ritalin per day, or 10 to 15 mg. per day of amphetamine), and over a period of nine to twenty-four months. These are sizable effects which, if persistent over a number of years, would significantly stunt a child's growth. Moreover, this finding raises the possibility that other aspects of physical maturation might be affected, such as the development of sexual characteristics. Physicians will be reluctant to prescribe drugs that may slow physical development in children who are not well developed in the first place, and who think poorly of themselves for this reason.

Misuse of Stimulants

Physicians who prescribe drugs may not keep a close enough check on how the child does. Dennis, eight, was brought to his pediatrician because of his troubles with school work. He became introverted and withdrawn at the smallest dosage of stimulant drugs, still was not doing his school work, and yet was kept on the drug for a year. Monroe, seven, received a stimulant drug for six months, with no apparent effect. Many doctors would like to help these children, but they do not have the sophistication or the interest to supervise a drug regime. On the other hand, they are pressured by parents and school people to prescribe these drugs.

Too many children are kept on drugs all day, every day, for years, until no one remembers what the youngster's real personality is like. Walter, sixteen, had been on drugs continuously for six years; he was trapped by this time, because both he and his family were afraid to rock the boat by stopping the pills. This story, which is not unusual, raises a disturbing ethical question. Parents and doctors may discuss the prescription of stimulants with an eight- or nine-year-old child (we think they should), but they can reasonably decide to give the drugs to a child of this age without his consent. Some years later when the same child is mature enough to decide for himself whether to take the drugs, his family and teachers are so used to his drug-influenced behavior that it may be very hard for him to stop.

This particular problem can be avoided by using drugs in a discriminating way. If they are to have this treatment, most children should be given drugs to cover them during school hours, and not at all during weekends or vacations. Misuse of drugs generally reflects a lack of proper caution and judgment on the part of parents, teachers, and doctors.

Questions about Responsible Use of Drugs

Suppose your doctor recommends that your hyperactive child be given stimulants specifically to help him to do better in school, that you are confident he will supervise the treatment carefully, and that he says you should plan for the phasing out of the drug before the child enters the seventh grade. Do you still hold back? We suggest that you should.

There is no evidence that hyperactive children learn good habits because they concentrate better and follow directions more readily when they are on drugs. It is widely assumed that over a long period pharmacological control of a child's behavior will lead to self-control, but the results of the follow-up studies we cited in Chapter 3 do not support this idea. It would be surprising if children did acquire new habits under the influence of drugs, because learning is so closely related to the specific stimuli (internal and external) experienced by the individual as he learns a new pattern of behavior. It is unlikely for this reason that a pattern he follows when he feels somewhat subdued after taking a stimulant will carry over to a time when he is his natural self, full of pep and mischief. Or, to put it another way, perhaps he has learned some control while on drugs, but it is not strong enough to restrain his natural behavior.

We think that parents should plan for the worst outcome while hoping for the best; they should assume that any good effect of the drug is temporary. They then have to consider what they can do to help their child learn to control his behavior, what they can expect from teachers along the same lines, and when is the best time to start working.

We have suggested answers to the question of *what* to do. How about the time? Our answer would be right now, as soon as you recognize the problem. If you temporize by giving your child drugs till he is about to go to junior high school, he will be that much older and stronger, you will be older and perhaps less energetic, and you and your child will be dealing with several teachers and an overworked counselor rather than one teacher and a principal who may have known your child for several years.

Perhaps you can compromise successfully between "no drugs" and "drugs for several years," but we have found that successful drug treatment is seductive. The effects can be remarkable and it is hard to give them up. Trying to change one's own behavior is laborious, and parents may not feel enough need to do so as long as their child is taking medicine.

Another difficult issue is that drugs allow the child, his parents, and teachers to "cop out" of responsibility. It is not uncommon to hear of a child excusing some bad behavior on the grounds that he had not taken his pill that day. It is common for parents to give an extra pill when their child is unusually difficult, or for a teacher to wonder out loud whether a child has taken his pill rather than asking herself what she might do to help him through a bad spell. Everybody tends to sit back and let the doctor take care of the problem, because his prescribing the drug implies that the problem is a medical one.

A reason commonly given for starting a child on drugs is that they will restore his self-confidence by allowing him the experience of success. In fact, the effects on a child's self-esteem are two-edged. Young children are so unself-conscious that they seem not to associate their new success with taking a drug, but they are not fools. Sooner or later they will remark, if you listen, that they are so dumb or so weird that they have to take pills "to be like everybody else."

Drugs and Society

From time immemorial people have taken drugs to drown their sorrows. Unhappy people have sought relief in the past from opium, cocaine, peyote, hashish, and alcohol. During the past twenty-five years, however, our pharmacopoeia has mushroomed incredibly: 90 per cent of all the drugs available today were unknown twenty-five years ago. This proliferation has been particularly noteworthy in psychopharmacology, *i.e.*, among drugs that relieve undesirable emotional states. We now have drugs that can eliminate anxiety, depression, and aggression, bolster people's morale and help them to feel happy and work better—and do all this without producing drastic side effects.

Our society has not yet resolved the questions that are raised by the availability of drugs that relieve everyday troubles. Is it better to take a tranquilizer every day and be able to proceed with the business of living than to end up a derelict on skid row? Is it better for a child to take a stimulant with breakfast and lunch every day than to fall behind in school, be rejected by his parents, and quarrel with his friends? No rational person would flatly recommend suffering over the reasonable use of drugs. Yet the question remains: To what degree should we attempt to work out our problems through rational analysis, emotional adjustment, and conscious attempts to change our approach to life, as opposed to buying solutions across the counter of a drugstore? Perhaps this question cannot have a general answer; some people can work out their problems themselves and others cannot. Yet there is a value judgment to be made, and the kind of judgment that is made by the majority of our population determines the kind of society we will have.

Right now our society seems to act more and more as though every problem has a pharmacological solution. To our way of thinking, too many people, including children, are taking too many drugs for too long a time. Recent surveys of drug use in the population at large show that about one out of four adults in the United States has used one or more kinds of psychotropic drugs in the year before being interviewed, and nearly half the adult population has taken a tranquilizer, sedative, or stimulant at some time in their lives. These people are not drug abusers; they are taking "legitimate" drugs, usually prescribed by physicians, for problems that often have nonphysiological causes and nonmedical solutions.

The American Medical Association in its official journal recently questioned the dangerous implications involved in the basic practice of many physicians who encourage patients "to rely on pills to solve psychological and social problems." Yet this same journal, along with many other respectable medical publications, is full of advertisements advising doctors to prescribe a broad armamentarium of chemicals for "the middle-aged housewife who can't stop feeling 'blue,' " for the "junior executive crushed by his repeated failure to be promoted and anxious about the future," and for "the young widow whose grief has persisted too long, is pessimistic and fearful about what lies ahead, has lost interest in everything."

Doctors and laymen alike are exhorted day in and day out to find the solutions for problems in bottles of medicine. The harried mother on the television screen hates her child—until she takes a tranquilizer that lets her deal with the child's demands. A book on child rearing suggests that a parent soothe a child having trouble falling asleep by giving him a baby aspirin. "It's not too important whether the aspirin really helps him get to sleep or not," says the author. "The *idea* that he is being helped may be enough to relax him and allow him to sleep. A sugar pill might be just as effective."

This undue emphasis on the use of medicine reaches children at an early age. The preschooler who watches his favorite children's shows on TV is told to take a daily vitamin pill, not about the benefits of a sound, nutritionally balanced diet. He and his parents learn from television, newspaper, and magazine ads about the benefits of cough syrups, chest rubs, and candy-flavored aspirin. The giving of medicine is equated with love. When Mommy loves her child, she gives him something to make him feel better.

Other cultural factors contribute to the increasing tendency to prescribe medicines for children with learning or behavior problems. For complex social and historical reasons, partly related to the smaller size of families, the affluence that allows us enough leisure time to take up the problems of individual children, and the demands our complex society makes on citizens who want to succeed in it, there has been a surge of interest in the emotional and learning problems of young children.

When parents have problems with their children, they usually go first to the doctor, expecting him to have all the answers. He has no simple solution, but he wants to help the families in his care. So, programmed as he is to think of problems in terms of diseases, and then in terms of drugs to cure the diseases, he reaches for his prescription pad. Such thinking on the part of the medical profession and the public at large does not allow for the fact that most children's learning and behavior problems do not fit the medical "disease model."

Should Your Child Be Receiving Medication?

We believe that children should not be given medicines for relief of symptoms without weighing the probable effects on the child's personal development over the years. Giving pills to children in order to change their behavior is a radical step, and one we think should be taken only when more conservative approaches have been tried and have failed.

By following the guidelines in this book, by consulting professional persons, and by talking in groups with other parents in the same boat, most parents can change their child's behavior and the family relationships within three to six months. If, after this time, things seem just as bad as ever—no matter how they have changed the pressures at home or at school, no matter how they have dealt with the school and with professional consultants, then it may be time to think about drugs.

A brief period of drugs may be indicated if a child's life is in hopeless turmoil or if he is terribly depressed—and nothing else seems to help. Medicines may make the difference between a child's attending school or not. Drugs may be indicated for children who have multiple handicaps or who show strong evidence of brain injury. The use of drugs for children is not an unmitigated evil. They do have their place in good treatment. Before a drug is prescribed for a child, however, it is incumbent upon the child's parents and physician to give great thought to the child's problems and to explore thoroughly other modes of treatment.

If Your Child Receives Stimulant Drugs

If your doctor does decide to prescribe stimulant drugs for your child, you and he should adhere to certain guidelines to insure maximal benefit and minimal risk.

1. The treatment should be considered a limited, temporary measure to help a child make a fresh start in school.

2. The pills are not a cure. They must be accompanied by other measures, such as a planned behavior-shaping program, supportive psychotherapy, and a prescriptive teaching program.

3. A child should receive drugs only after a careful pediatric examination and any other testing that may be indicated. The physician has to rely in great measure on reports from a child's parents and teachers about the child's behavior. If the parents report problems, but the teacher does not, or vice versa, the child should probably not be receiving drugs.

4. Parents should be in close contact with their child's physician at the beginning of a drug regime while the appropriate dosage is being developed. After the dosage is stabilized, they should be speaking to him at least every two or three months for the entire time that the child is receiving the drug.

5. Stimulant drugs should not be administered to a child be-

yond puberty, since it is at this age that an individual becomes aware of the drug's effects and may abuse it.

6. A parent should *never* give a child a drug without a doctor's knowledge or juggle the prescribed dosage. The stimulant drugs are powerful chemicals; their use and dosage must be strictly regulated by a medical person who knows the drug's potential and the patient's condition. A parent should not take it upon himself to give a child "a little Benzedrine" from time to time, on days when the child is acting up.

7. Both parents and physician should consider the child's feelings about taking medicine and should try to deal with them. Children often have fears and worries that they do not express. One youngster may feel, "Boy, I must be really sick if I have to take these pills all the time." An older child may worry that he will become a drug abuser. Parents and doctors can help to allay these fears by explaining to the child that these medicines help many children who have trouble concentrating (or sitting still, or whatever the child's biggest problem seems to be), that the children take them until they do not need them any more, that there is no danger of addiction if he follows the doctor's directions carefully. The word "medicine" should always be used, as opposed to "drug," which has, of course, a completely different connotation.

8. A child should not receive stimulant drugs until he is of grade school age. Giving a small child a potent chemical that has not been thoroughly tested for safety on children his age is unwise. Giving a drug to a fussy four-month-old baby because his mother is unable to cope with him and is threatening suicide is treating the wrong patient.

9. In most cases, a child should receive a drug only during school hours. He should not receive it after school, on weekends, or during school vacations. If life in the family is a nightmare because of the child's behavior, it may be necessary for him to take the drug on rare occasions during out-of-school hours in the interest of happier family relationships, but this is a poor substitute for parents learning how to handle the child on their own.

10. From time to time, possibly every couple of months, the child's medicine should be re-evaluated. Dosage may be diminished in an attempt to taper off gradually, or the drug should be withdrawn completely on school days during school hours to see whether the child still needs it. If the changes between a child's medicated self and nonmedicated self become less extreme as he learns new ways of controlling his behavior, it may be time to discontinue the drug altogether.

11. Some mechanics of administration:

- To avoid as much loss of appetite as possible, the child should take his medicine with breakfast and lunch.
- To avoid sleep problems, he should not take it any later than lunchtime.
- If the child eats lunch in school, he should go to the school nurse to take his noontime dose. He should not have the responsibility himself for taking his pill, nor should his teacher assume this responsibility.

PART IV

Stages Through Life

In our child rearing, we have failed to develop ideas as to
how to foster the child's inherent need to love someone, not
just his inherent need to be loved by someone.

—Irene Josselyn, in
Youth: Problems and Approaches

15   THE FIRST FIVE YEARS

"I knew while Curt was still in the womb that he was going to be
a pistol," said Curt's mother. "He bounced around so much inside
me that I would automatically put my hand over my abdomen to
keep him from popping out! After a while, it wasn't that joyful excitement of feeling a life move inside you; it was actually painful
the way he dug into my ribs and my breastbone."

Most of the children who will later be called "hyperactive" will
seem somewhat different to their parents during the first two years
of life, and some like Curt behave differently even before they are
born. Other children will seem quite normal and not bother their
parents until they go to nursery school or even until they first go
to grade school.

Kathryn Barnard, a nurse interested in the development of young
children, recently looked into the early histories of several school-
age children with adjustment and/or learning problems. She found
that most of their parents had felt early in their child's life that he
was different from the average child. At the time, parents' feelings
were often only vague questions based on differences they observed
in their child's eating and sleeping patterns and in his inability to
adjust to environmental changes. Yet their concern stayed with
them. The parents had taken these children to the doctor for minor
illnesses more often than they had taken their other children, apparently hoping that the physician would recognize the "different-
ness" of this child and be able to give some guidance to the
parents.

In another study, 318 mothers of one-month-old, first-born children were asked to rate the way they thought the average baby responded in terms of crying, feeding, spitting up, elimination, predictability, and sleep, and then to rate the way their own baby responded. The answers were examined and then stored for four and a half years. At that time, 120 of these children were seen. Those whose mothers had rated them inferior to "the average baby" were more likely to have psychological or psychiatric problems. This may have reflected those mothers' unrealistic expectations and their ensuing disappointment in their children, or it may have represented the reality of these particular infants having been so different from the average baby that they had difficulty relating to their parents and making necessary life adjustments.

Some hyperactive children have eating and sleeping problems from birth. They are hard to satisfy and hard to live with. One father heard a baby in the hospital nursery who was "always screeching like an out-of-sync myna bird," and asked, "What poor devil will have to take that baby home?" Of course, the "poor devil" turned out to be himself, the baby kept up his screeching for the next three months, and the whole family was bleary-eyed. Fortunately, these parents realized that the reason their baby slept and ate so little was not because of anything the parents did or did not do, but because of the personality the baby had at birth. When parents can accept this truth, life is easier all around, because they do not add their own self-doubts to all of the practical difficulties of raising such a child. Parents who can accept their difficult child's personality and who can learn constructive ways of managing him from an early age will forestall years of emotional conflict.

Sleeping

The typical hyperactive baby "never" sleeps; the amount of time he is asleep is so brief compared with other babies that his parents feel he is always awake. The wakefulness itself bothers them less than the fact that even before the baby's eyes open, his mouth opens, too—and there goes that "out-of-sync myna bird" to get on everyone's nerves. Parents can take some measures to encourage babies to sleep more, and others to keep the babies happier when they are awake.

If at all possible, the baby should be in a room of his own. Even if the family lives in a tiny apartment with one bedroom, it is best to roll the infant's crib out into the living room at night to get him out of his parents' room. Parents should have ready access to a young baby, but to be warm and loving they need to get some rest themselves.

Try to accustom the baby to sleeping through household noises, but if he wakes up at every little sound, provide a quiet environment for him: put a note on the door asking people to knock rather than ring, turn down the telephone bell, close the windows.

Kathryn Barnard, R.N., investigated the sleep habits of premature infants and looked for ways of increasing their quiet sleep. The babies were placed in rockers built into their isolettes, and small speakers that emitted a recorded heartbeat sound were attached to the isolettes. Controlled studies showed that the rocking movements and the heartbeats helped the babies sleep better and longer.

Of course, mothers have rocked their babies at the breast from time immemorial. This study offers proof that the mothers knew best all along. It also points up the advantages of modern technology in helping those babies who need more rocking than the most devoted parents can give. The nursery sections of department stores sell a set of four springs that can be attached to the legs of the baby's crib. As the baby moves around, the springs make the bed rock; so the baby actually rocks himself. These stores also sell an electric gadget that simulates a heartbeat and can be put in the baby's room.

Some babies cry a lot, seemingly from boredom; from an early age they need a lot of stimulation. A mobile over a baby's bed may engage his interest. Other infants like to be put in a semi-reclining seat and brought out with the rest of the family (when everyone is awake) or in front of a softly playing television set.

As the baby grows into a toddler, he may still sleep less than the average child. This has one advantage, especially in families in which both husband and wife work: the later the baby stays up at night, the more he will be able to see of both his parents. Parents should not try to deprive a small child of his nap in an attempt to get him to sleep earlier at night. Most children naturally outgrow their naps when they do not need them any more. When they give them up before they are really ready, they become overtired and overstimulated and are likely to be cranky in the late afternoon and early evening, setting off negative responses from their parents and interfering with their smooth transition to sleep in the evening.

Hyperactive children thrive on routine in all aspects of their lives. Children who have regular routines for napping and sleeping will be able to make their transitions more easily than those who never know what to expect.

On page 170 (Chapter 10) we discuss the problems of the toddler who wakes up regularly in the middle of the night. Once parents have allowed their young child to get up, come into their room and either wake them up or crawl into bed with them, on a regular basis, it is very hard to break the habit. It is far better to prevent these patterns by being firm at the outset.

Eating

"Priscilla wanted to nurse practically all day long. I believe in demand feeding, so I was always on call for her. But when I developed a cracked nipple from nursing around the clock, I realized I was overdoing things," said one mother. Feeding on demand works well for many children who have an inborn body clock: they eat, then sleep for a few hours, then are ready to eat again. For the baby who is very wakeful and fretful, however, demand feeding makes far too many demands on the parent. A baby like this gets along better with some sort of schedule. While a parent should not try to keep one eye on the clock and another on the baby, some kind of rough schedule will keep a wakeful, demanding baby from running the household and running his parents ragged. Parents have to do right by their infants, but they also have to do right by themselves.

These children are often colicky babies, who for no apparent reason cry piteously, sometimes drawing up their legs in pain. The colic attack may come at the same time every day, usually in the early evening. Some parents find that holding the baby on the left side, so that he can hear the parental heartbeat, is helpful. In any case, the colic usually disappears spontaneously at about three months of age.

These babies are often frustrating to feed, especially to breastfeed. They have trouble taking hold of the nipple; when they do latch on, they suckle for a minute, fall asleep, and then wake up starved half an hour later. The baby seems to thwart the mother's every effort to give of herself to him; she sees this as a rejection by her own child and feels angry and resentful. If she can accept her baby's difficult nature for what it is and avoid taking it personally, she will not feel like a failure. If she decides to stop nursing the baby because of his erratic habits, she should not feel guilty. Breastfeeding is beautiful when a mother and baby can enjoy the experience together. When the going is too difficult, however, the baby will be better cared for by a happy, relaxed, bottle-feeding mother than by a tense and anxious nursing mother.

Feeding problems continue when the baby adds solid foods to his diet. He may refuse every new food and have to be offered the same food several times before he is willing to accept it. He may eat better in a high chair, or else held in his parent's arms, with his arms tucked under the adult's arms to prevent their flailing around and knocking the food about the room. As soon as possible, he should be given finger foods that he can pick up himself. "Timmy fed himself from the age of five months," said the mother of one hyperactive boy. "I never did know how much he got and how much the dog got from whatever Timmy dropped on the floor. He seemed to enjoy his mealtimes a lot more than when I fed him, and he seemed healthy enough, so I figured that what I didn't know didn't hurt either of us."

Most children's appetite decreases at about the age of two. As long as the doctor says a child is doing well, his parents should not worry about his lack of appetite and should not make an issue about eating. They should offer nourishing foods and stay away from "junk" snacks. They should maintain regular routines, which are just as important for establishing good eating habits as they are for stabilizing the life of the hyperactive child.

Crying

Sometimes parents feel that nothing they can do will stop a baby's crying. They pick him up, they walk him, they rock him, and yet he continues to howl. The parents feel inadequate and rejected. They must tell themselves that some babies are born hard to please, and that there is no reason for them to reproach themselves if they have done what is reasonable to meet the baby's needs. They must also remember that crying is a baby's only way to attract attention. Just as they would not always gratify an older child's wish immediately, they should not go to their baby at once whenever he cries. The baby will come to no harm if he has to wait until his mother or father has finished doing something important, or gotten ready to attend to him.

The kind of incessant crying that is a "problem" is crying that persists after a baby has been fed, changed, held, cuddled, and rocked until both parents are exhausted.

"Bobby cried from the moment he was born," said his father. "I couldn't wait for him to speak in sentences, so I could ask him 'Why are you crying?' Well, I waited two and a half years for the answer, but it finally came out as 'I don't know.'" The truth was that Bobby didn't know why he cried so much. More prone to tears and excitable reactions than other children, Bobby needed his parents' acceptance of his more demanding personality; he also needed their help in learning adaptability and control.

One mother was determined that her restless, crying baby would learn how to accept and enjoy parental affection. The only time Tammy would lie still was when she was being nursed or when one of her parents was dancing around holding the infant. Tammy's mother launched a systematic training program. Immediately after nursing the baby, Tammy's mother would rock her and sing to her—activities that had seemed to make the baby squirm more than ever. At first, the mother did this for only one minute before putting Tammy down. Then she rocked and nursed Tammy for two minutes. Since Tammy had just been fed, she lay quietly in her mother's arms for these brief periods. Eventually her mother worked the rocking sessions up to ten minutes, which seemed to be the baby's limit for lying still. The training program enabled the baby to accept this display of parental love and provided a way for both parents to soothe and comfort the baby. Tammy developed into an affectionate little girl who thrived on physical contact.

Temper Tantrums

Some suggestions for eliminating tantrums are given on page 139 (Chapter 10). These same basic principles work with very young children, as we can see from hearing about Michael. At the age of twenty months Michael was demanding that whoever put him to bed stay in his room until after he went to sleep. Since this sometimes took up to two hours, Michael's parents had become understandably annoyed. Yet they continued to give in to the baby's demands, because every time they tried walking out of his bedroom before he was asleep, he would scream so loudly and so long that they would come back.

After several months of this tyranny, Michael's parents consulted their physician, who advised them to put the child to bed and to tell Michael pleasantly that they would leave the room so that he could fall asleep, that they would remain close by, but that they would not come back into his room until the morning. The adult was then to leave the room and keep his word. The first time Michael's father did this, the baby screamed for an hour before falling asleep. The second time he cried for fifteen minutes; the third for ten minutes. By the eighth time Michael was put to bed in this cheerful but firm manner, he was not fussing at all. On three or four occasions during the next several months, Michael would again start to cry before going to sleep; when he realized that this was not bringing any results, he stopped. From then on, Michael went to sleep quietly and happily. His parents were more pleasant to him once they had broken his control over them.

Children do not need to be punished for showing temper. They simply have to learn that this sort of behavior will not get them what they want. Once they realize this, they will give up the tantrums. Sometimes a child has to be removed from the rest of the family so that he will be deprived of an audience and so that everyone else will not be disturbed. This should be considered less as punishment and more as a positive means of eliminating tantrum behavior.

Once a child can express his rage and anger in words, he should be encouraged to do this instead of acting out his hostile feelings. Even before the child can express himself well, his parents should demonstrate their understanding of his feelings in simple language. "We know you don't want us to go out," they might say. "We know you get angry when we go out without you. But Mrs. Everest is here to take good care of you, and we *are* going out. We'll see you later." Parents can acknowledge and respect their children's feelings without being ruled by them.

Rhythmic Habits

Many babies and toddlers engage in what seems incessant body rocking, head banging, foot kicking, and head rolling. These habits usually appear during the first year, last for several months, and then disappear. Some children find these rhythmic habits good tension releasers. As long as a child is not harming himself and is still taking part in normal activities, there is nothing to worry about. If the child is hurting himself or if the habit goes on for hours or persists over a long period of time, it is wise to seek professional advice. If a habit bothers you so much that you feel you have to do something, wait until the child stops. When he pauses for a breather, give him your full attention and offer him some other interesting and enjoyable activity. Do not punish him for the habit or attend to him while he is doing what you want him to stop.

Aggressive Behavior

When small children bite adults or other children, push down other children, pinch baby sisters or brothers, or engage in other aggressive behavior, parents must put a stop to it. They should let a child know that they accept and sympathize with his angry feelings, but that they cannot let him act out these feelings by hurting other people.

Parents should make extra efforts to praise a child warmly when he does get along well with other children and adults. He should receive notice for good behavior.

The aggressive, hurtful behavior cannot be ignored without appearing to be condoned. When a child's behavior goes beyond reasonable limits, he should be removed from the situation immediately. When he runs down the street pushing all the little children off their tricycles, he should be taken back into the house right away and told, "Since you cannot play nicely with the other children, you may not go out today." When he harasses his baby sister, he should be isolated for a short time and made to understand that no matter how angry he may be at the baby, he will not be allowed to hurt her. (The baby should be kept in a place where she will be safe from attack.) When the child bites or hits a parent, the parent should immediately leave the room.

Calming Influences

It is important to develop ways of calming a child who is wound up and out of control. Some youngsters find relaxation in a bath. "On really bad days, Seth is the cleanest kid in town," says Seth's father. "Since a bath seems to be the only thing that really calms him, he sometimes gets three baths a day." Other children find a release from tension in a parent's full attention, either lying down together on a bed, reading, or listening to records together, or being rocked on a comforting lap. For other ways to soothe excitable children, see pages 138–139 (Chapter 10).

Outlets for Physical Activity

Extremely active from birth, Charles broke three cribs by rocking in them so that they skidded across the room and eventually gave way. (His habit of kicking out the slats speeded up the process of deterioration.) While unusual wear and tear is inevitable with hyperactive children, a few suggestions for diminishing the rate of destruction are given on page 156 (Chapter 10).

The child should have many opportunities to discharge energy. Housework has to take second place while this child is young, so that he can be taken to the park to run. A back yard with a high fence and simple climbing equipment allows a child to spend time outdoors every day. The youngster should be kept as busy as possible inside the house—fetching things, sorting laundry, "washing" dishes, "helping" to cook, exercising the dog, and so forth.

Tricia has always loved and needed physical challenges. When she was three, her mother went out to buy her a tricycle. Against the advice of the salesman, she insisted on getting a big three-wheel chain bicycle as opposed to the usual kiddie trike. Tricia relished mastering this big new toy and spent many happy hours riding it. At four, Tricia was enrolled in a tumbling class at the "Y." She then went on to swimming, dancing, softball, and, in fact, just about every community program that fostered movement. Generally the youngest child in the group, she thrived on the activity.

Running Away

Hyperactive children of this age will frequently run away from their mothers when they are in the supermarket, or, more seriously, when they are in a department store, and they can get truly lost. They will also take off out of the house or from the yard and disappear, leaving the mother frantic when she discovers that they are gone. A fenced yard with a lock on the gate will give Mother greater peace of mind, but the fence will have to be quite a tall one. It is also wise to have locks on the inside of all doors that open out of the house, which the child cannot reach, at least without attracting the attention of whoever is in the house. The parents should make it clear to the child that he is not allowed out of the yard or out of the house without somebody else being with him. This rule should be firmly enforced. Mothers are sensible not to go to the supermarket on their own with such a child but to ask an older child from the neighborhood to go with them, if there is nobody else at home. It is much better for a mother not to go alone with such a child to large stores or shopping malls because of the danger of the child becoming lost. If she wants to take the child, then the father should go along, too.

Accident Prevention

More prone to accidents, active and impulsive children need more supervision from a very early age. No infant, especially a very active one, should be left alone on an unprotected surface. (At the age of one week, Jay was moving all the way up and down his crib; it would have been unthinkable to leave him alone for a second.) From an early age, an active baby should be wearing a harness to keep him in his carriage. (At three months, Joel pulled himself up in his carriage and turned it over.) As soon as a baby can pull himself up to his knees, his parents should put a "crib extender" on the bed, to make the sides higher and more difficult to scale. (At six months, Judy did a flip out of bed, landed on her head, and took her first—of many—trips to the emergency room.)

Toilet Training

A child who does not have the patience to sit on the toilet until he performs, who expresses his defiance by refusing to go in the potty, and who cannot see what all the fuss is about is going to be difficult to toilet-train. It is best not to think about training a child until he is staying dry for a couple of hours at a time and until he has real control over his bowel movements. This will probably be some time after two years of age. Once parents are sure the child is physically and psychologically ready, they can begin the training by putting the youngster in pants instead of diapers (emphasizing that *"big* boys and girls wear pants"). When the child does have an accident, he should change his pants himself.

One parent successfully trained a resistant child by setting up an intensive two-week training period. During these two weeks, the mother made no plans other than to train three-year-old Teddy. Since his elimination held to no regular pattern, she took him to the toilet every hour and had him sit there for two minutes. When he performed at all, she praised him warmly. When he did not, or when he had an accident in his pants, she ignored it— aside from cleaning him. By the end of the two weeks, Teddy was exercising full control of both urine and bowels.

Another child who had resisted training eventually responded to rewards. Three-year-old Roddy was told he would receive a popsicle every time he made a bowel movement in the toilet. During the next week, he made two movements in the potty; he received much praise each time, along with his popsicle. Roddy's mother and father continued to give the child a popsicle every time he performed, until, within a month, he was not soiling his pants at all. One day the parents deliberately allowed themselves to run out of popsicles. When Roddy asked for one, he was told that they did not have any but that they would get more at the store. The parents "forgot" to buy the popsicles for a few days, but Roddy continued to move his bowels in the toilet without seeming to miss the popsicles.

Parents should not feel too discouraged if they have trouble in getting a hyperactive child to be dry at night. Enuresis is quite commonly associated with hyperactivity for reasons that we do not yet understand. At a later age than the toddler stage, when the child himself is really interested in being dry at night so that he can go visit with his friends or go to camp, there are effective ways to help him learn to be dry at night (see page 153).

Speech and Language Development

Hyperactive children quite often have speech that is unclear and difficult to understand or that seems to develop more slowly than is normal. This is an important problem, because the child's development of language skills plays a key role in his learning to control his own behavior and to get along with other children. Faulty language development may also set the stage for later learning problems in school. If other people have difficulty in understanding a child of this age—for example, nursery school teachers—or if parents feel that a child's speech is developing more slowly than that of their other children, then they would be wise to have the child evaluated by a speech and hearing clinic. At such a clinic they may be reassured that there is no serious problem that should be treated or they may be given some common-sense advice about how to encourage the child's development of language skills.

Nursery School

For many hyperactive children nursery school at an early age is a godsend. It is a blessing to their parents, since it gives them a rest from the demands of this physically and psychologically demanding child. And it is a boon to the child, since it exposes him to a variety of interesting activities, adds structure to his life, keeps him busy, and gives him early experience in getting along with other children. When you enroll your child in nursery school, tell the director of the school or the child's teacher a little bit about your child's personality. If he is aggressive at home, tell them. If you have developed effective ways of managing him, tell them. The better your communication is with the nursery school, the more your child will get out of his time there.

Drugs

In Chapter 14, we stated that drugs are hardly ever indicated for preschool children.

In certain rare instances, when the parents have faithfully implemented all the suggestions offered on page 170 (Chapter 10) and a small child is still having such severe sleep problems that he and the rest of the family are truly suffering, it may be advisable to give the child a drug to help him sleep through the night. This should be considered only as a last resort, when all else has failed.

Stimulants are commonly prescribed for three- and four-year-olds, but we believe that drugs are only appropriate when a preschool child is so severely affected, possibly because of brain injury, that anything resembling a normal life for him and his family is impossible.

Fathers and Mothers of Young Hyperactive Children

The father who assumes a strong role in the care of his child will be able to know and understand this child better. In too many families the mother, who spends most of her day with the child, recognizes at an early age that this youngster has a special kind of personality and special needs, while the father persists in thinking that "he's just all boy" and "all he needs is a good whaling to straighten him out." When a father invests time with his children, he becomes more understanding and intuitive about them, with good results all around.

Another benefit from Father's involvement in raising children is that the mother is thereby relieved of the sole, or at least prime, responsibility for child care. In the traditional family, in which the father works at a full-time job and the mother is home with the children every day, she assumes a disproportionate share of responsibility for the way the children turn out. When there are problems, everyone looks at her: she must have done something wrong; it is all her fault. Her guilt turns into resentment against the child who has made her fail as a mother, and her relationship with her child steadily deteriorates. When both parents share more equally in the children's upbringing, each can shoulder some of the responsibility, as well as sharing in the pleasures.

To provide other gratifications in her life and to avoid undue intensity of the mother-child relationship, a woman should have some commitment aside from her family—a part-time or full-time job, some creative endeavor, some meaningful involvement in community affairs. Perhaps the father can juggle his working hours so that he can be home with the child when the mother is out. If not, the parents must search for an exceptional baby-sitter—a person who is warm and sensitive and able to relate well to an energetic and demanding child.

When asked whether she had any words of advice for other parents, the mother of two hyperactive boys said, "Space your family!" This woman had always dreamed of having several children close together. Despite the fact that her first child was a handful right from birth, she became pregnant again when the baby was three months old, thinking it was "just a stage." The second child was practically a carbon copy of the first. The next five years were particularly difficult for this family, since neither of the boys was able to get the individual attention he required, and both parents felt continually under pressure. The parents of a particularly demanding baby or toddler usually do both themselves and the child a favor when they put off having more children until they feel they can cope with the needs of the one they already have.

> One of the great needs of an adolescent is the security gained
> from a firm word that is not a paralyzingly firm word.
>
> —Irene Josselyn, in
> *Youth: Problems and Approaches*

16   THE HYPERACTIVE ADOLESCENT

A Teen-ager, Only More So

A hyperactive teen-ager needs even more love and acceptance from
his parents than his peers do; having been at odds with society
for years, he has greater doubts about his identity and future.
Since he is still impulsive and looking for excitement, he also needs
more discipline. This requires great finesse from the parents, since
his shaky self-confidence makes it so hard for him to accept their
supervision. Parents should try their best to listen, to trust, to
build self-confidence, to set limits, and to enjoy their child who is
almost grown up. We have already described the technique of
active listening devised by Carl Rogers (page 66). Parents who
use this daily with their teen-agers need not worry about a "com-
munications gap."

Your hyperactive teen-ager is basically a decent person, in spite
of the trouble he causes. He is not headed for jail or the unem-
ployment office. You have done your best for him. So, believe
that he will come out all right in spite of all the hard times you
have. Show that you believe in him by acting as though you expect good behavior, not bad. Children and adolescents tend to act
as they feel people expect they will; in an atmosphere of trust they
do better. Research in English high schools has shown that delin-
quency is most prevalent in schools that have a repressive, authoritarian atmosphere.

Dignity

Teen-agers crave respect and dignity. They hate to be lumped in as "one of the children." If the family is going visiting with another family, it is better to invite your teen-age children to sit with the adults and participate in the adult conversation, instead of sending them off with the younger chldren. This may be a small demonstration of respect, but it means a lot to the adolescent. They tend to make outrageous statements, but if you treat their words as seriously as they were offered, you will keep communication open.

In matters of individual taste, parents should stay off their children's backs. Parents have no business telling their teen-age children how they should look and how they should dress. Hair and dress are powerful symbolic issues that help teen-agers to secure an identity among their peers. Parents can discourage an adolescent from exploiting these issues simply by not paying any attention. They need to give way on trivial things like the length of a boy's hair or the propensity of a girl to wear jeans instead of dresses. They should, instead, concentrate on important items such as staying in school, keeping away from drugs and liquor, and driving carefully.

Young people have an overwhelming desire for privacy. Parents of an adolescent who has already been in trouble are sorely tempted to find out what they can about his activities by whatever means. They may listen in on his telephone conversations, read his mail, rummage through his room looking for drugs, and check up on him all the time by calling friends and neighbors. By showing their mistrust, they will probably push him in the wrong direction. The child will think, "My parents believe the worst of me, anyway. So why shouldn't I live down to their expectations?" It is better for parents to exercise reasonably firm control, to talk openly about their concerns, and to believe in their child as a fundamentally decent person. When parents do suspect wrongdoing, they should confront their child—but give him the benefit of the doubt.

Friends

Parents should take as positive an attitude as possible toward their child's friends, just as they need to show trust in the child himself. A positive regard for the friends, no matter how strange and surprising they may seem to the parents, will promote the best behavior, just as suspicion generates the worst.

While parents cannot dictate what friends their children will make, they can regulate to some extent what their children do. Parents who consistently enforce relatively firm rules about where their children may go and what time they have to be home will, to a certain extent, affect the company they keep. The crowd who wants to stay out until all hours is not going to hang around with the youngster whose parents come out looking for him if he is not home in time. Most important, parents who have done a good job of involving their children in worthwhile activities will have set the stage for their children to make the right sort of friends.

A Sense of Worth

A job is one of the best ways to develop a young person's sense of worth. It allows him later hours for a respectable reason, provides a feeling of independence through the paycheck, and makes him feel more like the adult that he almost is. Working for a drive-in hamburger stand, helping out at a gas station, selling after school in the five-and-dime store, or caring for the children of a working mother every day after school are all good possibilities.

Adolescents should also share in the work of the family. Aside from shouldering their fair load, such involvement makes them more self-reliant and better able to care for themselves. Teen-age boys and girls alike should have a regular responsibility for preparing family meals, doing yard work, and keeping their own rooms and their own clothes clean.

Adolescents should be encouraged to develop their special interests or skills. A youngster who is really good in sports, animal care, music, bicycling, or mountain climbing, or who is really knowledgeable about cameras, politics, or auto mechanics boosts his self-esteem. He will gain the confidence that comes from knowing he can do at least one thing well and will be more sanguine about being able to find an adult vocation. He will also have a vehicle for keeping busy and channeling some of his energies into socially approved outlets. A hyperactive young person should be steered toward action-oriented activities that will take up the entire summer and be a regular part of his weekly life during the school year. Hyperactive teen-agers often have a way with younger children. They well remember the pains and conflicts of their earlier years and are compassionate with children going through the same thing. For this reason they make particularly capable camp counselors, junior leaders, baby-sitters, and tutors.

Limits

Though teen-agers will protest the most reasonable rules, they appreciate them as helping to control their behavior and as signs that their parents care for them. Limits have to be more or less in key with the mores of the community. Important rules should be set down early before infractions have become a major problem. Parents should insist on reasonable hours for coming home at night, on regular attendance at school with at least passing grades, on the performance of household chores, on reasonable social behavior within the home, including civility to other family members, on not coming home under the influence of drugs or alcohol, and on obtaining specific permission before using the family car.

If rules are broken, parents should attach penalties that mean something to the youngster: deprivation of use of the family car, not being able to go out at night, or deprivation of allowance.

Earlier in this book we urged parents not to cut off their child's allowance as punishment. But in "last ditch" situations, it is entirely appropriate for parents to withdraw a teen-ager's allowance.

When a sixteen- or seventeen-year-old boy proposes to drop out of school and make it on his own, there may be no good reason for his parents to continue to support him as they would if he were continuing in high school or going on to college. The move toward independence can be a healthy step if the adolescent proposes to pay for board and lodging on his own and actually finds a job that will support him.

Parents cannot, and should not, try to watch a teen-ager every hour of the day, but they should make it their business to know where their child is, what he is doing, and with whom he is doing it. (Ideally, parents should have set some fairly firm rules along these lines when their children were younger. Even if they have been lax in the early years, there is no reason why they cannot lay down rules now.) Teen-agers should be expected to tell their parents where they are going to be. If their plans change at the last minute, they should call home—no matter what time of the day or night—to inform their parents as to their whereabouts. From time to time, the parents should telephone to be sure their child actually is where he said he would be. When they do call, they should not be blatant about "checking up" on their youngster in an atmosphere of suspicion and mistrust but should have some perfectly sensible reason for calling, such as delivering a telephone message that they thought might be important or reporting a change in their own plans.

Young people should have firm time limits for coming home—after school, after a neighborhood movie, or after a party. In general, it is reasonable to expect a teen-ager to be home by ten o'clock in the evening on school nights and by midnight on weekends, unless there is some good reason for staying out later.

Parents should not let a teen-ager go to spend the night with a friend unless the parents know both the friend and the friend's family. Parents who are interested in their children should not feel embarrassed about calling up the family of the host child and making plans to meet them before their child is allowed to spend the night. (If the other parents are just as interested, they will welcome the call and the visit; if not, you would not want your child to be there.) Parents should not allow a child to invite a friend to sleep over if they are going to be out quite late, nor should they allow their child to sleep out if no adults are to be home. When adolescents are invited to slumber parties, nights out, weekend camping trips, and so forth, parents should make it their business to find out what kind of adult supervision there is going to be. If they have doubts about the kind of supervision or the standards in the home to which their child is invited, they should not hesitate to say "no." It is foolhardy to leave teen-agers alone in the house for days at a time.

School

It is a source of amazement to parents and teachers alike when they realize that a hyperactive child who has been inattentive all through grade school and hardly ever turned in required work has somehow learned the skills he needs to get through secondary school. To everyone's relief, many such youths show an interest in school and a taste for hard work when they reach high school. They may become even more interested in school because of extra-curricular activities like the school newspaper, the photography club, talent shows, or some other non-academic pursuit.

Other hyperactive children have been at odds with school authorities all along, and never become really interested in school. They run with a crowd of young people who are either in trouble themselves or teetering on the edge. Parents, teachers, and counselors watch with sinking hearts as these youngsters move into the impersonal world of the secondary school. Yet, with understanding and help, these youngsters can at least graduate. If the schools they attend provide a varied curriculum that includes vocational subjects and work-study programs, if their parents are firm in seeing that they realize certain minimum goals in schoolwork, and if teachers and counselors recognize the malaise of the restless, distractible, disaffected student and make extra efforts on their behalf, these youngsters can make it.

School Attendance

Authorities may be quite passive about students' skipping classes or playing hooky, though this is a dangerous habit. Parents may not hear from the school until the child has been missed several times. Parents and school people ought to keep a close check on attendance as soon as a child has begun to cut classes. Teachers should inform the counselor when a child is absent from class and efforts should be made to find him. Parents may have to deliver a child to school in person. Tough penalties should be invoked for this flagrant violation of society's rules: grounding, loss of car privileges, or extra chores.

The Guidance Counselor

The guidance counselor becomes the key person in the life of the hyperactive junior high school student. A skillful, sensitive counselor can become the best friend and ally of the child and his parents. Now that the child no longer has one teacher who knows him well, the counselor is the only person who can get to know the whole child and help him co-ordinate the various aspects of his school life. The counselor can mediate misunderstandings between a child and his teachers, provide sympathy and support when he needs a morale boost, and keep the child from using his problems to evade reasonable obligations.

As soon as the child enters junior high, his parents should meet with the counselor to talk about the child, the special problems he is likely to have, and the special attention he may need. They should set up an arrangement whereby they find out from the counselor, who has found out from the child's teachers, what homework is being assigned each week. Knowing precisely what is expected of their child, they will be in a better position to see that he does his work.

They should also discuss with the counselor the need for flexibility in the curriculum and in the amount and type of work set for their child. Many hyperactive youngsters despise vocal music, are bored by foreign languages, but love art and shop. It may be worthwhile to sacrifice some of the requirements for college to keep a hyperactive adolescent really interested and involved in school. Fortunately, a growing number of colleges are becoming more flexible about their entrance requirements; the fact that your child does not take the standard requirements for foreign languages or sciences will not necessarily keep him out of college.

Realistic Expectations

In secondary school realistic goals are just as—if not more—important as in the elementary school. Even if he has done well in school, the academic world and the sedentary life may not have much appeal for a hyperactive teen-ager. A young person like this may benefit from taking part in a work-study program, by which he attends classes part-time and works part-time at a trade or vocation he can pursue after graduation.

Realistic goals may involve the parents' accepting the fact that their child will not make it in a competitive, academically superior college or that he is not interested enough to get the grades that would qualify him. Post-high-school training may involve vocational training—welding, lithography, or business school. It may mean going to a two-year community college, from which he will emerge with a technical or vocational education. Or it may involve attending a college that no one in the family or in one's circle of friends ever heard of, but one that may offer the child an education tailor-made for his interests and his abilities.*

* The Association for Children with Learning Disabilities has compiled a directory of four-year and two-year colleges and post-high school training programs whose admission policies admit young people with learning

Going Away to School

Sometimes a teen-ager comes to a dead end in his school, in his home, and in his community. He has alienated people who could help him, he is in with a crowd of youngsters who are in just as much hot water as himself, and he does not seem able to change course. He would do better to live with friendly relatives in the country and go to school there, or perhaps he should go to a residential school. A young person has a better chance of finding himself if he can leave the scene of so many failures and make a fresh start in a small community, with people who love and understand him and will work with him, and where the pressure for academic success is tailored to his abilities. A good residential school may offer a sort of real-life, continuing, group-therapy experience that helps a student to become self-reliant, disciplined, and able to live democratically with other people.

Drinking and Drugs

The hyperactive teen-ager is likely to be more adventurous than the average youngster and more rebellious against authority. It would not be surprising, then, if he were more likely to sneak a drink or a few puffs of marijuana at an early age. Parents need not become hysterical if they discover such experimentation, but they must not take it lightly. They should carefully investigate signs that their child has been using drugs or has been drinking, especially to the point of drunkenness.

Close supervision of a child's activities should restrain his behavior in regard to drugs and drinking. Parents who know where their child is, who permit him to be only in well-supervised situations, and who oversee his activities will be discouraging this sort

---

disabilities and whose curriculums can be modified for those students when accepted. The directory is available for $1.50 from ACLD, 2200 Brownsville Road, Pittsburgh, Pa. 15210.

of experimentation. While parents should not expect the worst, they should take steps to prevent it. They should keep liquor and such medicines as stimulants or tranquilizers in locked cupboards. They should know how much beer is in the refrigerator, how much medicine is in the bathroom, and what the levels should be on the Scotch bottles.

Sex

Hyperactive youngsters may be interested in sex at an early age. Parents of a girl tend to be particularly concerned about their daughter's sexual activity, because they are afraid that she will "get a reputation" and not be accepted by the more achieving boys and girls in the neighborhood, and because they are afraid that she will become pregnant.

They must try to avoid being too preoccupied with a girl's sexual behavior. Their own attention will promote it, and their efforts to control it by unduly close supervision will radiate mistrust. The best way for parents to counteract undue sexual activity in a young girl is to concentrate on other spheres of her life.

A hyperactive girl may have a very low sense of self-esteem and feel that no one would pay her any attention for herself. Therefore, she tends to play up her sexual attractiveness, since she knows that this is one sure-fire way of getting attention from the boys. Her parents should try to build her self-confidence by persuading her to take part in activities such as gymnastics, horseback riding, camp counseling, being a lifeguard, and pursuing artistic, musical, and crafts activities. A girl can rarely get into too much trouble at the "Y" or at a well-run, well-supervised camp. More important, she will have fun, be able to develop her skills, and take part in constructive group activities.

A girl who is sexually active should be encouraged to visit a gynecologist, who can examine her and give her advice on contraception. There is no reason to believe that a girl will become more promiscuous because she is protected against becoming pregnant. The refusal to give her the facts and means of contraception will probably not hinder her sexual activity; it will increase her chances for getting pregnant. Some girls actually want to become pregnant for a variety of complicated psychological reasons. These girls need psychological counseling as much as—or more than—medical advice.

Getting Outside Help

When life with an adolescent becomes virtually unbearable—when he is defying his parents at every turn, staying out all night, running around with people who reinforce his own antisocial tendencies, taking drugs, drinking, not attending school—the parents must recogize their inability to deal with the problem alone. They must seek help. Usually, the adolescent himself recognizes that he is in a bind he cannot get out of. It would hurt his pride too much to admit this, and so he will probably forcefully protest any form of outside intervention. In his heart, however, he is likely to be relieved both at this evidence that his parents care about him and also at the prospect of getting out of the mess his life is in.

The troubled adolescent and his family may find help through one of the following resources: family service agencies, mental health clinics, family guidance clinics, school guidance programs, church- or synagogue-sponsored youth programs, community drug counseling programs, and the like. They might try to enlist the support and help of an individual who knows and is respected by their youngster. This person might be a relative or friend of the family, the family doctor, the leader of a community project, a clergyman, a teacher, or a camp director.

Some form of counseling, given by a psychologist, school guidance counselor, or psychiatrist, may be helpful. One kind that is especially effective with adolescents is family therapy, in which the parents—and sometimes the other children in the family—participate, along with the adolescent himself. Such counseling sessions help family members to recognize the problems in their home, to see how each of them is contributing to these problems, and to agree upon mutually acceptable rules and ways of handling situations. Another type of counseling that works well with adolescents is the group session. Since this is an age when a person is especially susceptible to the influence of his peers, other young people may do more to influence an adolescent's behavior than his parents or a therapist.

Drugs

A substantial number of hyperactive children enter adolescence plagued with the restlessness, distractibility, and fidgetiness that gave them trouble all through grade school. Still unable to concentrate for any length of time, they do poorly in junior high and high school. It is tempting to think about prescribing stimulant drugs to help these youngsters achieve some success in school, but the price seems too high.

First, there is the risk of drug abuse. As a child grows into a teen-ager, he becomes aware of his feelings and how his mind works. He realizes what the drugs are doing to him, and he thinks about the possibility of manipulating these effects. On a day when he has a test, he may take more than his usual dose, and have a wild "high." He may trade pills with other youngsters, or sell to them, and thus get involved in the drug "scene."

As dangerous as the threat of drug abuse is, it is not the most important reason for not giving teen-agers psychotropic medication. A teen-ager is on the threshold of adulthood. He has to learn to direct his own destiny. If he depends on drugs to control his behavior, he may never learn how to do it himself. He may well head into adult life depending on drugs for basic everyday functioning. Neither he nor his family will be able to deal with his real, unmedicated personality.

Juvenile Court

Desperate problems call for drastic solutions. When an adolescent seems headed for certain trouble, and none of the above resources have helped, the parents who have lost control of a teenager have a valuable resource—the juvenile court. By going there informally, they can get help in preventing trouble. It is better for a young person to get help from the authorities before he is in serious trouble with the law.

The youngster will be assigned to a probation officer who is likely to be an interested person with particular talent for working with young people. He will see the youth regularly, get to know him, and try to develop a friendly, helping relationship. He will not immediately use his authority, but if the boy does not fulfill the minimum standards of behavior and school performance set for him, the officer can recommend that the juvenile court judge order that the boy go to a residential school or home (not a state institution). The intervention of a probation officer has brought many a troubled youth to consider what he has been doing with his life and how he wants it to turn out. A probation officer can be a powerful ally to the child and the family, especially when a child has gotten into some kind of delinquent behavior, like smoking marijuana, running away from home, or shoplifting.

The adolescent years are stormy for many young people, especially for those who are hyperactive. Yet no matter how bad things may be, parents need not despair. It is not too late to help their troubled adolescent. Many youths who were thought by parents, teachers, and even professional persons to be beyond redemption have been reached and have been able to turn themselves around to become happy, productive people.

The sea has fish for every man.
                    —Proverb

17   ALL'S WELL THAT ENDS WELL

We do not know for sure what kind of men and women hyperactive children grow up to be, because the appropriate research has yet to be done. We can do little more than go on our impressions of the fathers and mothers we have met who thought they had been hyperactive, apparently with good reason. They seem to be restless, energetic, outgoing people who have succeeded in their careers in spite of poor performance in school. They are salesmen, construction engineers, store managers, pilots, firemen, military men, truck drivers, lawyers, and doctors. Certain jobs seem to attract men and women with a "hyperactive" temperament. Sales work and politics require endless energy, an extroverted manner, and quick decisions. Adventurous work such as flying or soldiering has a special appeal, and so does work that allows a lot of individual freedom, such as show business, art, and photography. Adult life offers the hyperactive person a variety of opportunities that suits his personality, in contrast to the extraordinary uniformity that is expected during school years.

We would like to illustrate this point with brief histories of two Americans who were outstandingly successful after a very poor start in life. They were probably hyperactive, but in addition they had to face much less understanding than is available now.

In 1853, a six-year-old boy named Tom set a fire inside his father's barn, "just to see what it would do." Although the flames spread rapidly, the fire was discovered and put out before it did serious damage. No one was injured—except Tom, who received a public whipping for his mischief. Tom was the despair of his parents, who were always rescuing him from one scrape or another. They were used to having to be on the alert to fish him out of a canal; to pull him out of the pit of a grain elevator, where he had almost smothered; to dress the nasty scratches he received after he had tied the tails of two tomcats together. As if his mischief were not bad enough, Tom's father was disappointed because his son was not so bright as he would have hoped. The boy's father complained that his son, who pestered everyone with his "foolish" questions, "seemed wanting in ordinary good sense."

When Tom entered school at the age of eight, his teacher agreed with his father. After three months of being at the foot of the class, Tom overheard his teacher describe him as "addled," and say that it would not be worthwhile to keep him in school any longer. Hurt and angry, Tom burst into tears and ran home to tell his mother about his school problems, which he had so far kept to himself. In later years, Tom was to write: "Then I found out what a good thing a mother was. She came out as my strong defender. Mother love was aroused, mother pride wounded to the quick. She brought me back to the school and angrily told the teacher that he didn't know what he was talking about, that I had more brains than he himself, and a lot more talk like that. In fact, she was the most enthusiastic champion a boy ever had, and I determined right then that I would be worthy of her and show her that her confidence was not misplaced. My mother was the making of me."

Tom's mother, a former teacher, taught the boy herself, and he never went back to school. His lack of formal education showed up in later years in his inability to spell or to handle the niceties of English grammar and syntax. Yet this "addled" boy went on to invent the electric light bulb, the phonograph, and motion pictures, and to become famous as Thomas Alva Edison, the "wizard of Menlo Park."

The controversial politician who became governor of Louisiana and then United States Senator was superactive all his life. Before he could walk (which he did at the early age of nine months), he was constantly on the go. One of his favorite amusements, described by T. Harry Williams in his book *Huey Long,* involved rolling off the front porch, crawling to the gate, climbing up and somehow unlatching it, and crawling out to sit in the road. Once he learned to walk, he was everywhere. When the first train chugged into the little town of Winnfield, Louisiana, eight-year-old Huey crawled underneath it to inspect it more closely; the train had to be held up until they got him out again. When a relative told his mother that a good whipping would cure him of the habit of crawling under trains (which he continued to do at every opportunity), she replied that she would have to whip him to death to stop him.

As a boy, Huey was said to have "a feverish and almost abnormal energy, united with an encompassing curiosity." He was always on the run, never still. His father used to say that Huey would jump in the well to see what it was like if it wasn't kept covered. Huey's intelligence was recognized at an early age, but so were other things about him. One schoolmate described him as "belligerent, ornery, disputatious, officious, bossy, a show-off." Among the townspeople he was known as a "pesterance." He continued to be brash, smart-alecky, and a show-off, never hesitating to offer his elders his political opinions or his advice on the fine points of winning a game of checkers. Huey's personality was no different at school, leading to consistently deplorable grades in deportment. Yet he managed to have himself skipped a grade. When Huey decided that he knew everything that was going to be taught in the seventh grade, he presented himself at the beginning of the term to the eighth-grade teacher. He passed the casual examination she set him and won permission to enter her class. He did not stick around long enough to graduate from high school.

From boyhood and throughout his life, Huey Long was enormously egotistical. He had to dominate everyone around him and every situation he was in; he would do almost anything to get attention, no matter how unfavorable, and when he did not like the rules, he made up his own. He knew how to manipulate people with audacity and with laughter. Says T. Harry Williams, "These are qualities that make an ordinary person the opposite of endearing—but in a politician they are called genius."

Another illustration comes from the world of music. Sergei Rachmaninoff remembered having been punished a great deal as a child. One of his early punishments was to make him sit under the piano. As a nine-year-old in St. Petersburg, he was usually ice-skating, stealing rides on trolley cars, or wandering around the city when he was supposed to be at the Conservatory. Considering the few times he graced the Conservatory with his presence, it is not surprising that he received low grades. With a stroke of the pen he changed them into more respectable marks before showing them to his grandmother, with whom he lived. The boy loved best their summers in the country, where he swam, boated, and roamed through the woods to his heart's content.

The director of the Conservatory, and practically everyone else who knew Sergei, considered him lazy, mischievous, and completely lacking in discipline. He admitted this himself in later years, as he reminisced of the times his sister, who had a beautiful voice, had wanted him to accompany her on the piano. "The result was not.very satisfactory, for I was too self-willed to consider the feelings of the singer; I simply played as it pleased me and left the singer to follow as best she could. These attempts to perform together often ended in my sister's exclaiming, 'Oh, get out!' and boxing my ears."

Yet, at twelve, Sergei was studying with an excellent teacher, who forced him to follow a schedule that involved three hours of piano practice every day, except Sunday. The rigid discipline seemed to suit the youth, for he became earnest and unusually self-controlled. He was also enjoying another side to his master's teachings; at fifteen, he was learning his way around night clubs, posh restaurants, and places where he could meet gypsies and women.

As successful as Rachmaninoff became—both in his private life, where he had a good marriage, and in his professional life, where he received world-wide acclaim as composer, conductor, and concert pianist—he never lost his gloomy outlook on life.

In *Cradles of Eminence,* a fascinating book by Victor and Mildred Goertzel, one can read about the childhood experiences of four hundred famous people. Many of these seem to have had difficult times growing up, particularly in school. Winston Churchill, Albert Einstein, Henry Ford, Adlai Stevenson, Sarah Bernhardt, and the explorer, Fridtjof Nansen, all had their problems.

No sensible parent will say, "Since so many famous people had trouble in school and at home and even with the law, why should I worry about my child? He'll turn out all right somehow or other." It is reassuring to know that many eminent people overcame great problems in their early lives. It is more significant that many of these people attributed their success in life to a person or persons who believed in them and who helped them. That parents should believe in their hyperactive children is a cornerstone of this book.

EPILOGUE
A FINAL WORD TO PARENTS

The parents of a difficult child are so angry with him so much of the time that they inevitably feel guilty. Yet the day the parents can cast off this guilt is the day they can begin to help their child. Guilt makes parents defensive about any mistakes they may have made in the past, so that they are unable to concentrate on the present. Guilt makes people look for things to blame, instead of looking for real answers. Guilt makes parents reluctant to exercise the kind of discipline that gives children security, because it makes them too dependent on their children's approval. A child needs to be able to respect his parents more than he needs to like them. The child's respect for the way in which his parents organize their lives and help him organize his gives him confidence in his ability to cope with the outside world.

Parents, do not berate yourselves for what you have done in the past. You have not caused the problems of your hyperactive child. And if you feel that you have not done all you could to solve your problems, you must rest content with the awareness that we all do what seems best to us at the time. None of us is perfect, although as parents we can and should always try to make ourselves better than we are.

We hope that the suggestions we have offered in this book will help you to love and respect your child the way you really want to. We hope they will help you and your child to plan together for a happier and more fulfilling life.

REFERENCES

Page and Line   Chapter One: WHO IS THE HYPERACTIVE CHILD?

3:5   "The Story of Fidgety Philip" appears in *Struwwelpeter: Merry Stories and Funny Pictures,* written by Heinrich Hoffman in 1844 and now published by Frederick Warne & Co., New York.

3:8   Still, George F., "The Coulstonian Lectures on Some Abnormal Physical Conditions in Children," *The Lancet,* April 12, 1902, pp. 1008–12, April 19, 1902, pp. 1077–82, April 26, 1902, pp. 1163–68.

Chapter Two: HOW DID HE GET THIS WAY? SOME THEORIES OF THE ORIGIN OF HYPERACTIVITY

13:4   Ingram, T. T. S., "Specific Developmental Disorders of Speech in Childhood," *Brain,* Vol. 82, 450–467, 1959.

13:31   Ebaugh, Franklin G., "Neuropsychiatric Sequelae of Acute Epidemic Encephalitis in Children," *American Journal of Diseases in Children,* Vol. 25, 89–97, 1923.

14:29   Chess, Stella, "Diagnosis and Treatment of the Hyperactive Child," *New York State Journal of Medicine,* Vol. 60, 2379–85, 1960.

14:29   Stewart, Mark A., *et al.,* "The Hyperactive Child Syndrome," *American Journal of Orthopsychiatry,* Vol. 36, 861–67, 1966.

14:31   Minde, K., G. Webb and D. Sykes, "Studies on the Hyperactive Child VI: Prenatal and Paranatal Factors Associated with Hyperactivity," *Developmental Medicine and Child Neurology,* Vol. 10, 355–63, 1968.

15:4   Werner, Emmy, *et al.*, "Reproductive and Environmental Casualties: A Report on the 10-Year Follow-Up of the Children of the Kauai Pregnancy Study," *Pediatrics*, Vol. 42, 112–27, 1968.

15:19   Drillien, Cecil M., "The Incidence of Mental and Physical Handicaps in School Age Children of Very Low Birth Weight, II," *Pediatrics*, Vol. 39, 238–247, 1967.

17:10   Baldessarini, Ross J., "Pharmacology of the Amphetamines," *Pediatrics*, Vol. 49, 694–701, 1972.

18:1   Waldrop, Mary F., and Jacob D. Goering, "Hyperactivity and Minor Physical Anomalies in Elementary School Children," *American Journal of Orthopsychiatry*, Vol. 41, 602–607, 1971.

18:1   Waldrop, Mary Ford, and Charles F. Halverson, Jr., "Minor Physical Anomalies and Hyperactive Behavior in Young Children," in *The Exceptional Infant*, J. Hellmuth (ed.), Vol. 2, Bruner/Mazel, 1971.

19:14   Chess, *ibid.*

19:14   Stewart, *et al., ibid.*

19:14   Werner, *et al., ibid.*

Chapter Three: HYPERACTIVE AS A NORMAL VARIANT OF TEMPERAMENT

25:7   Thomas, Alexander, Stella Chess, and Herbert G. Birch, *Temperament and Behavior Disorders in Children*, New York University Press, New York, 1968.

26:6   Miller, Ray G., Jr., "Hyperactivity, Self-Concept, and Achievement," doctoral dissertation, St. Louis University, 1969.

26:10   Werner, *et al., ibid.*

27:10   Thomas, Chess and Birch, *ibid.*

28:15   Mendelson, Wallace, Noel Johnson, and Mark A. Stewart, "Hyperactive Children as Teenagers: A Follow-Up Study," *Journal of Nervous and Mental Diseases*, Vol. 153, 273–279, 1971.

28:17   Weiss, Gabrielle, *et al.*, "Studies on the Hyperactive Child: VIII. Five Year Follow-Up," *Archives of General Psychiatry*, Vol. 24, 409–14, 1971.

29:28   Morrison, James R., and Mark A. Stewart, "A Family Study of the Hyperactive Child Syndrome," *Biological Psychiatry*, Vol. 3, 189–95, 1971.

30:8   Cantwell, Dennis P., "Psychiatric Illness in the Families of Hyperactive Children," *Archives of General Psychiatry*, Vol. 27, 414–417, 1972.

Chapter Four: WHO CAN HELP?

34:1   Olds, Sally, "Is There a Tornado in the House?" *Today's Health,* Nov. 1969, p. 33.

52:17   Donofrio, Anthony F., "Child Psychotherapy—Help or Hindrance?" *Mental Hygiene,* Vol. 54, 510–15, 1970.

Chapter Five: HELPING YOUR CHILD TO LIKE HIMSELF

60:32   Coopersmith, Stanley, *The Antecedents of Self-Esteem,* W. H. Freeman and Co., San Francisco, 1967.

66:3   Rogers, Carl, *Client-Centered Psychotherapy: Its Current Practice, Implications, and Theory,* Houghton-Mifflin, Boston, 1951.

72:17   Armour, Richard, "Humor to the Rescue," *Parents' Magazine,* July, 1970, p. 48.

80:18   James, William, *Principles of Psychology* (2 vols.), Holt, New York, 1890.

85:5   Holt, John, *How Children Fail,* Pitman Publishing Co., New York, 1964.

Chapter Eight: RULES AND REGULATIONS

118:7   Smith, Judith M., and Donald E. P. Smith, *Child Management: A Program for Parents and Teachers,* Ann Arbor Publishers, Ann Arbor, Michigan, 1964.

Chapter Ten: SOME SPECIAL PROBLEMS AND WHAT TO DO ABOUT THEM

143:8   Blank, Marion, "The Treatment of Personality Variables in a Preschool Cognitive Program," in *Preschool Programs for the Disadvantaged,* Julian C. Stanley, ed., Johns Hopkins Press, Baltimore, 1972.

143:24   Palkes, Helen, Mark Stewart, and Boaz Kahana, "Porteus Maze Performance of Hyperactive Boys after Training in Self-Directed Verbal Commands," *Child Development,* Vol. 39, 817–26, 1968.

150:10   Matheny, Adam P., Jr., Anne M. Brown, and Ronald S. Wilson, "Behavioral Antecedents of Accidental Injuries in Early Childhood: A study of twins," *Journal of Pediatrics,* Vol. 79, 122–24, 1971.

150:10   Stewart, Mark A., Bradley T. Thach, and Miriam Ross Freidin, "Accidental Poisoning and the Hyperactive Child Syndrome: A Psychiatric Follow-Up Study of Accidentally Poisoned Children," *Diseases of the Nervous System,* Vol. 31, 403–407, 1970.

150:10   Sobel, Raymond, "Traditional Safety Measures and Accidental Poisoning in Childhood," *Pediatrics,* Vol. 44, 811–816, 1969.

153:15   Forsythe, W. I., and A. Redmond, "Enuresis and the Electric Alarm: Study of 200 Cases," *British Medical Journal,* Vol.: 1, 211–213, 1970.

153:23   Poussaint, Alvin F., and Keith S. Ditman, "A Controlled Study of Imipramine (Tofranil) in the Treatment of Childhood Enuresis," *Journal of Pediatrics,* Vol. 67, 283–290, 1965.

164:30   Holland, Cornelius J., "Elimination by the Parents of Firesetting Behavior in a 7 Year old Boy," *Behavior Research and Therapy,* Vol. 7, 135–137, 1969.

Chapter Eleven: SCHOOL PROBLEMS

191:footnote   Silberman, Charles, talk presented to Port Washington, New York Parent-Teachers Association, November 29, 1971.

210:11   Kingsley, Lowell V., "Parents Can Help With School Difficulties," *The Exceptional Parent,* Aug./Sept. 1971, pp. 13–15.

211:7   Douglas, J. W. B., *The Home and the School,* Macgibbon & Kee, London, 1966.

Chapter Twelve: THE POWER OF POSITIVE TEACHING

215:9   Lancaster, Joseph, *Improvements in Education, as It Respects the Industrious Classes of the Community,* Darton and Harvey, London, 1805.

216:28   O'Leary, K. Daniel, *et al.,* "The Effects of Loud and Soft Reprimands on the Behavior of Disruptive Students," *Exceptional Children,* Vol. 37, 145–55, 1970.

Chapter Fourteen: DRUGS AND THE HYPERACTIVE CHILD

236:7   Bradley, Charles, "The Behavior of Children Receiving Benzedrine," *American Journal of Psychiatry,* Vol. 94, 577–585, 1937.

236:25   Eisenberg, Leon, *et al.,* "A Psychopharmacologic Experiment in a Training School for Delinquent Boys: Methods, Problems, Findings," *American Journal of Orthopsychiatry,* Vol. 33, 431–47, 1963.

236:25   Conners, C. Keith, Leon Eisenberg, and Avner Barcai, "Effect of Dextroamphetamine on Children," *Archives of General Psychiatry,* Vol. 17, 478–485, 1967.

236:25   Weiss, Gabrielle, *et al.,* "Studies on the Hyperactive Child: V. The Effects of Dextroamphetamine and Chlorpromazine on Behavior and Intellectual Functioning,"

Journal of Child Psychology and Psychiatry, Vol. 9, 145–156, 1968.

236:25 Sprague, Robert L., Kenneth R. Barnes, and John S. Werry, "Methylphenidate and Thioridazine: Learning, Reaction Time, Activity, and Classroom Behavior in Disturbed Children," *American Journal of Orthopsychiatry*, Vol. 40, 615–28, 1970.

236:25 Sykes, Donald H., *et al.*, "Attention in Hyperactive Children and the Effect of Methylphenidate (Ritalin), *Journal of Child Psychology and Psychiatry*, Vol. 12, 129–139, 1971.

236:25 Campbell, Susan B., Virginia I. Douglas, and Gert Morgenstern, "Cognitive Styles in Hyperactive Children and the Effect of Methylphenidate," *Journal of Child Psychology and Psychiatry*, Vol. 12, 55–67, 1971.

238:15 Conrad, W. G., and J. Insel, "Anticipating the Response to Amphetamine Therapy in the Treatment of Hyperkinetic Children," *Pediatrics*, Vol. 40, 96–98, 1967.

238:20 Satterfield, James H., *et al.*, "Physiological Studies of the Hyperkinetic Child: I," *American Journal of Psychiatry*, Vol. 128, 102–108, 1972.

240:13 Safer, Daniel, Richard Allen, and Evelyn Barr, "Depression of Growth in Hyperactive Children on Stimulant Drugs," *New England Journal of Medicine*, Vol. 287, 217–220, 1972.

240:30 Laufer, Maurice W., "Long Term Management and Some Follow-up Findings on the Use of Drugs with Minimal Cerebral Syndromes," *Journal of Learning Disabilities*, Vol. 4, 55–58, 1971.

240:35 Laufer, Maurice W., personal communication, January 24, 1972.

Chapter Fifteen: THE FIRST FIVE YEARS

253:13 Barnard, Kathryn, and Bernice S. Collar, "Early Diagnosis, Interpretation, and Intervention: A Commentary on the Nurse's Role," paper presented to the New York Academy of Sciences Conference on Minimal Brain Dysfunction, Biltmore Hotel, New York, March 20–22, 1972.

254:1 *Ibid.*
255:15 *Ibid.*

Chapter Sixteen: THE HYPERACTIVE ADOLESCENT

268:20 Clegg, Alec, and Barbara Megson, *Children in Distress*. Penguin Books, Baltimore, 1968.

Chapter Seventeen: ALL'S WELL THAT ENDS WELL

281:22   Jones, Francis Arthur, *Thomas Alva Edison,* Crowell, New York, 1967.

281:22   Josephson, Matthew, *Edison,* McGraw-Hill, New York, 1959.

281:22   Compere, Mickie, *The Wizard of Menlo Park,* Scholastic Book Services, New York, 1964.

282:32   Williams, T. Harry, *Huey Long,* Knopf, New York, 1969.

284:4   Seroff, Victor I., *Rachmaninoff,* Simon and Schuster, New York, 1950.

285:4   Goertzel, Victor and Mildred G., *Cradles of Eminence,* Little, Brown, Boston, 1962.

INDEX

Academic development, 81–82
  stimulating, 202–205
Acceptance and love, 61–80
  adolescents, 268
  father's role, 70–71
  good qualities of child, 62
  listening to child, 65–66
  making friends, 76–78, 270
  open and honest communication, 64–65
  physical contact, 67, 107, 132
  relations with other adults, 78–80
  sense of humor, 71–73
  shared activities, 67–68
  sibling relationships, 73–76
  time spent with child, 67–70
Accident-proneness, 150–152
  preschoolers, 263
Achievement, sense of, 92
Adolescents, hyperactive, 28–29, 268–280
  action-oriented activities, 270–271
  desire for privacy, 269
  drinking and drugs, 276–277
  drug therapy, 279
  establishing limits, 271–273
  friends, 270
  jobs needed by, 270–271
  need for affection and love, 268
  need for respect and dignity, 269
  realistic expectations, 275
  rules and routines, 271–273
  school problems, 273–278
    residential schools, 276
    sexual behavior, 277–278
    sources of help for, 278–279
Adopted hyperactive children, 30
Adults
  handling complaints by, 79
  relationships with, 78–80
Adventurous behavior, 84, 91
Aggressive behavior, 92, 261
  fighting, 161–163
Allowances for children, 158–159
American Medical Association, 245
Amphetamines, 17, 235–237, 241
Approval, gestures of, 67, 107, 132
  See also Acceptance and love
Armour, Richard, 72
Association for Children with Learning Disabilities (ACLD), 47, 223, 227, 275n
Attention, 101–102
  being noticed for wrong thing, 126
  short span of, 118, 315–136
Authoritarianism, 92

Baby-sitting help, 69, 80, 149, 187
Barnard, Kathryn, 253, 255
Bed wetting, 152–153, 235, 264–265
Bedtime routine, 171–172
Behavior conditioning, 101–116

293

Behavior conditioning (*cont.*)
consequences of bad behavior, 130–131, 142, 156
guidelines for habit training, 128–132
punishment, 108–115
reward system, 101, 102–108
rules and regulations, 117–126
Behavior pattern of hyperactive child, 3–4
Bender Visual Motor Gestalt, 42–43
Benton Visual Retention Test, 43
Bernhardt, Sarah, 285
Birch, Herbert G., 25, 27, 72*n*, 92
Blank, Marion, 143
Boarding schools, 230–231, 276
Boredom, 149, 198, 202
Boys, incidence of hyperactivity, 19–20
Bradley, Dr. Charles, 236–237
Brain, abnormalities of function, 4, 11–19
chemical imbalance, 16–19
errors of development, 12–13
injuries, 13–16
Brain-damage syndrome, 13

Calming influences, 147–149, 261–262
Camps and camping, 69–70
Cantwell, Dr. Dennis, 30
Career opportunities, 281
Causes of hyperactivity, 11–24
abnormalities of brain function, 11–19
emotional disturbance, 20–23
home environment, 23–24
implications for parents, 31–33
inborn temperament, 25–33
pregnancy and delivery problems, 14–15, 32
prenatal development, 14–15, 18–19, 32
sex-related factors, 19–20
Cheating problem, 169–170
Chess, Stella, 25, 27, 72*n*, 92
Child-rearing methods, 91–100
establishing priorities, 94
first five years, 253–269
habit-training guidelines, 128–132
minimum of discussion, 99

parental expectations, 95–100
rewards and punishments, 102–115
rules and regulations, 117–126
Children and infants, 253–267
accident prevention, 263
aggressive behavior, 261
calming influences, 261–262
crying, 258–259
drug therapy, 266
eating problems, 256–258
indications of hyperactivity, 36
nursery schools, 265–266
rhythmic habits, 260–261
role of parents, 266–267
running away, 262–263
sleeping problems, 254–256
temper tantrums, 259–260
toilet training, 263–265
Chip-on-the-shoulder attitude, 153–154
Chores, responsibility for, 157–159
Chromosomal abnormality, 18–19
Churchill, Winston, 185, 285
Clothing and dress, 156, 173–174
Clumsiness, 154–156
College and vocational training, 275
Competence, 80–85
academic, 81–82
in sports and games, 82–85
Conrad, W. Glenn, 238
Consequences of behavior, 130–131, 142, 156
Contract system, 107, 129–132
in school, 212–214
sample contract, 213
Coopersmith, Dr. Stanley, 59–60, 70–71, 85–86, 112
Counseling, professional, 35, 52–53, 278
adolescents, 278–279
family therapy, 278
group therapy, 279
indications for, 36–37, 181–183
for parents, 49–50, 278
by pediatrician or family doctor, 37–39
by psychiatrists, 40–41
by psychologists, 39–40
Crib rocking, 262
Crying problems, 258–259

Cyclo-teacher, 209

Day-care arrangements, 184–185
Destructiveness, 156–157
Directions, listening to, 144
Discipline, 86, 110–111
    See also Punishment, Reward system, Habit-training programs
Distractibility, 4, 5–6, 135–136
Donofrio, Anthony F., 52
Drinking problems, 276–277
Drug abuse, 240–241, 276–277, 279
Drug therapy, 16–17, 55, 232–249
    adolescents, 279
    amphetamines, 17, 235–237, 241
    anticonvulsants, 234
    antidepressants, 234–235
    benzedrine, 236
    central nervous system stimulants, 235–236
    ethical and responsible use, 242–244
    methylphenidate (Ritalin), 235, 237, 239–241
    preschool children, 266
    risk of drug abuse, 276–277, 279
    social and cultural factors, 244–246
    stimulant medication, 17, 235–242
    decision to use, 246–247
    drug abuse and, 240–241
    guidelines for use, 247–249
    long-term use, 239–241
    misuse of, 241–242
    mode of action, 237–238
    predictability, 238
    side effects, 238–239
    tolerance to, 239
    tranquilizers and sedatives, 233–234

Eating problems, 160–161
    breastfeeding, 257
    preschoolers, 256–258
Ebaugh, Dr. Franklin G., 13–14
Edison, Thomas Alva, 281–282
Einstein, Albert, 285
Electroencephalograms (EEG), 46
Emotional disturbance, 3
    hyperactivity and, 20–23

Encephalitis, 14
Encounter groups, 67
Enuresis, *see* Bed wetting
Epilepsy, 46
Ethical and moral standards, 61, 85–86
Excitability, 4, 6–7, 137–140
    avoidance of situations, 137
    preparations for situations, 137–138
    recognition of imminent explosion, 138–139
Expectations, realistic, 92–100, 275
    establishing priorities, 94
    parental, 95–100

Failure, methods of handling, 85, 191
Families of hyperactive children, 29–31
    incidence of hyperactivity, 29–31
    shared activities, 67–68, 149, 203
    sibling relationships, 73–76
    See also Home environment
Family Service Association of America, 40
Father's role, 67, 70–71
    preschool children, 266–267
Fighting, problem of, 161–163
Fire-setting problem, 163–166
Flash cards, 209
Follow-up studies, 28
Ford, Henry, 285
Friends and friendships, 8, 76–78, 270

Gateway School, New York City, 154
Genetic studies, 18–19, 32
Getting ready on time, 166–167
Goertzel, Victor and Mildred, 285
Guidance counselors, 274–275
Guilt feelings, 32–33, 184, 267, 286

Habit-training programs, 104–105, 127–134
    child's motivation, 128
    consistency, 131
    defining the problem, 128
    doing chores, 158–159
    family discussions, 129

Habit-training programs (*cont.*)
　getting ready on time, 166–167
　guidelines, 128–132
　improving table manners, 160–161
　instituting reward system, 129–134
　responsibility for consequences of behavior, 130–131, 142, 156
Halverson, Charles F., Jr., 18
Handwriting difficulties, 155, 219
Hawaiian children, study of, 15, 26
Holland, Cornelius J., 164–165
Holt, John, 85
Home environment, 21–24
　atmosphere, 23–24, 59
　bedtime routine, 171–172
　democratic atmosphere, 87–88
　doing chores, 157–159
　establishing healthy climate, 91–100
　family discussions, 88
　father's role, 71, 266–267
　meeting child halfway, 96–98
　positive mental attitude, 98–100
　rules and regulations, 91–92
　safety precautions, 150–151
　separate bedrooms, 75–76, 170
　setting reasonable expectations, 92–100
　shared activities, 67–68, 149, 203
　sibling relationships, 73–76
　structure and routines, 86–87, 91–92, 95–96
　well-disciplined, 85–86, 202
Homework, 206–208, 218–219
　writing and checking work, 205
Humor, importance of, 71–73
Hyperactivity
　causes of, 11–19
　characteristics, 4–7
　definition, 3–4
　early onset of symptoms, 26–27
　effects on child and parents, 7–10
　indications of, 36–37
　theories of, 11–24
"Hyper-parenting," 9–10, 31
Hyperthyroidism, 4
Hypoglycemia, 24

Illinois Test for Psycholinguistic Abilities (ITPA), 43

Impatience, 93, 140–141
Impulsiveness, 4, 6, 93, 118, 141–147
　learning to control, 24, 141–147
　taking time to think, 143
Infants, *see* Children and infants
Insel, Jonathan, 238
Interrupting conversations, 179–181
Irritability, 93
Isolating child, 110–111

James, William, 80
Jastak Wide Range Achievement Test, 42
Juvenile court, seeking assistance from, 280

Kingsley, Lowell V., 210

Language skills, 202–203, 265
Laufer, Dr. Maurice, 240
Learning centers, 48
Learning disabilities, 3, 15, 194, 222
Listening to child, 65–66
　active listening technique, 74–75, 268
　use of "sympathetic grunt," 66
Locke, John, 117
Long, Huey, 282–283
Lying, problem of, 167–169
　fanciful tales and, 167–168
　rewards for honesty, 168–169

Matches, playing with, 163–166
Maze game, 143–146
Medical examinations, 4, 37
Medications, *see* Drug therapy
Motivations, 102
Motor abilities, 155–156
Musical competence, 83–84

Nagging, avoidance of, 99
Nansen, Fridtjof, 285
National Association for Mental Health, 40
National Institute of Mental Health (NIMH), 18
Neurological examinations, 16, 44–45
Neurologists, 44–46
Norepinephrine, 17

Nursery schools, 265–266

Overactivity, 4, 5, 147–149
    calming influences, 261–262

Page, William, 66
Parent discussion groups, 47, 50–52, 188
Parent-Teacher Associations, 210–211
Parents
    attitudes toward child, 98–100, 182, 184, 285
    building child's self-esteem, 59–90, 285
    conflict between child and, 21–22
    counseling and psychotherapy for, 49–50
    effect of hyperactivity on, 7–10, 23
    expectations and tolerance, 4, 95–100, 147, 201–202, 275
    guilt feelings, 32–33, 184, 267, 286
    helping child cope, 32–33, 286
    "hyper-parenting," 9–10, 31
    meeting child halfway, 96–98
    positive mental attitude, 98–100
    of preschool children, 266–267
    quality of parenting, 9–10, 31, 183–184
    school problems and, 195–201
        helping child, 201–211
    self-acceptance, 63
    self-esteem, 89–90
    shouting at, talking back and interrupting 179–181
    single parent, 186–188
    sources of help for, 34–55
    spending time away from child, 68–70
    spending time with child, 67–68
    supervising activities, 94–95, 150
    working mothers, 183–186
Pediatricians, consulting, 37–39
Perceptual handicaps, 3
Permissiveness, 23, 86
Perseverance, lack of, 135–136
Personality traits, 4–7
    inborn temperament, 25–33
Pets, caring for, 78, 157

Physical activity, outlets for, 155, 262
Physical contact, need for, 66–67, 107, 132
Physical education programs, 155
Physical examinations, 37
Poisons and poisoning, 151
Power and self-esteem, 61, 87–89
    home atmosphere, 87–88
Praise, use of, 65
    gestures of approval, 66–67, 107, 132
    reinforcing good behavior, 102–103
Prenatal development problems, 14–15, 18–19
Preschool children, 253–267
    See also Children and infants
Prevalence of hyperactivity, 19–20, 26
Private schools, 225–230
    evaluating, 228–230
    financing education, 225–227
    "free" or "open," 228
    residential, 4, 230–231, 276
    selecting, 227–228
Problem-solving games, 143–144
Professional counseling, *see* Counseling
Promptness, getting ready on time, 166–167
Psychiatrists, 39–40
    professional counseling, 40–41
Psychologists, 39–40
    professional counseling, 41–44
    tests given by, 42–43, 200–201, 212
Psychotherapy
    for hyperactive child, 52–53
    for parents, 49–50
Punishment, 109–116
    for breaking rules, 122–123
    isolation, 110–111
    limitations of, 111–113
    reinforcing bad behavior, 112
    rewards versus, 115–116
    scolding, 114–115
    spanking, 113–114
    withdrawal of privileges, 109–110

Rachmaninoff, Sergei, 284–285

Reading abilities, 218–219
Reading and books, 204–205
Recreational programs, 69, 185
Rejection, child's feelings of, 8–10
Remediation programs, 53–54, 210, 223
Residential placement, 4, 230–231, 276
Restlessness, 4, 147–149
Reward system, 75, 91, 105–115
  for beginnings of change, 107–108
  changing behavior in small steps, 108, 130
  contract system, 107, 129–132
  for effort, not results, 106–107
  example of, 132–134
  for following rules, 123–124
  gestures of approval, 107
  for good behavior, 101
  habit-training program, 128–134
  for improvements, 174
  intermittent reinforcement, 130–131
  material rewards, 104
  operation of, 105–108
  punishment versus, 115–116
  reinforcing good behavior, 102–103, 130–131
  social rewards, 104–105, 107, 115, 130
  token system, 105–108
  used by teachers, 215–216
Rhythmic habits, 260–261
Ritalin, 235, 237, 239–241
Rogers, Carl, 65–66, 268
Routine and schedules, 24, 95–96, 173
Rules and regulations, 117–126
  consistency in enforcement, 118, 121–122, 159
  establishing priorities, 94
  helping child to understand, 120–121
  importance of, 118
  making check list of, 125
  reasonableness of, 118, 119–120
  rewards and punishments, 122–125
  supervision, 94–95
  testing of, 124–125

Running away, 262–263

Safer, Dr. Daniel, 241
Safety education, 151–152
Satterfield, Dr. James H., 238
School problems, 9, 191–211
  academic competence, 81–82
  adolescents, 273–278
    guidance counselors, 274–275
  attendance, 274
  behavior problems, 195
  child's personality and, 193–194, 254
  early entrance or skipping, 198
  homework, 206–208
  individualized learning programs, 193
  language skills, 202–203
  nature of, 192–194
  nursery, 265–266
  parents and, 195–201
    being assertive, 198–199
    helping child, 201–211
  physical activities, 217–218
  private schools, 199, 225–230, 276
  psychological tests, 200–201
  remediation programs, 53–54, 210, 223
  special education, 222–231
  structured programs, 198–199
  tutoring, 208–210
Scolding child, 114–115
Self-esteem, developing, 59–90
  acceptance and love, 61–80
  competence, 61, 80–85
  parental, 89–90
  power, 61, 68–69
  virtue, 85–86
Sex-linked factors, 19–20
Sexual behavior, 277–278
Shared activities, 67–68, 149, 203
Sharing belongings, 178–179
Sibling relationships, 73–76
Sleep problems, 170–173, 254–256
  room of one's own, 75–76, 170
Sloppiness, 173–174
Soiling, 174–175
Sources of help, 34–55
  drug therapy, 55
  educational consultants, 44
  indications for, 36–37

neurologists, 44–46
for parents, 47–52
psychiatrists, 40–41
psychologists, 41–44
psychotherapy, 49–50, 52–53
Spanking, 113–114
Special education programs, 222–231
neighborhood schools, 222–224
Speech problems, 13, 47, 194, 265
Sports and games, 82–85
poor sportsmanship, 169–170
Stanford-Binet Intelligence Scale, 42
Stealing problem, 175–176
Still, Dr. George F., 3, 13, 23
Stimulant medication, *see* Drug therapy
Strecker, Dr. Edward A., 13–14
Sullenness, 126
Supervising activities, 94–95, 150
Table manners, 160–161
Talking back, 179–181
Talkativeness, problem, 93, 177–178
Teachers and teaching, 9, 22, 212–221
attitudes toward child, 81, 195, 219–221

individualized teaching, 44, 212–215
reading, 218–219
special education, 222–223
support for, 54–55
Teaching machines, 209
Television viewing, 203–204, 245–246
withdrawal of privilege, 109
Temper tantrums, 109, 126, 139, 180, 259–260
Temperament, inborn, 25–33
Thomas, Alexander, 25, 27, 72n, 92
Toilet training, 263–265
Toys and playthings, 156–157

Verbal abuse, 179–181
Virtue and self-esteem, 85–86
Vocational training, 275

Waldrop, Mary Ford, 18
Wechsler Intelligence Scale for Children (WISC), 42
Weiss, Gabrielle, 28
Wepman Test for Auditory Discrimination, 43
Williams, T. Harry, 283–284
Working mothers, 183–186

73 74 75 76 77 10 9 8 7 6 5 4 3